Terrorism Research and Analysis Project (TRAP):

A Collection of Research Ideas, Thoughts, and Perspectives

Volume I

Editors: Andrew J. Bringuel, II, M.A.
Jenelle C. Janowicz, M.F.S.
Abelardo C. Valida, Ph.D.
Edna F. Reid, D.L.S.

Cover art used with permission from SA Erich H. Wagner
Graphic Artist (Cover): Dawn Guinn

The contributions of all article authors are views expressed solely by those authors as works of scholarship and professional expertise; these texts do not necessarily reflect the views of Department of Justice, the Federal Bureau of Investigation, any other agency of the U.S. government, or any author-associated educational institution or company.

ISBN 978-0-16-087083-5

For sale by the Superintendent of Documents, U.S. Government Printing Office
Internet: bookstore.gpo.gov Phone: toll free (866) 512-1800; DC area (202) 512-1800
Fax: (202) 512-2104 Mail: Stop IDCC, Washington, DC 20402-0001

ISBN 978-0-16-087083-5

Acknowledgments

I would wish to recognize, with great gratitude, the expert advice and assistance of the following reviewers:

Steven Colon, Senior Instructor FBI BSU
Jeffrey Green, Special Agent FBI Fly Team
Tiffany Hill, Supervisory Special Agent FBI BSU
Jean Larned, Senior Instructor FBI BSU
Grant Rogers, Supervisory Special Agent FBI DTOPS

Editing this volume could not have been complete without the knowledge, hard work, and dedication provided by Jenelle Janowicz, Abelardo Valida, and Edna Reid who were responsible for putting everything together. Thank you all for giving generously of your time and talents to this project.

Additionally, I would like to thank fellow author Special Agent Erich Wagner for contributing his artwork for the book's cover and Ms. Dawn Guinn from the FBI's Behavioral Science Unit for her talented design work regarding the cover's layout. I would also like to thank my wife, Jenelle, for her understanding, support, and hours of listening to me explain the concept of TRAP. Grateful acknowledgment also goes to the FBI HQ Print Shop for their unwavering support to help bring this book into fruition.

Finally, all members of the Terrorism Research & Analysis Project (TRAP) would like to dedicate this 1st volume of essays to our late friend and colleague Arthur E. (Buddy) Westveer. His laugh, fellowship and advice will be missed by all who knew him.

A.J.B.

Table of Contents

Acknowledgments iii

List of Abbreviations v

Foreword ix

Introduction 1

I. Radical Islam's Manipulation of the Media 3

II. Actors Analysis & Capacity of Knowledge 31

III. Incorporating Contextual Sensitivity and Meta-Cognition into Intelligence and Law Enforcement Training 73

IV. Spotting and Assessing Potential Confidential Human Sources Using the Group Analysis Protocol (GAP) 111

V. Terrorism and Counterfeiting: A Synopsis of Critical Issues and Research Opportunities 149

VI. Behavioral clues to deception in counter-terrorism situations: Critique and prospectus 189

VII. The Role of Emotion in Predicting Violence 231

VIII. Animal and environmental rights extremists and crime: Setting forth a research agenda 259

IX. The False Allure of Torture 293

X. What is Lone Wolf Terrorism?: A Research Note 311

XI. Right-Wing Extremism and Military Service 341

XII. Making Bullets Dance: Drugs and "Small Players" in Small Wars 365

Contributing Authors 451

Index 463

List of Abbreviations

4GW	4th Generation Warfare
ACC	Australian Crime Commission
ACH	Analysis of Competing Hypotheses
ADL	Anti-Defamation League
ANA	Afghan National Army
ANP	Afghan National Police
AQI	Al Qaeda in Iraq
ATS	American Terrorism Study
CAD	Community, autonomy, divinity
CAPPS	Computer Assisted Passenger Prescreening System
CERT	Computer Expression Recognition Tool
C-GIRH	Cultural Generic Information Requirements Handbook
CHS	confidential human sources
CIA	Central Intelligence Agency
CMC	computer mediated communications
CNN	Cable News Network
CNVGM	criminal non-violent group member
CNVRTB	criminal non-violent radical true believer
COE	current operational environment
CVGM	criminal violent group member
CVRTB	criminal violent radical true believer

DDR	disarmament, demobilization, and reintegration
DHS	Department of Homeland Security
ECDB	Extremist Crime Database
ELF	Earth Liberation Front
ELF	Environmental Liberation Front
EMPCOA	Enemy's Most Probable Courses of Action
ETT	Embedded Training Team
FACS	Facial Action Coding System
FARC	*Fuerzas Armadas Revolucionarias de Colombia* (Revolutionary Armed Forces of Colombia)
FBI	Federal Bureau of Investigation
FM	Field Manual
GAO	Government Accountability Office
GAP	Group Analysis Protocol
GI	group identity
GM	Group Member
GTD	Global Terrorism Database
HPM	Human Performance Modification
HUMINT	HUMan INTelligence
IED	improvised explosive device
IMU	Islamic Movement of Uzbekistan
INTERPOL	International Criminal Police Organization
KGB	*Komitet Gosudarstvennoy Bezopasnosti* (Committee for State Security)

KKK	Ku Klux Klan
KLA	Kosovo Liberation Army
LEOs	law enforcement officers
MIT	Massachusetts Institute of Technology
NGO	non-government organization
OECD	Organization for Economic Cooperation and Development
OIF	Operation Iraqi Freedom
POW	Prisoner-of-War
ROE	Rules of Engagement
RRT	Rapid Recognition Training
RTB	Radical True Believer
SCGM	suicidal criminal group member
SCVRTB	suicidal criminal violent radical true believer
SNA	Social Network Analysis
SPLC	Southern Poverty Law Center
TOIBG	Terrorists and Other Ideologically Based Groups
TRAP	Terrorism Research and Analysis Project
TTP	tactics, techniques and procedures
VGM	violent group member
VRTB	violent radical true believer
WMD	Weapon of mass destruction

WPP	White Patriot Party
WTC	World Trade Center

Foreword

In 2009 after a casual conversation between an FBI Agent and an academic studying terrorism issues the topic of applied research came up and the idea of putting together a working group devoted to improving the response to terrorist threats by understanding their interests, methods, and behaviors.

The Terrorism Research and Analysis Project (TRAP) working group was established in 2009 with the first working group drawn from academia, law enforcement, and non-government organizations (NGOs) to discuss and research issues involving the understanding of terrorism and appropriate government response practices. The TRAP meetings are funded by the FBI's Behavioral Science Unit (BSU) and the research supported by various academic and/or government entities. Group members receive no salary and are only compensated for their travel and hotel expenses.

The goals for the first working group were to establish a mission statement and objectives for 2009/2010 including the publishing of 12 TRAP essays related to terrorism and to identify areas for field research that would have direct application to the field. The working group exceeded the goal regarding the essays and in the spring of 2010 received approval for the first field research study regarding human source development. Over the summer of 2010 meetings between several interested agencies led to the first GAP field research working group meeting September 2010. Data collection is planned for January 2011 with a completion date of 2013. Together TRAP proved that a consortium from academia, law enforcement, and NGOs can work together in a unique partnership.

TRAP would like to thank the continued work, dedication, and sacrifice made by all group members. The membership of the working group continues to grow and the second TRAP conference resulted in identifying another group of essays including one on establishing a "vetted-traveler" process to enhance security at airports in the United States. The group is now in the process of writing the second volume identifying the problems, solutions, and needs of the community.

As a note to the reader, you will notice that the only common thread among these essays is that there is no common thread. They all involve the topic of terrorism; many explore a number of research questions and suggest more research needs to be conducted.

It is TRAP's mission, "To develop research, advance knowledge, analyze and interpret terrorism data to understand the psychological, technical, and operational behaviors of terrorists and their organizations in order to construct methodologies and tools for defeating terrorism." The working group will continue to study, research, and develop tools to improve and enhance the government's response to terrorist actions.

SSA Andrew Bringuel
Program Manager for TRAP

Introduction

There are no shortages of books related to terrorism and terrorism response and no shortage of bright people trying to figure out the terrorist's motivations, targets, and tripping points. The idea of creating a working group comprised of academics, government law enforcement, and non-government organizations interested in identifying community needs and developing research-based analytic and investigative aids proved to be an interesting exercise. The idea took shape with the development of the Terrorism Research and Analysis Project (TRAP) and the hosting of the first TRAP working group.

This first volume of essays expressing ideas, thoughts, and perspectives regarding terrorism related topics is intended to provoke thought rather than provide answers. The idea behind the working group was to first identify a need, and then to determine if the need could be better served by a research-based analytic tool, investigative aids, or improved training. The mandate to the TRAP members was write with a practical purpose in mind. TRAP authors were asked to ask a question and determine if additional research is needed to improve the government's understanding of terrorism or improve the response to the threat.

These first essays represent the first volume of work from TRAP members and from it several field research studies have begun. It is hoped that this work represents an interactive process with the reader. The author's contact information is provided for the purpose of opening dialogues with readers. Questions, comments, and research interests should be directed to the author.

The contributions of all article authors are views expressed solely by those authors as works of scholarship and professional expertise; these texts do not necessarily reflect the views of the Department of Justice, Federal Bureau of Investigation, any other agency of the U.S. government, or any author associated educational institution or company.

I. Radical Islam's Manipulation of the Media

Jeffrey F. Addicott

Center for Terrorism Law, St. Mary's University School of Law

Nathanial T. Fulmer

Center for Terrorism Law, St. Mary's University School of Law

Robert C. Gunn

Center for Terrorism Law, St. Mary's University School of Law

Abstract

This article explores how radical Islamic terrorists have used the media to produce negative propaganda which drastically impedes victory in the War on Terror. Unfortunately, the media has - either unwittingly or negligently - often aided the goals of terrorism. The authors explore scenarios such as the United States' experiences at Abu Ghraib and the detention facility at Guantanamo Bay as examples of this phenomenon. The article gives recent historical perspectives on the manipulation of the media by terrorists and points to the lessons learned. In addition, the article proposes ways to mitigate the influence of negative propaganda and proposes proactive measures the United States should take to combat the propaganda of its terrorist enemies. While the United States government ultimately has a limited ability to control what terrorist propaganda is reported, the government does have complete control over the lawfulness of their actions and their efforts to educate both the media and the public regarding the proper rule of law and their adherence to the law.

Introduction

The War on Terror (now called "overseas contingency operations" by the Obama Administration) is not just about putting steel on a target; it is also a propaganda war. Al-Qa'eda and al-Qa'eda-styled radical Islamic terror groups are keenly aware of how invaluable a weapon propaganda can be to influence public opinion. They have shown great aptitude at manipulating the media to advance their causes by portraying the United States and other democratic governments fighting terrorism as acting outside of moral and legal bounds. The purpose of this article is to explore how the media operates to produce propaganda which drastically impedes victory in the War on Terror and to suggest ways to mitigate that influence.

As the United States passes the 8th anniversary of the 9/11 terrorist attacks, the War on Terror wages on against "Taliban, al-Qaeda, or associated forces" listed as unlawful enemy combatants in the, 2006 Military Commission Act.[1] A cornerstone of this global war is the intense effort by the radical Islamic extremists to diminish public support by driving the media to report fabricated stories concerning abuses of human rights and violations of the law of war. Terrorists are adept at distorting news reports and, far too often, they find willing voices in the media ready to assist.

---

[1] Military Commissions Act of 2006, Publ. L. No. 109-336, 120 Stat. 2600 (2006).

The freedom of the press is a central foundation of a free people. But, the press has often abused its freedom by imposing a worldview rather than objectively reporting the news. Unfortunately, the news is frequently used to promote an ideological agenda that conditions the thinking of its audience. Polls consistently demonstrate that the vast majority of people that make up news organizations self-identify as political liberals and therefore it is not surprising that some advocate a liberal value system which may minimize the contributions and necessity of the military establishment.[2] This phenomenon includes both the American military as well as the militaries of other democracies. For example, according to Colonel Richard Kemp's October, 2009 testimony before the United Nations concerning the Israeli Defense Force's (IDF) conduct in the, 2008 Gaza conflict: "It is the automatic Pavlovian presumption by many in the international media, and international human rights groups, that the IDF are in the wrong, that they are abusing human rights."[3]

Of course, the major recipient of media distortion is the United States military. Just days before the, 2009 anniversary of

---

[2] *See* BERNARD GOLDBERG, BIAS A CBS INSIDER EXPOSES HOW THE MEDIA DISTORT THE NEWS (2002) ("The old argument that the networks and other 'media elites' have a liberal bias is so blatantly true that it's hardly worth discussing anymore").

[3] Press Release, Human Rights Council, Human Rights Council Endorses Recommendations in Report of Fact-finding Mission Led by Justice Goldstone and Calls for their Implementation, U.N. (Oct. 16, 2009) (http://www.unhchr.ch/huricane/huricane.nsf/view01/256468C04BA76568C1257651004F7DA0?opendocument).

9/11, many world media networks enthusiastically reported that U.S. troops improperly "raided" an Afghan hospital.[4] The internationally reported story, substantiated only by a charity group called the Swedish Committee for Afghanistan, completely failed to mention the full set of facts associated with the incident – American soldiers were chasing insurgents who recently detonated an improvised explosive device (IED), the American soldiers had strong reason to believe that an insurgent commander was hiding in the hospital, the American soldiers entered the hospital with permission from the staff, and the soldiers worked in coordination with local military and law enforcement.[5] Such misleading media reports occur frequently and highlight how the media can aid terrorists in waging their propaganda battle. Sadly, far too much of the modern media either fails to diligently investigate a given report or covers stories from a single viewpoint. While some news reports are prejudiced because of reporter bias, others are driven by sensationalism to bolster sales.[6]

---

[4] *See* Jonathan Burch, *Aid group says U.S. troops raid Afghan hospital*, Sept. 2009, http://www.reuters.com/article/worldNews/idUSTRE5850OH20090906?feedType=RSS&feedName=worldNews.

[5] *See* Justin Fishel, Jennifer Griffen & the Associated Press, *U.S. Military Challenge Allegations of Misconduct at Afghan Hospital,* Sept. 2009, http://www.foxnews.com/story/0,2933,547481,00.html.

[6] Paul Wilkinson, *The Media and Terrorism: A Reassessment*, Terrorism and Political Violence, Vol. 9, No. 2, 52 (1997).

Terrorism is a "psychological weapon" employed to produce widespread fear.[7] An ancient Chinese proverb states that "the goal of the terrorist is to kill one and frighten 10,000." Terrorist acts are premeditated and designed to create a climate of extreme fear directed at a target much greater than the immediate victims.[8] Not surprisingly, terrorists rely upon the media to reach their audience to produce the desired fear and influence opinion. Realizing the power of the media to sway public opinion, terrorists attempt to manipulate the media to disseminate propaganda to portray their opponent as the "violator of the law." Without question the media is a powerful tool used by terrorists to spread fear and propaganda aimed at discouraging and delegitimizing their adversary.

The exposure provided by the media to terrorists is indispensable to their objectives and has been described as the "oxygen of publicity" by the former British Prime Minister, Margaret Thatcher.[9] While the media does not normally share the objectives of terrorists, they do benefit substantially from sensationalized stories produced by the actions and claims of terrorists.[10] Therefore, the relationship that exists between terrorists and some factions of the media can become one of

---

[7] *Id.* at 54.
[8] *Id.* at 51, 54, 57.
[9] *Id.* at 53.
[10] *Id.* at 52.

mutual dependence, each relying on the other to aid in furthering their objectives.[11]

The modern media is a fiercely competitive market with constant pressure to break a story first and in the most dramatic fashion.[12] Obviously terrorism and terrorist propaganda often provide these media sources with the exciting story they are looking for to boost viewership and revenues.[13] The economic incentive to report stories related to terrorism quickly and dramatically does not encourage quality investigation and source verification.[14] This situation provides terrorists with the opportunity to manipulate news stories and exploit the power of the mass media. Additionally, as the methods and affordability of communication technologies expand, the individuals reporting stories are not necessarily traditional media sources.[15] Unfortunately, these new media sources often operate with even lower quality standards. While, the media is certainly not controlled by terrorists, terrorists are keen to manipulate the media to further their objectives in return for revenue-generating-news.[16]

---

[11] Adam Lockyer, *The Relationship between the Media and Terrorism,* 1 (2003); *Id.* at 54.
[12] Lockyer, *supra* note 11, at 1; Wilkinson, s*upra* note 6, at 54.
[13] Wilkinson, *supra* note 6, at 52.
[14] *See id.* at 57 (discussing coverage of pseudo-events).
[15] Charles J. Dunlap, *Lawfare: A Decisive Element of 21st – Century Conflicts?*, JFQ/ Issue 54, 3d quarter, 34-35 (2009).
[16] Wilkinson*, supra* note 6, at 53.

A democratic government cannot wage a successful war without dedicated public support.[17] Accordingly, this support can erode or even reverse rapidly if constituents sense the war is being conducted unjustly.[18] As a nation governed by the rule of law, it is vital that America validate - for itself and for the civilized world - the legitimacy of its War on Terror by the manner in which it conducts combat activity. Clearly, the United States cannot claim that its forces are the "good guys" unless the rules of armed conflict are meticulously observed. No doubt, the attention of the world has shifted from the murderous machinations of the al-Qa'eda and their like, to an extreme focus on how well the United States and its allies adhere to all aspects of the rule of law in battling these people. For better or worse, this phenomenon is a reality. No media outlet shows interest regarding the fact that the "bad guys" behave in gross violation of the law of war. After all, that is precisely why they are the "bad guys." On the other hand, the world has an intense interest in how the "good guys" perform. If a State claims that their cause is just, they must act accordingly.[19] Public support for war erodes quickly within a democracy when the citizens on the home front perceive that their

---

[17] Dunlap, *supra* note 15, at 35.
[18] *Id.* at 35.
[19] JEFFREY ADDICOTT, TERRORISM LAW: MATERIALS, CASES, COMMENTS 195 (Lawyer and Judges Publishing Company, Inc., 5th ed. 2009).

soldiers may be disregarding the law of war and acting like the "bad guys."

The modern media is a powerful weapon that can influence public opinion almost instantaneously with regard to whether the United States and its allies are abiding by the law of war and waging a *jus en bello* against terrorism. To a large degree, from Valley Forge (1778) to the present time, the United States military can take full credit for a commendable record in its adherence to the law of war. This is because of its commitment to institutionalizing certain truisms which might be encapsulated in the old saying that "[a] right thing must be done in a right way or it is wrong." Thus, defeating the enemy - a right thing - must be done under the law of war - in a right way - or the entire activity is wrong.[20] However, the aberrations of bad conduct provide powerful lessons for how damaging such acts can be once the mass media informs the home front and the world of what has occurred. The infamous prison abuse scandal of Abu Ghraib by which the abuses by a few American guards were parlayed into the false conclusion that American soldiers regularly abuse all detainees, recalls the same propaganda lessons associated with the My Lai massacre during the Viet Nam War.[21]

---

[20] *Id.* at 192.
[21] *Id.* at 194.

On March 16, 1968, an American combat task force of the 23rd Infantry Division murdered well over 300 unarmed South Vietnamese civilians at My Lai. Despite an initial cover-up by some in the military, the enormity of the atrocity made it unlikely that it could long be kept secret.[22] Color photographs appeared in the December, 1969 issue of *Life* magazine.[23] Needless to say, the public reaction was one of disbelief; no one believed that a massacre of that magnitude could have been committed by American soldiers and concealed for over a year.[24] The initial military cover-up only provided the media with a more sensationalized version of the war crime to present to its audience.

Like the Islamic terrorist groups, the North Vietnamese Communists waged the Vietnam War with clear objectives in mind and a clear sense of how to use media to their advantage. The Communists relied heavily on all forms of propaganda, placing special emphasis on the ambiguity of words to erode the will of the United States to continue the war.[25] Al-Qa'eda has been similarly successful in its use of violence and propaganda.[26] Before his death by U.S. forces in June, 2006, al-Qa'eda chief in Iraq Abu Musab al-Zarqawi managed to organize attacks on Shias and their

---

[22] *Id.* at 199.

[23] Ronald L. Haeberle, *The Massacre at Mylai*, Life, Dec. 5, 1969 at 36.

[24] *Id.* at 200-201.

[25] *Id.* at 208.

[26] *See* Maddy Sauer, *The Hunt for American al Qaeda,* June 2008, http://abcnews.go.com/Blotter/story?id=5026716 (An example of al-Qa'eda's concerted propaganda efforts).

holy places of worship that were played up in the media with such great vigor that many in America pronounced a defeat for the United States.[27]

On the other hand, the United States military operates in a world where any transgression it commits will be covered tenfold in comparison to any crime perpetrated by its enemies whether it be the Viet Cong or al-Qa'eda. American violations in Vietnam absolutely pale in comparison to the thousands upon thousands of command directed slaughters that were committed by the communist regime of then, North Vietnam and their Viet Cong allies.[28] However, media rarely frames war crimes by the United

---

[27] *See* Joel Roberts, *Senator Reid On Iraq: "This War is Lost"*, April 2007, http://www.cbsnews.com/stories/2007/04/20/politics/main2709229.shtml (Senator Harry Reid stated on April 19, 2007: "I believe myself that the secretary of state, secretary of defense and — you have to make your own decisions as to what the president knows — (know) this war is lost and the surge is not accomplishing anything as indicated by the extreme violence in Iraq yesterday").

[28] *See* Addicott, *supra* note 19, at 198 (As Professor Rudy Rummel noted: "The American record in Vietnam with regard to observance of the law of war is not a succession of war crimes and does not support charges of a systematic and willful violation of existing agreements for standards of human decency in time of war, as many critics of American involvement have alleged. Such charges were based on a distorted picture of the actual battlefield situation, on ignorance of existing rules of engagement, and on a tendency to construe every mistake of judgment as a wanton breach of the law of war." In the estimate of Rummel, North Vietnam sponsored the slaughter of over one and a quarter million of its own people from 1945 to 1987. Included in this figure, since the fall of South Vietnam in 1975, are over 250,000 boat people and 250,000 other civilians who were either ruthlessly murdered outright or who perished in communist death camps set up to "re-educate" non-communists).

States military and its allies in this context. In the end, a "good guy" doing a bad thing always makes for the "best" news.

The United States experienced the truth of this aphorism during the War on Terror, in the media coverage of the prison scandal at Abu Ghraib in, 2004. The successful invasion of Iraq in, 2003 by United States and its allies was followed by a deadly insurgency.[29] Coalition forces and Iraqi civilians were targeted for murder by various groups of sectarian guerrilla fighters, common criminals, and al-Qa'eda linked terrorists.[30] The rising intensity of the insurgency in mid, 2003 also mandated that the large number of detainees had to be categorized and housed. The establishment of detention facilities to house the detainees was aggravated by their sheer number. This required the coalition forces to utilize Saddam-era prison structures including the prison at Abu Ghraib, located about, 20 miles west of Baghdad. Abu Ghraib soon became the largest U.S. run detention facility and, at a high point in the tempo of operations, housed up to 7,000 detainees in October, 2003.[31] Within this 280 acre complex was the infamous

---

[29] *See* James Glanz and Tom Shanker, *Iraq Study Sees Rebels' Attacks as Widespread*, N.Y. Times, Sep. 29, 2004 at http://www.nytimes.com/2004/09/29/international/middleeast/29attacks.html.

[30] *Id.*

[31] See Christine Hauser, *U.S. Releases More Prisoners from Abu Ghraib*, N.Y. Times, Oct. 31, 2009 at http://www.nytimes.com/2004/05/28/international/middleeast/28CND-PRIS.html.

Tier 1 (cellblock 1a), a small, two-story isolation wing and the site of the prisoner abuse at Abu Ghraib. Photographs taken by fellow soldiers first aired in, 2004 on a CBS show called *60 Minutes II*.[32] The widely circulated photos showed a handful of U.S. military police soldiers engaged in a variety of abusive and sexually sadistic acts against mostly blindfolded Iraqi detainees.[33] Among other things, the photos showed naked prisoners stacked in pyramids, connected by wires, on a dog leash, and threatened by dogs. In addition, a handful of U.S. military police charged in the abuse scandal had forced naked prisoners to simulate sex acts.[34]

The abuses at Abu Ghraib should not have happened, but the damage to American credibility and the War on Terror was largely caused by the massive and unrelenting news coverage.[35] Indeed, the false picture that was painted by the media was that the conduct at Abu Ghraib was not the exception but the rule for all detainees. There can be no question that the feeding frenzy by the media did more damage to the war effort than a 1,000 suicide bombers. Amazingly, the *New York Times* put the Abu Ghraib

---

[32] *60 Minutes II* (CBS News Television Broadcast Apr. 28, 2004).

[33] *See* Seymour M. Hersh, *Torture at Abu Ghraib*, The New Yorker, May 10, 2004.

[34] Addicott, *supra* note 19, at 264-265.

[35] *See* Thomas Sowell, *The Media Frenzy over Abu Ghraib Military Prison in Iraq*, Capitalism Magazine, May 11, 2004 at http://www.capmag.com/article.asp?ID=3681; *Abu Ghraib Accountability: An Overhyped Story, Not Whitewash,* The Wall Street Journal, Apr. 27, 2005, at http://www.opinionjournal.com/editorial/feature.html?id=110006612.

story on its front page for 32 consecutive days,[36] causing many to erroneously conclude that the Abu Ghraib incident was proof that America tortures or mistreats detainees regularly.[37] Lost in a large amount of the media coverage was the fact that the military self-reported the abuses which occurred at Abu Ghraib,[38] that the military prosecuted and convicted the Abu Ghraib offenders,[39] and that the tactical chain of command was relieved for dereliction of duty.[40]

When one considers that the number of detainees in the War on Terror - including Afghanistan, Iraq, and other operations - is over 50,000, it is unrealistic to expect that abuses by individual soldiers acting in their individual capacity will not occur. Violations of rules occur in every human endeavor, to include war. The investigations which followed Abu Ghraib found that there was no official policy, either written or oral, to torture or abuse

---

[36] Peter Collier, *American Honor,* May 2007, http://online.wsj.com/article/SB118014402282815483.html?mod=googlenews_wsj.

[37] *See* Robert Winnett, *Torture Row: Judges Accuse U.S. of Coverup*, Feb. 2009, http://www.telegraph.co.uk/news/majornews/4517343/Torture-row-Judges-accuse-US-of-cover-up.html; *See* David Morgan, *Red Cross: Torture Committed at CIA Sites*, March 2009, http://www.cbsnews.com/stories/2009/03/16/terror/main4869240.shtml.

[38] *See* Sowell, *supra* note 35 ("The story of what happened at Abu Ghraib prison was told by the American military authorities months ago. This was not some cover-up that the media exposed. What the media did, irresponsibly, was send inflammatory photographs around the world").

[39] *See* Associated Press, *Fast Facts: Abu Ghraib Convicetions,* Sept. 2005, http://www.foxnews.com/story/0,2933,170603,00.html.

[40] *Abuse and the Army*, The Wall Street Journal, May 6, 2004 at A18.

prisoners. According to the Schlesinger Report, the most far reaching investigation to date and the one which the *Wall Street Journal* deemed the "definitive assessment of what went wrong,"[41] no approved procedures called for or allowed the kinds of abuse that in fact occurred.[42] In fact, the Schlesinger Report found no evidence of a policy of abuse promulgated by senior officials or military authorities.[43]

While each and every case of abuse is repulsive to American standards of decency and justice, the terrorists have certainly become "media-savvy" in their quest to parlay these individual cases into marketable propaganda. Despite the facts set out in the Schlesinger Report, media outlets for months on end did not adequately report the facts but chose to publish front page stories of the abuse photos. The consequences were predictable - many people that were opposed to the United States were quick to exploit the individual cases of abuse at Abu Ghraib by painting the entire conduct of all American soldiers as immoral and illegal.[44]

Terrorists have used the media to exploit the phenomenon known as "imputed responsibility" against the United States and

---

[41] *A Rumsfeld Vindication*, The Wall Street Journal, Aug. 26, 2004 at A12.
[42] The Schlesinger Report: An Investigation of Abu Ghraib, Independent Panel to Review Department of Defense Detention Operations, James R. Schlesinger, Chairman (Aug. 2004) at http://fl1.findlaw.com/news.findlaw.com/hdocs/docs/dod/abughraibrpt.pdf.
[43] *Id.*
[44] Addicott, *supra* note 19, at 278.

coalition partners.[45] The term recognizes the fact that the acts of a few soldiers who engage in egregious abuses of the law of war are immediately imputed to the entire military establishment. For instance, although a handful of individuals murdered innocent civilians at My Lai, significant segments of the public soon viewed all American soldiers in Vietnam as "baby killers."[46] To a large degree, the mass media feeds this phenomenon, as reflected by almost every Hollywood movie concerning the Vietnam War.[47] In American cinema, the soldier is routinely depicted as engaging in abuses of the law of war or ingesting large quantities of illegal drugs. The fact that the vast majority of American soldiers did neither is not shown.[48] More recently, the exploitation of Abu Ghraib by terrorists through media coverage has allowed that incident "to become the perfect effect-based, asymmetrical operation that continues to present difficulties for American forces."[49] With the media deck stacked against the U.S. military, the best way for it to win the propaganda war on the home front is

---

[45] *See* WILLIAM C. BURTON, BURTON'S LEGAL THESAURUS 304 (Brian Burton ed., McGraw Hill 4th ed. 2007) (1980) ("Impute" can mean to "apply, ascribe, attach, attribute, attribute vicariously, blame, charge to, etc").

[46] *See* Jamie Holguin, *Vietnam War's Legacy Still Felt*, March 2005, http://www.cbsnews.com/stories/2005/03/02/eveningnews/main677645.shtml. *See also* Vietnam Veterans of America, Chapter 951, http://www.vva951.org/baby-killers.html (a veteran's personal account of being called a "baby killer").

[47] *See* Apocalypse Now (Paramount Pictures, 1979); Platoon (Hemdale Film Corporation, 1986).

[48] Addicott, *supra* note 19, at 211.

[49] Dunlap, *supra* note 15, at 34.

to make every effort to see that abuses do not occur and, if they do, promptly investigate and punish those proven to be guilty.

Ironically, sometimes the media coverage simply reflects a reality that is itself harmful to United States interests. For instance, some would argue that a significant public relations victory for the terrorists occurred when the Obama Administration announced its decision to close the detention facility at Guantanamo Bay Naval Base (GITMO) within a year.[50] Unlike the abuses at Abu Ghraib by a few renegade soldiers, the United States has no actions to atone for concerning GITMO. Simply put, the announcement of GITMO's closing was a public relations disaster since it only fueled the already false perception that America had either tortured detainees or engaged in illegal conduct by merely exercising its right under the law of war to detain them.[51] Since the detention of Taliban, al-Qa'eda, and associated forces at GITMO as enemy combatants is legal under the law of

---

[50] Executive Order – Review and Disposition of Individuals Detained at the Guantanamo Bay Naval Base and Closure of Detention Facilities (Jan. 2009).

[51] U.N. Econ. & Soc. Council [ECOSOC], Comm'n on Human Rights, *Situation of Detainees at Guantanamo Bay*, U.N. Doc. E/CN.4/2006/120 (Feb. 15, 2006) (Report of the Chairperson of the Working Group on Arbitrary Detention, Ms. Leila Zerrougi; the Special Rapporteur on the independence of judges and lawyers, Mr. Leander Despoil; the Special Rapporteur on torture and other cruel, inhuman or degrading treatment or punishment, Mr. Manfred Nowak; the Special Rapporteur on freedom of religion or belief, Ms. Asma Jahangir and the Special Rapporteur on the right of everyone to the enjoyment of the highest attainable standard of physical and mental health, Mr. Paul Hunt).

war,[52] America has the right to detain enemy combatants indefinitely until the war is over in order to prevent them from rejoining the conflict. As to the treatment of detainees, the United States military has run the detention facility with the utmost professionalism creating a humane, legal, and transparent environment.[53] Despite these realities, GITMO became the epicenter for unrelenting waves of duplicitous propaganda by terrorist enemies and ideologues fixated with portraying America as the "bad guy." Certainly, if the Obama Administration is successful in shutting down the detention facility at GITMO, the negative distortions regarding detention operations will not end. Instead, America's enemies will redouble their propaganda efforts.

---

[52] Traditional law of war authority allows a government to hold enemy combatants until the end of hostilities. *See* Article 118 of Common Article 3 of the Geneva Conventions of 1949. This designation was codified by the Military Commissions Act (MCA), *see supra* note 1. The MCA clearly defines an unlawful enemy combatant as either a person who has engaged in hostilities or who has purposefully and materially supported hostilities against the United States or its co-belligerents who is not a lawful enemy combatant (including a person who is part of the al-Qa'eda, or associated forces). Under the Third Geneva Convention, prisoner of war status is only conferred on persons who are: "Members of other militias and members of other volunteer corps, including those of organized resistance movements, belonging to a Party to the conflict and operating in or outside their own territory, even if this territory is occupied, provided that such militias or volunteer corps, including such organized resistance movements, fulfill the following conditions:

> (a) that of being commanded by a person responsible for his subordinates;
> (b) that of having a fixed distinctive sign recognizable at a distance;
> (c) that of carrying arms openly;
> (d) that of conducting their operations in accordance with the laws and customs

of war." *Id.*

[53] Jeffrey Addicott, "Closing GITMO Would be a Mistake," San Antonio Express-News, 19 January 2009, Sec. B.

Terrorists have also benefited from the overly intense media scrutiny of the techniques used by American interrogators.[54] The almost unanimous allegations of torture by more than 500 detainees released from GITMO have all proved to be spurious (not all liars are terrorists, but all terrorists are liars). The few instances of enhanced interrogation techniques that were used by the Central Intelligence (CIA) Agency personnel were carefully reviewed by the Department of Justice[55] to ensure that the practices did not violate the Torture Convention.[56]

---

[54] See *A Rumsfeld Vindication*, supra note 41, at A12 (discussing how the media frenzy over the torture issue caused a retreat in interrogation techniques used by U.S. forces which diminished their ability to combat the insurgency in Iraq).

[55] Memos for John A Rizzo Senior Deputy General Counsel, Central Intelligence Agency, May 30 2005 at http://documents.nytimes.com/justice-department-memos-on-interrogation-techniques#p=1

[56] Convention against Torture and Other Cruel, Inhuman or Degrading Treatment or Punishment. U.N. Res. 39/46 (1984). Without question, the Torture Convention devotes far more attention to crafting the meaning of the term torture, which it defined as:

> [A]ny act by which severe pain or suffering, whether physical or mental, is intentionally inflicted on a person for such purposes as obtaining from him or a third person information or a confession, punishing him for an act he or a third person has committed or is suspected of having committed, or intimidating or coercing him or a third person, or for any reason based on discrimination of any kind, when such pain or suffering is inflicted by or at the instigation of … a public official or other person acting in an official capacity. It does not include pain or suffering arising only from, inherent in or incidental to lawful sanctions.

According to the Torture Convention, for torture to exist in the context of an interrogation the following criteria must be present: (1) the behavior must be based on an intentional act; (2) it must be performed by a State agent; (3) the behavior must cause severe pain or suffering to body or mind; and (4) it must be

Still, media sources exhibit little understanding of the treaties and judicial precedents which legally define terms such as "torture" or "illegal rendition."[57] Suggestions of torture generally come from media reports based on unnamed sources and anecdotal evidence. For example, in March, 2002 the *Washington Post* used an unnamed source to suggest that the United States had turned over dozens of terror suspects to countries such as Egypt and Jordan for interrogations involving torture.[58] Rendition is a common practice which is only improper under international law if, for instance, the United States knowingly delivers a suspect to a

---

accomplished with the intent to gain information or a confession. In adopting the Torture Convention, the United States Senate provided the following reservations which require specific intent and better define the concept of mental suffering:

[T]he United States understands that, in order to constitute torture, an act must be specifically intended to inflict severe physical or mental pain or suffering and that mental pain or suffering refers to prolonged mental harm caused by or resulting from: (1) the intentional infliction or threatened infliction of severe physical pain or suffering; (2) the administration or application, or threatened administration or application, of mind altering substances or other procedures calculated to disrupt profoundly the senses or the personality; (3) the threat of imminent death; or (4) the threat that another person will imminently be subjected to death, severe physical pain or suffering, or the administration or application of mind altering substances or other procedures calculated to disrupt profoundly the senses or personality.

[57] *See, e.g.,* Professor Addicott's May 2009 testimony before the Senate Committee on the Judiciary, Subcommittee on Administrative Oversight and the Courts hearing entitled: "*What Went Wrong Torture and the Office of the Legal Counsel in the Bush Administration*," Washington, DC. Text can be viewed in entirety at: http://jurist.law.pitt.edu/paperchase/2009/05/bush-era-interrogation-techniques.php (arguing that water-boarding as practiced by the CIA did not constitute torture under the Torture Convention).

[58] Rajiv Chandrasekaran and Peter Finn, *US Behind Secret Transfer of Terror Suspects*, Washington Post, Mar. 22, 2002 at A01.

nation that it has substantial grounds to believe engages in "a consistent pattern of gross, flagrant or mass violations of human rights."[59] While an "unnamed source" in a media article may view a particular country as a nation that satisfies this test, it is ultimately a question for the government of the United States and the international community to answer. Without more evidence than that provided by unnamed sources, it is impossible to accurately gauge what interrogation methods are being used in a particular State.[60] Terrorists greatly benefit from stories insinuating torture or illegal rendition from media sources that use little real evidence or understanding of the law to substantiate their claims.

Perhaps the favorite topic for media bias in reporting involves the matter of civilian casualties from combat operations.[61] As coalition forces continue to preserve stability in Iraq and fight a

---

[59] Article 3(2) of the Convention against Torture and Other Cruel, Inhuman or Degrading Treatment or Punishment, U.N. res. 39/46 (1984).

[60] Addicott, *supra* note 19, at 245.

[61] *See 'Dozens Dead' in US Drone Strike,* June 2009, http://news.bbc.co.uk/2/hi/8115814.stm; *See Suicide Bomber, Suspected U.S. Drone Strike Pakistan,* April 2009, http://www.usatoday.com/news/world/2009-04-04-us-pakistan-attack_N.htm; *See US Drone Strikes May Brake International Law: UN*, Oct. 2009, http://www.google.com/hostednews/afp/article/ALeqM5iUaMrNjdCeSmf_4__CYrSIe26SBg; *See* Michael Rowland, *Civilian Deaths Spark US Air Strike Rethink,* May 2009, http://www.abc.net.au/news/stories/2009/05/15/2571775.htm; *See* Lisa Schirch, *The Costs of Drone Strikes,* Oct. 2009, http://www.huffingtonpost.com/lisa-schirch/the-costs-of-drone-strike_b_319318.html; *See* Amir Mir, *60 U.S. Drone Attacks Kill 687 Civilians in Pakistan,* April 2009, http://www.tehrantimes.com/Index_view.asp?code=192181.

resurgent Taliban and al-Qa'eda in Afghanistan, false and exaggerated media reports regarding collateral damage to civilians sometimes serve to energize the terror groups and frustrate coalition objectives.[62] These negative reports are often aggressively exploited by the terrorists in order to effectuate their propaganda campaign to turn public support and divert attention from the successes of collation forces. Manipulation of the modern media by terrorists has actually intensified alongside with the great advancements in weapons technology used to direct force on targets in the most discriminating fashion possible to avoid civilian targets. Despite advances in precision munitions and aerial surveillance technologies, the terrorists have successfully manipulated the modern media to report that these weapons are being used in an inhuman manner.[63] In fact, it is well known that the Taliban and al-Qa'eda - like Hamas in the Gaza and Hezbollah in Lebanon - deliberately increase the risk to civilians by locating themselves among them.[64] Al-Qa'eda and Taliban forces purposefully attempt to stir public anger against the practice of aerial bombing, which the Afghan people have considered barbaric since the British first bombed Kabul as part of the Third Anglo

---

[62] Dunlap, *supra* note 15, at 36.
[63] *Id.* at 36; *Cf. Predators and Civilians: An Intelligence Report Shows How Effective Drone Attacks Are,* (2009), http://online.wsj.com/article/SB124743959026229517.html.
[64] Dunlap, *supra* note 15, at 36.

War in, 1919.[65] As precision weapons increasingly threaten the terrorists, they have responded by intensifying their propaganda campaign to sway public support.

The Israeli military has also encountered similar tactics by the terrorist organizations of Hezbollah during the, 2006 Lebanon War and more recently the, 2008 military self-defense moves against Hamas in the Gaza strip. When Israel conducted operations in Gaza during, 2008, Israeli officials complained that Hamas' weapons and supplies were discovered under mosques, in schools, and under civilian homes. Israeli intelligence also reported that the leadership of Hamas had taken refuge beneath the largest hospital in Gaza.[66] In short, radical Islamic terror groups hope for civilian casualties which they can then use for their own propaganda efforts through the media.

Winning the public support battle is a vital component of the American war effort and requires a concentrated public relations offensive. The United States can help the public to delegitimize the terrorists themselves by better use of the media.[67] As the propaganda war becomes an increasingly important dimension of the terrorist's offensive, counter measures become absolutely essential. The cost of losing the propaganda battle will

---

[65] Stephen Tanner, "Indomitable Afghanistan," *Military History*, August/September, 2009, 33-35.
[66] Dunlap, *supra* note 15, at 36.
[67] *Id.* at 36.

result in diminished support from the home front, deficiencies in war funding, and difficulties for the military in recruiting volunteers. In addition, coalition partner nations may not commit to long-term strategies for ultimate victory, thus reliving the cardinal mistakes of Vietnam. The most effective approach to addressing the phenomena of media bias is through proactive measures. First, the American government must push for commitments from the major media sources to report with integrity. Thomas Jefferson once observed that "truth will prevail if left to herself; that she is the proper and sufficient antagonist to error, and has nothing to fear from conflict unless disarmed of her natural weapons, free argument and debate."[68] While this advice speaks against censorship as a means to controlling what is reported by the media, it also recognizes that the government must enter the debate to encourage the media to accurately report stories so that the truth will be apparent.

Second, efforts to educate the media as to what the law of war does and does not require is an essential element to promoting integrity in reporting.[69] Building working relationships with the media in advance will facilitate this education and foster a clear understanding of operational objectives and strategy.[70] If the media is apprised of factual information in advance, the likelihood of

---

[68] Wilkinson, *supra* note 6, at 62.
[69] Dunlap, *supra* note 15, at 35, 37.
[70] *Id.* at 37.

thorough investigation, evenhanded reporting, and reporting for the sake of exposing the truth is increased. Such relationships will hopefully encourage the media to report for motives other than just creating greater revenue. Ideally, the media should be embraced as a major tool to combat terrorism and gain public support rather than functioning as an unwitting instrument to advance the propaganda of terrorist enemies.[71]

Third, efforts to inform the public regarding the legitimacy of military operations are always necessary, including greater operational transparency. Successfully combating the terrorist's propaganda war by revealing how America's military conducts operations will allow for combat forces to focus on their tactical advantages on the battlefield. Operational transparency will underscore the legitimacy of military operations and allow for the public to comprehend the necessity for the lawful use of force.

Fourth, American military forces must exhibit their adherence to the law of war through the media to combat propaganda efforts by the terrorists. Informing the public about the law of war and acceptable tactics is crucial. This effort will remind the world that terrorists are the ruthless killers and abusers of human rights and not coalition forces.[72] This message must always be delivered in a way that effectively communicates with

---

[71] Wilkinson, *supra* note 6, at 60; Dunlap, *supra* note 15, at 35.
[72] Jaap de Hoop Scheffer, *Afghanistan: We Can Do Better*, The Washington Post, January 18, 2009, at B7.

the culture of the target audience. While it is impossible to control what the modern media reports, coalition forces have complete control over their own efforts to inform the public and media about their adherence to the law of war.

Ensuring that military operations continue to be in conformity with the law of war is paramount to all other concerns.[73] The conception that the law of war is simply an impediment to effective military operations is a strategy for defeat.[74] The mistakes of My Lai and Abu Ghraib must be avoided at all costs. Commanders in the field must be intensely aware that "CNN is watching" and continue to develop tactics which promote compliance with the rule of law.[75] Troops on the frontlines must be fully conscious of the applicable law of war and adhere to them even in the heat of combat.[76] Winning public support requires many simultaneous actions in the propaganda war, but none is more central to success than conducting operations in a lawful manner.

---

[73] Dunlap, *supra* note 15, at 38.
[74] *Id.* at 37.
[75] *Id.* at 37; *Cf.* THE MEDIA AND THE WAR ON TERRORISM 63 (Stephen Hess & Marvin Kalb eds., 2003) (discussing the "CNN Effect" of continuous media coverage during war).
[76] Dunlap, *supra* note 15, at 37

References

Bernard Goldberg, Bias: A CBS Insider Exposes How the Media Distort the (News Regenery Publishing, Inc., 2002).

Jeffrey Addicott, Terrorism Law: Materials, Cases, Comments (Lawyer and Judges Publishing Company, Inc., 6th ed., 2011).

Ronald J. Sievert, Defense, Liberty and the Constitution: Exploring the Critical National Security Issues of our Time (William S. Hein & Co. Inc., 2005).

The Media and the War on Terrorism (Stephen Hess & Marvin Kalb eds., Brookings Institution Press, 2003).

The Ashgate Research Companion to Political Leadership (Joseph Masciulli, Mikhail A. Molchanov, and W. Andy Knight eds., Ashgate, 2009).

9/11 Commission Report: Final Report of the National Commission on Terrorist Attacks upon the United States (Barnes & Noble, 2004).

II. Actors Analysis & Capacity of Knowledge

Claudia Baisini
Swedish National Defense College

Pete Simi
University of Nebraska

Abstract

The operational environment in which Law Enforcement operates presents challenges that span from global terrorism to a very multifaceted domestic situation, composed of several sub groups, each with its own micro culture, rules, values, and mindset. Such mindsets cannot be understood through the same frame of reference that works for us. Law Enforcement is an organization that traditionally is known for having strong organizational culture, strengthened by stories, myths, routines, a certain discourse, and so forth. Such artifacts are very positive organizational attributes, but also contribute to reinforce biases and categorizations; the lenses through which agents interpret a case. Awareness of such lenses and their impact is needed, in order to learn the "terrorist mindset". Armed Forces all over the Western world are facing the same challenges; Counterinsurgency operations are conflicts where the human dimension is very intense, soldiers are increasingly engaged in policing and Investigative activities, and understanding the mindset of the actors in the Operational Environment is paramount. A complex and dynamic environment cannot be simplified or met with linear and templates and classifications; its complexity and versatile nature must be appreciated and reflected it in the way we approach it.

To tackle this problem, the Swedish Armed Forces have developed a concept called "Red & Green/Profiling, a method to learn and understand the logics that guide these actors' mindset.

Introduction

Law enforcement personnel, in general, and counter-terrorism personnel, in particular, are responsible for investigating and assessing the relative threat of individuals and groups who perceive the world in seemingly bizarre and irrational ways. Terrorism is typically differentiated from "normal"[77] violence because terrorists are motivated by a political/social/religious ideology and intend to further their cause through the use of such violence. It is not surprising that government officials including law enforcement perceive terrorists and extremists through a frame of reference that likens them to an "alien force" and/or a "demonic entity" (e.g., President Bush's reference to the "axis of evil"). Yet a frame of reference that defines "good" and "evil" in overly simplistic ways prevents a deeper understanding of "why, when, where, and how" terrorism may occur. These are ultimately the questions that law enforcement is charged with answering. These are also the questions that need to be answered in order to prevent future acts of terrorism.

The global dimension of today's terrorist threat underscores what has always been an important element of effective threat

1 Sudnow, David (1965) 'Normal crimes: sociological features of a penal code in a public defender's office', Social Problems 12: 255-76.

assessment: namely, contextual factors matter and should be part of the assessment protocol. The environment in which police operate is multifaceted and national culture comprises several sub groups, each with its own micro culture, rules, values, and frame of reference. This is even more evident in the case of international threats. When we approach extremist groups, the tendency is to apply our own frame of reference to understand and interpret "them." The tendency to do this results in a mismatch; different groups do not necessarily think according to the same "set of rules."

The tendency to use our own frame of reference to understand terrorist threats and other "outsiders" is reinforced by our primary group (e.g., family, peers) and secondary groups (e.g., media etc.). A critical dimension for law enforcement professionals in terms of developing and reinforcing their frame of reference is the organizational culture they belong to. Law enforcement typically has a strong organizational culture that, like all culture, is strengthened by stories, myths, routines, and a specific discourse[78]. These elements are the signs of a strong culture which, in turn, contribute to reinforcing the existing one. While useful, these characteristics may also reinforce biases and inaccurate categorizations. Such biases and categorizations become the lens through which agents interpret a case. In other

---

[78] Geertz, C. (1973) *The Interpretation of Cultures*, Basic Books

words, organizational culture is an asset, but if not managed effectively may hinder approaching a case from other perspectives and learning about the "terrorist mindset."

The Swedish Armed Forces Red & Green Concept[79]

Military forces all over the western world are facing challenges that are very similar to local and national law enforcement. Counterinsurgency operations involve conflicts where the human dimension is very intense and understanding the mindset of the actors within the operational environment is critical. A complex and dynamic environment, such as the ones that are faced by military forces and law enforcement, cannot be met with linear templates and classification. We must appreciate the complexity and multifaceted nature of the environment and reflect it in the way we approach it. As Ashby well illustrates in the Law of Requisite Variety: *"in active regulation only variety can destroy variety [...]. Since the variety of perturbations a system can potentially be confronted with is unlimited, we should always try*

---

[79] The name of the concept is under consideration and is unknown whether it will be changed. It must be said that there are not clearly defined templates to classify actors as Green or Red, and there shall not be. In order to avoid falling into the pitfall of categorization, which is what the method tries to overcome, other names are being considered, particularly Context Based Actors Analysis/Assessment.

maximize its internal variety (or diversity), so as to be optimally prepared for any foreseeable or unforeseeable contingency"[80].

To tackle this problem, the Swedish Armed Forces are developing a concept called Red & Green/Profiling[81], a method to understand the mindset of relevant actors in an operation area. Red & Green Teaming is a term that has been used in the military world during the past years, usually less focused on understanding actors' mindset, rather on developing potential courses of action (particularly Red).

The Swedish Armed Forces Red & Green Concept is taking a step further compared to earlier efforts. Given the complexity and multifaceted nature of the operational environment, and its actors, the revised concept focuses attention on seeking to understand the actors' frames of references in order to come closer to how they might think, what they might want, how they could interpret our actions, and how ***else*** we could interpret their beliefs and action. This, in turn, lays a better ground for the development of potential Red or Green Course of Action.

---

[80] Principia Cybernetica Web http://pespmc1.vub.ac.be/REQVAR.HTML and Morgan, G. (1998) *Images of Organization*. SAGE Publications Inc.

[81] Red stands traditionally for "enemy" or "hostile" while Green is for "neutral." It must be highlighted that the status of actors can change throughout the conflict, even throughout one day Green can become Red and vice versa, depending also on the perspective of observation. In fact, the name Red & Green is more something that has been inherited, rather than something that has a practical bearing on how the analysis is conducted.

In order to do this, the group must first realize that they interpret the world according to their own categories and that such categories do not necessarily fit the operational environment. Participants must therefore learn what the relevant categories are within the operational context that motivates the actors under study. Next, participants help the planning group by providing such new categories through role playing of the actors and challenging the planners to re-think; some actors do not think according to the same rules as the planners.

The Red & Green group is available to the planners at any time during the planning process and can be called to answer questions or challenge Blue assumptions. Ultimately, the Red & Green purpose is that of generating "rethinking" among the planners and, therefore, contributes to their *Learning* of the Operational Environment. [82]

Theoretical Framework of Red & Green Concept

The theoretical framework of the Red & Green Concept relies upon social constructivism, organizational theories of

---

[82] The importance of learning and understanding the Operational Environment is a critical issue in US and NATO new Doctrinal Publications, particularly referred to Counterinsurgency; this sort of conflict demands, among other factors, that military personnel assume a more police-oriented role. See: **US Army Field Manual FM 3-07** Stability Operations, October 2008; **US Army Field Manual FM 3-24 / US Marine Corps MCWP 3-33.5 Counterinsurgency**, December 2006; TRADOC Pamphlet 525-5-500 **Commander's Appreciation and Campaign Design** (CACD), January 2008.

learning, knowledge creation and organizational culture.[83] The method has also been enriched by inputs from crime investigation, particularly in cooperation with FBI Behavioral Science Unit (BSU), at the FBI Academy, Quantico Virginia.

Constructivism

According to constructivism, cognition is not a representation of a reality that is "out there," rather it is a creation and construction. Knowledge is shared among people and tied to their perceptions and experiences. According to Roseneau (1992), "we will come to create the world in ways that are unique to ourselves"[84]. Furthermore, social constructivism focuses on the relational dimension, stating that all knowledge, even knowledge that involves the most basic daily routine, is a consequence of *social interaction*. In other words, knowledge is influenced by the interactions between individuals (and by the interaction of people with things, as Latour, Callon, and Woolgar suggest in Actor Network Theory).[85]

Knowledge is contextual because it "depends on (it is constructed by) each person's way of relating to the specific

---

[83] Heuer, R. (2006), Kotter, J (1996), Morgan, G. (1998), Weick, K. (1995, 2003), Argyris & Schön (1978, 1996)
[84] In Baisini, C. and Deinlen, E. (2002) *Knowledge in Knowledge Intensive Organizations. The Case of Crime Investigation and Consulting Firms.* Gothenburg School of Economics and Law, Graduated Business School, Master Thesis Series.
[85] Law, John (1999) *Actor Network Theory and After*, Blackwell and Sociological Review, (co-edited with John Hassard), Oxford

event"[86] and by that person's interaction with others. This phenomenon can be perceived as a system of functions, as each person applies his/her own categories to the interpretation (sensemaking) of an event. Furthermore, the interaction among people creates an ***enriching*** flow of exchange or flow of knowledge. The person's categories of interpretation *are influenced* (constructed) by the social interaction with others (and their categories) but also contribute to *construct* the categories that are relevant for the group within different social contexts.

Environments continuously change as do personal experiences and insight. Another dimension of a social constructivist perspective involves the central role of perceptions. Thus the same person may perceive the same event in different ways depending on the context. Kurt Lewin[87] exemplifies this in his equation where he states that "Behavior" is a function of "Person" and her/his "Environment" [B=f(P, E)][88].

We need to understand and implement Lewin's equation in order to come closer to understanding how the terrorist thinks. Because the environment is dynamic and such conditions change, we need to focus on understanding how the environment has shaped a particular person/group and how he/she relates to his/her context.

---

[86] Baisini & Deinlein (2002) Ibidem.

[87] Lewin, K. (1951) *Field theory in social science; selected theoretical papers.* D. Cartwright (ed.). New York: Harper & Row

[88] Lewin, K. (1935) *A dynamic theory of personality.* New York: McGraw-Hill

The starting point for assessing how environments shape people is by focusing on our own circumstances; namely examining the organizations that we belong to and reflecting on how our own mindset has been shaped by the interactions that we experience in various social settings. Too often the focus is on the "other" and on trying to interpret their thinking and actions; the "other" cannot be understood without better understanding of the self. When agents look at the other, they look at the actors' through their own way of interpreting the world, which reflects their own categories and logics. *In this sense, the agent "constructs" his/her understanding of the terrorist the very moment he/she starts reviewing information and building opinions.*

It is therefore paramount that agents increase awareness of their own logics, categories, and how they interpret the world in order to use such information to learn about the terrorist's mindset. This is a twofold process. The first step of this method that will be presented in this essay involves self awareness, which aims to encourage the group to reflect about their own values, narratives, and categories that guide their understanding of the world. The initial part of the process is geared toward helping people identify their frame of reference. A person's frame of reference is constructed by their personal history and experiences within the larger collective of the group. Frame of reference is also influenced by a person's geographical location, group dynamics, and organizational culture. As individuals experience these external conditions, they begin to *internalize* these influences. Internalization is an active but ongoing process that permeates our daily lives, thus individuals are not fully aware of how and when internalization is shaping their view of the world. Culture is a part of what constructs these categories and, in turn, is constructed by them thru the interaction of people.

The deep and sometimes unseen effects of internalization are why it is so important to direct the group to reflect upon these categories and elevate them to a more conscious level; our frame of reference drives behavior and understanding. Because we are not fully aware or conscious of these categories, the categories appear clear and obvious. As a result, we take them for granted; however, what is obvious to us is not obvious to someone with different experiences, environments, geographical situations, cultures, and so forth.

The logics and mindset that we internalize are very hard to change especially since we do not frequently challenge these categories. This is what the field of organizational change has struggled with since the work of Kurt Lewin in the, 1930s.

Organizational Change and Learning

Organizational change represents one of the fields that have extensively focused on studying the dynamics of internalized and deeply rooted frames of reference and on learning. Organizational change and learning have a reciprocal relationship; neither one occurs without the other. Furthermore, organizational change theorists have struggled with answering the same questions as the Red & Green method presented here: How to move away from a deeply rooted mindset and learn about others'? How to learn new categories of interpretation of the world without being hindered by the "ruling" ones? How to take into consideration other "worldviews" and understand them so that we can design our mission accordingly and accomplish it?

The field of organizational change has been influenced by the work of Kurt Lewin; a German psychologist and member of the Gestalt School of Psychology who left Germany during WWII and moved to the US, where he continued his work which was sponsored by Office of Naval Research. Lewin was one of the first to study group dynamics and his work on sensitivity training, force field analysis, leadership, organizational culture, and change management provided the impetus for modern organizational theories of learning and change.

Lewin's model of change process in human systems can be described in the three steps of Unfreezing – Change – Refreezing, and is still used as a basis for change studies and learning.[89] The

[89] The Red & Green method presented in this essay strives at taking Lewin's model one step further and facilitate what Karl Weick calls *Continuous Change,* see Weick, K. and Quinn, R. (1999) *Organizational Change and Development, Episodic and Continuous*

key is that human change is a profound psychological dynamic process that involves painful unlearning, as one cognitively attempts to restructure one's thoughts, perceptions, feelings, and attitudes[90].

According to Lewin, the stability of human behavior is based on "quasi-stationary equilibria" supported by a large force field of driving and restraining forces. For change to occur, this force field has to be modified because only adding a driving force toward change often produces an immediate counterforce to maintain the equilibrium. This is the reason why the R&G method refers to these theories: it is not enough to tell people to "change your mindset, think more openly and more critically, try harder and find other categories and frames of reference." Despite trying to think differently, the forces of the internalized categories bring the system back to its own usual way of interpreting. The internalized categories feel "obvious" and "natural." In other words, the group tends to always return to its "own" frame of reference and interpret other actors according to such frame of reference. These observations led Lewin to the important insight that the equilibrium can more easily be moved by removing restraining forces.

Changing, Annual Review of Psychology, volume 50. This aspect of the concept is currently under development.

[90] Argyris, C. (1985), *Strategy, Change, and Defensive Routines*, Pitman

Unfortunately restraining forces are harder to get at because they are often personal psychological defense mechanisms or group norms ***embedded*** in the organizational or community culture. Externalizing and revising these forces is the aim of the self-awareness activity in the work of the Red & Green team[91].

Learning, Action Learning, and Rethinking

Learning is defined by Edgar Schein as a process of "cognitive restructuring"; labeled by others as frame braking or reframing. [92]By taking in new information, the person/group realizes that it can have one or more of the following impacts:

1) *Semantic redefinition*--we learn that words can mean something different from what we had assumed;
2) *Cognitive broadening*--we learn that a given concept can be much more broadly interpreted than what we had assumed;
3) *New standards of judgment or evaluation*--we learn that the anchors we used for judgment and comparison are not absolute and if we use a different anchor our scale of

---

[91] The full ramifications of such restraining forces were only understood after decades of frustrating encounters with resistance to change, and only then did we begin to pay attention to the work of cognitive psychologists on perceptual defenses, to what psychoanalysts and the Tavistock group were trying to show us with their work on denial, splitting and projection, and to Argyris's seminal work on defensive routines. Schein, E. H. (1992) *Organizational Culture and Leadership. 2d. Ed.* San Francisco, CA.: Jossey Bass; Argyris, C. (1990) *Overcoming Organizational Defenses*. Boston: Allyn & Bacon

[92] Schein, E. & Bennis, W. (1965) *Personal and Organizational Change through group methods,* John Wiley & Sons

judgments shifts.[93] Here the word "anchors" has the same meaning as the word "categories" or "frames of reference" used in the Red & Green method.

How can this be done? The key to this "unfreezing" process is moving away from the usual frame of reference. In order to achieve unfreezing, a system's equilibrium must be altered. This is the purpose of the activities in the Red & Green method; to destabilize the existing frame of reference and generate rethinking (Double Loop Learning, see below).

Furthermore, the method rests on questioning system properties, according to the principles of *action learning*, an inquiry-based process of group problem solving, team building, leadership development and organizational learning (Kramer, 2007;, 2008)[94]. The philosophy behind action learning method is based on the work of the Austrian psychoanalyst, Otto Rank.

"The heart of action learning is asking wicked questions to promote the unlearning or letting go of taken-for-granted assumptions and beliefs. Questions allow group members to 'step out' of the frame of the prevailing ideology, reflect on their

---

[93] Schein & Bennis, Ibidem

[94] Kramer, Robert (2007). How Might Action Learning Be Used to Develop the Emotional Intelligence and Leadership Capacity of Public Administrators? *Journal of Public Affairs Education,* 13 (2), pp. 205-246 ; Kramer, Robert (2008). Learning How to Learn: Action Learning for Leadership Development. A chapter in Rick Morse (ed.) *Innovations in Public Leadership Development.* Washington DC: M.E. Sharpe and National Academy of Public Administration, pp. 296-326

assumptions and beliefs, and reframe their choices. The process of 'stepping out' of a frame, out of a form of knowing – a prevailing ideology – is analogous to the work of artists as they struggle to give birth to fresh ways of seeing the world, perspectives that allow them to see aspects of the world that no artists, including themselves, have ever seen before" as Rank wrote in *Art and Artist* (1932/1989, p. 70). [95]

Single and Double Loop Learning

Learning may reflect a change in behavior (single loop learning), or a change in behavior ***and*** of the criteria/paradigms that were regulating such behavior (double loop learning).[96] Red & Green method aims at generating Double Loop Learning as the purpose is moving away from the group's frame of reference and learning about the actors' frame of reference.

---

[95] Rank, Otto (1989) *Art and Artist: Creative urge and personality development*, Norton Paperback

[96] Argyris, C. and Schön, D. (1996) *Organizational learning II: Theory, method and practice,* Reading, Mass: Addison Wesley and Baisini, C and Deinlein, E (2002) *Knowledge in Knowledge Intensive Organizations, the case of Crime Investigation and Consulting Firms.* Masters Thesis. Gothenburg School of Economics and Law, Graduated Business School.

Cybernetics[97] suggests that a system operates in an intelligent manner when it monitors changes and prepares appropriate responses[98]. This presupposes that:

1. The system can sense and monitor significant aspects of the environment;
2. The system is able to relate this information to the norms that regulate the system's behavior;
3. The system is able to detect significant deviations from these norms; and
4. The system is able to initiate corrective actions when discrepancies are detected.

The norms that regulate the system's behavior limit the learning that takes place within this sort of system. If something happens outside the realm of these norms the system breaks down. Consider the following example: a house thermostat internally regulates itself based on predetermined norms (what temperature the housekeeper has chosen), but it cannot change such norms itself. In a sense the thermostat learns but only in a very mechanical way akin to single loop learning. More complex

[97] A discipline that originated in the 40s from the work of the MIT mathematician Norbert Wiener focused on studying the dynamics of communication and learning. See Baisini and Deinlein (2002) *Knowledge in Knowledge Intensive Organizations, the case of Crime Investigation and Consulting Firms.* Masters Thesis. Gothenburg School of Economics and Law, Graduated Business School.

[98] See also Morgan, G. (2006) *Images of Organization*, Sage for more about organizational learning.

systems, such as the human brain, have the capacity to change in a multiplicity of directions at a fundamental level.

The theory of Single and Double Loop Learning was developed by Chris Argyris from Harvard University and Donald Schön from Massachusetts Institute of Technology (MIT) and they have investigated these two learning processes in organizations. As mentioned earlier, change requires frustration and disconfirmation of the expected outcome. This is also the basis for Argyris and Schön's theory of learning. Single Loop Learning happens when an individual's action is not achieving the goal and the individual adjusts his/her behavior in order to increase the probability to achieve the goal as exemplified in the following steps:

1. sense, scan, and monitor the environment
2. compare this information against operating norms
3. initiate appropriate action (within the realm of the identified operating norms)

Double Loop Learning, on the other hand happens when the individual, who is confronted with an unmet goal and the frustration of disconfirmation, is able to move beyond the framework of his/her norms to seek a new way of solving the problem by challenging the existing norms that have regulated and informed the "failed" behavior:

1. sense, scan, and monitor the environment
2. compare this information against operating norms

2a. *Question* whether the operating norms are appropriate for the attainment of the goal

3. Initiate appropriate action.

The ability to achieve Double Loop Learning is what defines a learning organization. However, as operating norms are usually deeply rooted and internalized (tacit knowledge[99] and organizational culture), they are the hardest to detect and challenge.

The Red & Green method aims at generating double loop learning within the team by encouraging the group to reflect upon their operating norms (categories or frames of reference). The reflection process is intended push the operating norms to a more conscious level (self awareness activity). Through frustration and disconfirmation (the activity of "challenging hypotheses") the group must revise the initial operating norms and identify alternative ones (re-thinking). These alternatives should include the ones that belong to the actors' mindset. In order to hinder the pitfalls of tunnel vision and other cognitive biases, the group also works in an inductive way following multiple evidence and interpretation trails.

Furthermore, the role of the Red & Green team is that of facilitating double loop learning among the members of the Operational Planning Group by challenging their assumptions and

---

[99] Nonaka, I. and Takeuchi, H. (1995) *The Knowledge Creating Company*, Oxford University Press, Oxford

expectations and showing another way to look at things; the Red & Green actors' way.

The Importance of Discourse in Constructing Meaning

Understanding the predominant discourse within an organization is a way to gain insight about the organizational culture that drives it. What is the narrative, the story that this organization tells? Hence, what values and principles guide its understanding of reality and its behavior? This can help us unveil the espoused theory (the label and code of conduct that the organization officially adopts on posters) vs. the theory in use (what words are actually used by people on everyday basis, during coffee, training or in the locker room), and hence increase understanding of how the organizational values contribute to construct its story.

Among the overall aim of the Red & Green/Profiling method there is in fact that of encourage to look at these actors (may they be potential terrorists, representative of the Red Cross or a competitor in business) as bearer of a story. Coming closer to such story can be critical to understand the actor's mindset and behavior. *Schutz pointed out that it is impossible to understand human conduct while ignoring its intentions and it is impossible to understand human intentions while ignoring the settings in which they make sense.*[100] The prevalent discourse in the organization gives insight in such settings.

For instance, if the mission statement is focused on words such as trust and empowerment while the employees most recurrent discourse is about "avoiding mistakes" this tells us that there might be a discrepancy between what is stated and how actually things are carried out. This has practical relevance because the members of the team must be aware that, although slogans mention trust, their main concern is that of not making mistakes and that will be reflected in their behavior, which is how they conduct an investigation and how much initiative they take in being creative and let evidence guide them as opposed to feel pressure to close the case and, hence, force evidence to fit the quickest explanation.

Another example is referred to the meaning that is given to words, which is why the word discourse is used. Although we often use words that we believe have a universal bearing, these often assume different meanings depending on the context of the person using that word. Some years ago one of the authors conducted a study on Afghanistan for the National Defense College in Stockholm. One of the tasks was that of mapping the most important values that drive the sense-making and behavior of Swedish soldiers. One of the questions was "what is most

---

[100] In Czarniawska, B (2008) *Narratives in Social Science Research*, Sage.

important for you, in your life?" The same question was asked to Afghans, most of them people who had just left their Country and moved to Sweden. Among the most recurrent answers was the concept of "Freedom", common to Swedes and Afghans. At first sight one could draw the conclusion that we are not all that different and share the same main values. However, a second set of focused interviews revealed that what they meant with the word "freedom" did not have the same bearing.

While Swedes answered that freedom meant "to be able to wear what I want, to read what I want, to go where I want, and to say what I want", Afghans almost in unison explained that freedom means to have a job that assures a steady income so they can provide for the independence/self-sufficiency of their family.

This is important because it has consequences on how we conduct an operation. If we identify "Freedom" as a very relevant issue to gain population control in an area and act upon our idea of freedom, we would try to provide the people with possibility to wear what they want and to say what they want. However, this does not reflect *what freedom means to them*; hence it is not appropriate to the actual context.

Discourse is then important to understand the deepest values that drive the organization and its narrative. It has also practical bearing on the Red & Green Teaming activity in practice. One of the goals that this method wants to achieve is to facilitate the team thinking about the actor (shall it be a criminal, a potential terrorist, the Red Cross, or a business competitor) in terms of a story, a plot. *A plot is the basic means by which specific events, otherwise represented as a list of chronicles, are brought into one meaningful whole.*[101] The ultimate goal is that of making them see the shades and extra meaning that can be learned about these actors by looking at these elements and thinking according to competing interpretations, rather than thinking in a binary mode where there are only "yes or no" and "right or wrong" answers.

Ultimately, by arranging the elements they have in alternative plots they come to see the different facets, layers, and implications around a situation or an actor; they would come to get a better grip of its complexity. This gives them a broader and richer set of potential actions on how to choose their next step.

Mindedness and Mindfulness

Among the objectives that this method wants to achieve is the process of "Mindedness". This concept will be explained more in detail later; however, it is important here to make a distinction between mindedness and the, more popular within organizational studies, concept of Mindfulness. This not to say that the one should exclude the other, rather to suggest that they could very well reinforce each other; they are however not synonyms.

Mindfulness is referred to as a "*rich awareness of*

[101] Czarniawska, B. (2008) *Narratives in Social Science Research*, Sage.

discriminatory detail generated by organizational processes"[102] or *"Mindfulness as information processing is clear in Krieger's (2005) definition that mindfulness is a psychological state in which individuals engage in active information processing while performing their current tasks such that they are actively analyzing, categorizing, and making distinctions in data*".[103]

Another definition comes from Levinthal and Rerup, who describe it as "a high sensitivity of perception and high flexibility of behavior to respond to diverse, changing stimuli". [104] Mindfulness is a very relevant concept in Organizational Studies, and one that the organization must strive for, if it wants to win in resilience and learning.[105] The concept of Mindedness proposed with the Red & Green/Profiling method should rather be seen as one step to be taken in order to reach a mindful organization.

As will be soon explained, the main difference between the two, and what makes them complementary, is the fact that while mindfulness is directed *outwards*, to higher receptiveness and perception of the context or situation, Mindedness is directed inwards. Its purpose is that of increasing awareness of what we

---

[102] Weick, Sutcliffe, & Obstfeld. (1999). *Organizing for high reliability: Processes of collective mindfulness*. B. Staw,
R. Sutton, eds. Research in Organizational Behavior, Vol. 21.JAI, Greenwich, CT, 81–123

[103] In Weick & Sutcliffe (2006) *Mindfulness and the Quality of Organizational Attention*, Organization Science 17(4) July-August, pp 514-424 (p. 516).

[104] Levinthal & Rerup (2006) *Crossing and apparent chasm: Briding mindful and less-mindful perspectives on organizational learning*. Organization Science. 17(4) 503–514 (p. 505).

[105] See Weick & Sutcliffe studies on High Reliability Organizations.

bring with us when we look at the context: what is inside us that make us see and interpret the context as we do. According to the above mentioned theories of constructivism, there is no such thing as an objective reality: the very moment we look at something, relate to a situation, analyze a problem, what is inside us determines (constructs) how we perceive the object. Mindedness is here suggested to increase awareness of this dynamics. It should also be highlighted that this is not done according to a belief that if we know better what we bring to the picture then we can more exactly determine a situation more *objectively*; this is not an equation where we have a total (context) and, if we subtract from the total our own fame then we have as a result the pure truth. Far from this, what the method wants to achieve with the concept of Mindedness is an increased understanding of the dynamics involved in the act of "relating" to something, in order to provide the organization with increased flexibility of mind and broader and richer repertoires of interpretation and, hence, action.

Mindedness is a term borrowed from psychoanalytical theories and refers to the reflection upon the dynamics that happen inside, within oneself, and of how such dynamics influence ones feelings, perception and behavior. Mindedness, if achieved, is the increased awareness of such dynamics, which allows a broader repertoire to understand what happens outside *through the broader understanding of what happens inside*. It shall not be confused with reflection, another very important aspect of the method. According to Jordan *"Reflection, in a broad sense, denotes a practice of inquiry that is concerned with past, current or future phenomena, such as decisions, actions, processes and events. Reflection means engaging in comparison, considering alternatives, seeing things from various perspectives, and drawing inferences."* [106] Inquisitive thinking and reflection are milestones of the method, and they are used in order to achieve Mindedness: the fact that one reflects does not automatically lead to increased awareness of what has been reflected upon. Mindedness represents such awareness and the active "use" of it in the act of relating to situations.

Overview of the Method

The R&G/Profiling method[107] involves activities that are carried out in an iterative manner, often also in parallel. Overall, it is important to state that the sort of thinking the method seeks to generate is similar to that required within inductive qualitative research: to have an attitude that is receptive and open to "let the clues" lead the observer and let the story unravel as opposed to the observer deciding in advance where the clues will lead, and as a result, is blind to evidence that does not confirm such preconceived ideas. Furthermore, the method aims at facilitating an Inquisitive

---

[106] Jordan et al. (2009) *Reflection and Mindfulness in Organizations: Rationales and Possibilities for Integration*, Management Learning Anniversary Issue 40(4) 465-473 (p. 466) SAGE.

[107] Perhaps in the future it will be re-named Context Based Actors Analysis.

Thinking attitude, as base for learning.

The first phase is called "Discover Self Consciousness" where the group identifies its own frame of reference, biases, and the role played by their organization's culture. During each of the following activities there will be a "reconnection with Discover Self Consciousness". Here the group members use what they identified in the first step as a baseline to reflect upon how that is influencing their current work and, eventually, look for alternative ways. The activity "Develop Multiple Hypotheses" builds upon laying out a plurality of possible interpretations of the elements gathered thus far. Focusing on *multiple* hypotheses was chosen in order to counter one of the most common Cognitive Biases[108]: once a person has made up his/her mind about something that first impression is very hard to change, even in light of new and relevant information. The focus on *multiple* hypotheses forces the group to think in multiple trails from the beginning and tries to prevent them from focusing on one hypothesis, which would be harder to change. By keeping open and focused on a plurality of interpretations the team members consider alternatives beyond the first impression and prevent tunnel vision.

This activity is followed by "Challenging hypotheses"; here the group must avoid the natural tendency to search only for evidence that validates their hypotheses. Rather, they must

---

[108] See Heuer, R. Psychology of Intelligence Analysis.

challenge their hypotheses and search for negative evidence. The activity "Challenging Hypotheses" aims at generating the disconfirmation that was illustrated above in the theoretical framework and that is the ground for learning. By challenging their hypotheses, the group members also challenge the reasoning pattern that led them to this point and must re-think that pattern according to other mental models. Challenging hypotheses is done according to principles of argumentation and inquisition; the main tool used for that are the FBI Analytical Strategies, including Analysis of Competing Hypotheses. During this phase several "reconnections" with self consciousness take place. This because awareness of how much our own frame influences what we see must be always high. "*We can have very good argumentation and inquisition methods, and Analysis of Competing Hypothesis is excellent, and we have very intelligent and bright people carrying it out. However, they think within their own mental models and do not move from there. If the input to a good analysis is completely compliant with our own framing, the analysis can be very good, however it is almost useless. If we cannot manage to shift from it and embrace other logics to develop our hypotheses and our arguments, we will not come to understand more about these people's mindset or the Operational environment*". [109] The next

[109] From an interview with a DIA officer about the importance to train people to stretch their way of thinking.

activity aimed at activating re-thinking and reflection in action is the so-called "Reverse Discourse." Here the group must focus on their own discourse and identify their predominant narratives. Furthermore, once they have identified such predominant discourse, they choose the words that are most used to describe a hypothesis and substitute these words with others that have a similar, yet slightly different, meaning. This is done to show them that often the words chosen to describe a situation are inherited from the dominant group or organizational culture and by continuing to use such words without questioning their meanings; the group reinforces biases that are underlying the predominant discourse. Reverse discourse facilitates critical thinking in the group as members reflect upon the words they chose and the meaning they give them. This part of the process illustrates how choosing slightly different words changes their meaning.

Simultaneous to these activities, group members start a parallel activity called "Following Multiple Lines of Inquiry." During this phase, members are required to start guessing how the different hypotheses that have survived can be combined into different plots or stories. If we consider the single hypotheses as Lego blocks, the different lines of inquiry would be different constructions that can be built with these blocks.

The activities illustrated above, that will be described more in detail in the next paragraph, are designed to bring about two main cognitive processes in the group: Mindedness and Rethinking.

Mindedness

The term Mindedness is abbreviated from the psychological term "psychological mindedness"[110], and here is used to indicate the process of deep awareness of one's own frames of reference and primary categories. Increased awareness over the processes that drive the group's understanding provides a baseline for Double Loop Learning; rethinking should be facilitated when one knows what should be re-thought. We present a modified definition of the term psychological mindedness. Psychological mindedness includes "*the [subject's] desire to learn the possible meanings and causes of his/her internal and external experiences as well as the [subject's] ability to look inwards to internal factors rather than only outwards to environmental factors… [and] to potentially conceptualize the relationship between thoughts, feelings, and actions*".[111]

Insight in the operating rules and categories that drive the group's thinking and understanding, contributes to the group's ability to identify the complexity that exists within others' frames of reference.

---

[110] referred to within psychoanalytical literature. See Bachrach, H.M. & Leaff, L.A. (1978) *"Analyzability": A Systematic Review of the Clinical and Quantitative Literature,* Journal of the American Psychoanalytic Association, 26, 881-920

[111] Mc Callum, M. & Piper, W.E *Psychological Mindedness and Emotional Intelligence* in Bar-On, R. & Parker, J.D.A. (2000) *The Handbook of Emotional Intelligence*, Jossey-Bass

Re-thinking:

The method aims at generating disconfirmation of pre-conceived ideas and revising of the categories that guided such ideas, particularly during the activity called "Challenging Hypotheses." Re-thinking is the base of learning and R&G method attempts to achieve Double Loop Learning[112]. Overall, the higher goal is that of bringing the group closer to understanding actors according to different categories and logics than their own. Understanding such categories requires they shift aside from their paradigms and learn other alternative ones. This is what is referred to as Double Loop Learning.

The method attempts at facilitating re-thinking by supporting the players in the following activities:

- keep an open mindset by working on *multiple* hypotheses from the very beginning
- be critical towards such hypotheses and challenge them; be prepared to think again
- experience frustration and disconfirmation of what they took for granted
- reflect upon what categories drive their frame of reference
- reflect upon how/if such categories influence the hypotheses they developed

---

[112] As defined by Argyris & Schön, see above in this essay.

- reflect upon the dominant discourse within the group and how/if that influences their understanding of the actors, try changing it
- think about *other* categories, the ones that drive R&G actors'

The predominant categories that are natural for the group may be leading the group toward mirror imaging and interpreting the actors according to logics that do not belong to them. The team then must rethink the categories they applied to the interpretation of these actors. In other words, they shall not only change the single hypothesis, but also the frame of reference that led to the development of that hypothesis and the logic behind it. In this sense R&G aims at generating learning.

This is one of the reasons why diversity in the group is recommended: the chances of confrontation and understanding among different viewpoints are increased if the group is composed of people who come from different backgrounds in terms of life experiences, branch of the organization they belong to, personality, and so forth.

The R&G Activities

The different activities that constitute the method are briefly illustrated below. It is worth mentioning that all activities include exercises that are generated to facilitate the mental processes that are wished for.

Explore/Discover Self Consciousness

We have a tendency to focus on the "object", the actor that we are investigating. But we often forget that, as mentioned earlier, according to social constructivism we construct the meaning we give to our context in relation to our experiences, such as social interaction, discourse, and narratives. Hence, the meaning we give to things depends to a large extent on our experiences. So, if we want to learn about the actor, we should start with understanding in what way our biases and capacity of knowledge influence, limit, and construct our views. We refer here to the points of reference the group has; through what filter and frame of reference the group interprets and gives meaning to facts and happenings. In order to "unfreeze" such frame of reference, it must be clear what the frame of reference consists of, what are the "operating norms" that we attempt to shift from. Particularly important, and difficult to highlight, are the operating norms that are internalized and deeply rooted, those that are so "obvious" that nobody pays attention to them. This is an activity that involves individuals and the group, as the group is an entity on its own and, through very peculiar group dynamics, creates its own view and frame of reference.

For such norms to emerge, group members must be more aware of what drives their understanding and what their operating norms are. They must also gain insight in their organization and how that influences their thinking, what is the *espoused theory* in the organization and, most important, what are the *theories in use*[113]?

Consciousness is a term used in personality psychology to describe one of the four processes that lay the foundation of personality[114] and it is described as "*a person's awareness of the rest of the mind*". [115] It is a precondition for change; by being conscious of the self, the environment, and the environment's dynamics and reactions, the mind monitors opportunities for change. Above all, the question is; how can we shift aside from what we are not conscious of?

It is important to highlight that this is not an activity that is relegated to a specific phase; it starts as a first step before the other "profiling" activities are started, but then the group goes back in what is called "reconnect with self consciousness", as a reminder and continuous cross check of "how much of itself the group is putting into its interpretation of the actor's mindset." It is an activity that is intertwined throughout the whole process.

Develop Multiple Hypotheses

This activity aims at making the players aware that there is not only one way to read events and information and making them

---

[113] Czarniawska, B. (2005) *A Theory of Organizing*, Studentlitteratur

[114] The other three processes are motivation, emotion and cognition. See Mayer, J.D and Hanson, E. (1995) *Mood Congruent Judgment over time.* Personality and Social Psychology Bulletin, 21, 237-244

[115] Mayer, J.D, Salovey, P. and Caruso, D. *Emotional Intelligence as Zeitgeist, as Personality, and as Mental Ability* in Bar-On, R. and Parker, J.D.A. (2000) *The Handbook of Emotional Intelligence,* Jossey-Bass

consider a broad range of possible interpretations, particularly the most unthinkable and, apparently, illogical. Focusing from the beginning on multiple hypotheses is an attempt to diminish the risk of tunnel vision and monolithic thinking: particularly the pitfalls that come with Cognitive bias as mentioned earlier in reference to Richard Heuer's work. Furthermore, pushing the team members to think about the unthinkable (what is unthinkable to them) aims at broadening their view and confronting them with the fact that what they may consider logical is not a universal "truth."

Challenging Hypotheses

This activity aims at generating the frustration and "disconfirmation" necessary for the cognitive process of re-thinking to occur, which is the condition for learning. Develop a more thorough understanding of the actors and the team members themselves by thinking over what led to the generation of such hypotheses and, eventually, "change course". The discussion generated by tension between thesis and antithesis leads aims at unfolding new elements and interpretations, and to pay attention to what is missing, as it happens in the "dance" between prosecution and defense in a trial. Challenging occurs through use of the FBI 6 Analytic Strategies[116]

Reverse Discourse

[116] FBI Academy, BSU.

The language used to define or describe something contributes to construct the meaning given to that "something". If we refer to someone as one who has a well establish habit it implies a certain meaning we give to this person habit. If we chose the word "obsession", that loads the statement with a different meaning. This activity aims at increasing awareness of how the words that are chosen influence the meaning that is given to things, and to play with changing such words and see how/if the meaning changes. Ultimately, this activity aims at increasing elasticity and flexibility in how players approach the issue.

Follow Multiple Lines of Inquiry

Unfold *several* story lines, several plots in which the elements of the puzzle could fit together. The different hypotheses can be seen as building blocks of the actors' narrative. Purpose of this activity is also to avoid tunnel vision and make sure that the group keep their eyes open and see that the building blocks can be combined in multiple ways and, hence, tell different stories. Each story is a way to interpret the actor: what he/she is coming from, how that has affected him/her, what drivers are his/her drivers and motives, and, last but not least, what is his/her frame of reference.

Furthermore, this activity contributes to the further development of multiple hypotheses, in synergy: by Following Multiple Lines of Inquiry the group gets insight about their building blocks, developing multiple hypotheses. It is a goal that within this activity the group looks at the different pieces and at how they can be combined, in other words they look at the overall picture and its components, at the macro and micro level, the two continuously informing each other, as the hypotheses are constituent parts of the different plots, but gaining insight over the different plots can inform new ways to go in developing multiple hypotheses.

Summary

In this essay we have presented some implications of organizatio-nal theory and constructivism on law enforcement work. Our environment, in which the organization we belong to plays a large role, shapes how we see and interpret things, which in turn shapes the environment in an ongoing process. Biases are unavoidable and, the authors would like to add, they are a very positive feature because they are an expression of identity, as individuals and as organizations. However, they also constitute the filter through which we interpret the world. The authors suggested a method that is being developed by the Swedish Armed Forces that aims at learning the frame of reference of actors that are relevant for military operations and law enforcement (Terrorism as an example). The method aims at generating increased awareness of own biases and the role plaid by them and then engage in learning about other frames. The traditional theories of

Organizational change talk about the necessity of *unlearning*[117]: one needs to *unlearn* the existing frame in order to change it. We argue that not only unlearning is not necessary, but it would be damaging: the own framing and biases constitute what gives meaning to what the group has to interpret. What we suggest is using the increased awareness of such framing (that the method aims at generating) in order to stretch its boundaries across other frames or sets of rules. Words such as *stretching, enriching, or transforming* would be more appropriate to describe the processes described here than *unlearning*.

Focus is laid upon generating a flexible and creative way of approaching the actor: discover its narrative, the plot. This also is done to foster a way of thinking, more holistic than deterministic. Each activity in the method is thought to generate a specific type of learning; Meta-Cognition or learning to learn.

[117] Schein, E. (1972). *Professional Education, some new directions*, Mc-Graw Hill.

References

Argyris, C. (1985), Strategy, Change, and Defensive Routines, Pitman.

Argyris, C. (1990) Overcoming Organizational Defenses, Boston: Allyn & Bacon.

Argyris, C. and Schön, D. (1996) Organizational learning II: Theory, method and practice, Reading, Mass: Addison Wesley.

Bachrach, H.M. & Leaff, L.A. (1978) "Analyzability": A Systematic Review of the Clinical and Quantitative Literature, Journal of the American Psychoanalytic Association, 26, 881-920.

Baisini, C. and Deinlein, E. (2002) Knowledge in Knowledge Intensive Organizations, the case of Crime Investigation and Consulting Firms, Master's Thesis, Gothenburg School of Economics and Law, Graduate Business School.

Czarniawska, B. (2005) A Theory of Organizing, Studentlitteratur.

Czarniawska, B. (2008) Narratives in Social Science Research, Sage.

Heuer, R. (2007) Psychology of Intelligence Analysis.

Jordan et al. (2009) Reflection and Mindfulness in Organizations: Rationales and Possibilities for Integration, Management Learning Anniversary Issue 40(4) 465-473 (p. 466). SAGE Pubs.

Kramer, R. (2007). How Might Action Learning Be Used to Develop the Emotional Intelligence and Leadership Capacity of Public Administrators? Journal of Public Affairs Education,13 (2), pp. 205-246.

Kramer, R. (2008). Learning How to Learn: Action Learning for Leadership Development. A chapter in Rick Morse (ed.) Innovations in Public Leadership Development,

Washington DC: M.E. Sharpe and National Academy of Public Administration, pp. 296-326.

Law, J. (1999) Actor Network Theory and After, Blackwell and Sociological Review, (co-edited with John Hassard), Oxford.

Levinthal & Rerup (2006) Crossing and apparent chasm: Briding mindful and less-mindful perspectives on organizational learning, Organization Science, 17(4): 503–514.

Lewin, K. (1951) Field theory in social science: Selected theoretical papers. In D. Cartwright (ed.) New York: Harper & Row.

Lewin, K. (1935) A dynamic theory of personality. New York: McGraw-Hill.

Mayer, J.D and Hanson, E. (1995). Mood Congruent Judgment over time, Personality and Social Psychology Bulletin, 21, 237-244.

Mayer, J.D, Salovey, P., and Caruso, D. (2000). Emotional Intelligence as Zeitgeist, as Personality, and as Mental Ability in Bar-On, R. and Parker, J.D.A. (eds.) The Handbook of Emotional Intelligence, Jossey-Bass.

Mc Callum, M. and Piper, W.E. (2000). Psychological Mindedness and Emotional Intelligence in Bar-On, R. & Parker, J.D.A. The Handbook of Emotional Intelligence, Jossey-Bass.

Morgan, G. (2006). Images of Organization, Sage.

Nonaka, I. And Takeuchi, H. (1995). The Knowledge Creating Company, Oxford University Press, Oxford.

Rank, Otto. (1989). Art and Artist: Creative urge and personality development, Norton Paperback.

Schein, E. H. (1992) Organizational Culture and Leadership. 2d. Ed. San Francisco, CA.: Jossey Bass.

Schein, E. & Bennis, W. (1965). Personal and Organizational Change through group methods, John Wiley & Sons.

Schein, E. (1972). Professional Education, some new directions. Mc-Graw Hill.

Sudnow, D. (1965). Normal crimes: sociological features of a penal code in a public defender's office. Social Problems (12) 255-276.

Weick, Sutcliffe, and Obstfeld. (1999). Organizing for high reliability: Processes of collective mindfulness. In Staw, B. and Sutton, R. (eds.) Research in Organizational Behavior, Vol. 21. JAI, Greenwich, CT, 81–123.

Weick, K. and Sutcliffe, K. (2006) Mindfulness and the Quality of Organizational Attention. Organization Science 17(4) July-August, pp. 514-424.

Weick, K. and Sutcliffe, K. (2007). Managing the Unexpected: Resilient Performance in an Age of Uncertainty. Jossey-Bass.

Weick, K. and Quinn, R. (1999). Organizational Change and Development, Episodic and Continuous Changing, Annual Review of Psychology (50)

Manuals

US Army Field Manual FM 3-07 Stability Operations, October, 2008.

US Army Field Manual FM 3-24 / US Marine Corps MCWP 3-33.5 Counterinsurgency, December, 2006.

TRADOC Pamphlet 525-5-500 Commander’s Appreciation and Campaign Design (CACD), January, 2008.

III. Incorporating Contextual Sensitivity and Meta-Cognition into Intelligence and Law Enforcement Training

Claudia Baisini

Swedish National Defense College

Erik Bjurström

Mälardalen University

Don Gemeinhardt

RTI International

James M. Nyce

Ball State University

Abstract

In this essay we discuss the implications that "tunnel vision" can have for Law Enforcement and by extension any intelligence gathering organization. We review some important theories of intuition and decision making connected to perception and visual cognition. We will argue that intuition and perception are informed by the observer's set of anchors that constitute his/her frame of reference, including group and social dynamics. Often standard practice is to shape assessments so they confirm (fit into) normal institutional practices and pipeline(s). The principles discussed allow for assessments that are less influenced by factors of this kind. To do this, one must learn how to "unfreeze" anchors and foster meta-cognition (learning how to learn). We argue that such principles, ones valuable to all levels of intelligence assessment, can be taught, as well as enhanced observation skills and meta-cognition.

Introduction

In this essay we look at the implications that "tunnel vision" has for law enforcement. We first review those theories of intuition and intuitive decision making that take seriously perception and visual cognition. We will show that intuition and perception are guided by the observer's set of anchors that constitute his/her frame of reference, including group dynamics. The issues that tunnel vision raise concern law enforcement and relate to a number of issues common to any intelligence gathering organization. Often intelligence is "tailored" to fit into the pipeline(s) more often than an assessment considered on its own merits. The principles that can "unfreeze" such assessments will take us to a discussion of perceptual anchors and meta-cognition (learning how to learn) and observable or visual cognition. The results can be valuable to all levels of the intelligence enterprise.

The environment in which police forces operate is changing; Globalization has brought the world within the domestic boundaries. It has also increased outreach to areas and subjects police forces previously have had little experience or competence in. This requires law enforcement personnel to be able to switch different frames of reference, in order to understand the mindset of the individuals they are investigating. This issue is even more important when we think about countering international terrorism.

An example known to most of us is the increase in the Hispanic population in the US. The resulting cultural change in the US is a factor that police officers must be familiar with and be able to respond to. The same is true with US-Muslim population. The ability to work within different cultures to develop leads, arrests and evidence means that situational awareness, critical to an officer's safety, has to improve too. The expanding intelligence need of today's police or intelligence forces to assess and prevent crimes requires that staff understand the motivations and processes individuals from different cultures may have.

However, if individuals acted consistently culturally defined group by group, analysis would only require understanding the norms and routine behavior of that group. However, social science has largely failed in its attempts to deliver predictability, which should be seen as an achievement in that it has lead to alternative approaches to understand human action[118], and variations in practice[119]. This, what has often been called e.g. "practice theory"[120], challenges earlier behaviorist theories[121], theories that emphasize the collective and routine-bound action in

---

[118] Czarniawska (2004) "*Narratives in Social Science Research"* London, SAGE.
[119] Lounsbury (2007) "Institutional Rationality and Practice Variation: New Directions in the Institutional Analysis of Practice", *Accounting, Organizations and Society*.
[120] Whittington (2006) "Completing the Practice Turn in Strategy Research", *Organization Studies*, Vol. 27, No. 5, pp. 613-634; Schatzki (2005) "The Sites of Organization", *Organization Studies*, Vol. 26, No. 3, pp. 465-484.
[121] Kolb & Kolb (2009) "The Learning Way – Meta-cognitive Aspect of Experiental Learning", *Simulation & Gaming*, Vol. 40, No. 3, pp. 297-327.

organizations and society[122]. Acknowledging the human capacity for self-reflection has profound consequences for the social sciences.

The critical point here is to what extent and under what conditions do human actors have the capacity for self-reflection and thereby can question the role that tradition, context and constraint have in situation-specific decision-making. Here, scientific results and theories point in contradictory directions; the debate within organization theory is still open. On one hand, traditional organization theory and more recent social theories as well as recent sociology of knowledge stress the ***illusion** of individual, rational choice* and instead highlight the influence that social groups and even artifacts have on cognition.[123] On the other hand, the acknowledgement of individuals' capacity to reflect upon situations and even on own thoughts certainly challenge any ideas of predicting behavior. Taking context into account may provide important clues for understanding the logic of social action. However, human action or its rationale cannot be derived directly from any general set of rules for behavior, but must instead take into account the individual's capacity for intuition and empathy, i.e. the ability not only to see, but also to feel the world and the situation from somebody else's perspective.

---

[122] Simon (1947) *"Administrative Behavior"* New York: Free Press; Cyert & March (1963) *"A Behavioural Theory of the Firm"*, Cambridge, MA, Basil Blackwell.
[123] C.f. Whittington (2006), Schatzki (2005).

Clearly, any interpretation of human action involves both conscious analysis and emotional involvement in the situation. However, especially when confronting different cultures, drawing upon own, past experience in other contexts can mislead one's interpretation. Nevertheless, especially in critical, time dependent situations where solutions do not come easily, relying on analysis alone may prove to be insufficient. Pina e Cunha & Chia[124] argue that while deliberate, analytical, data-driven processes may guide development, disruptive breakthroughs into the new is often sensed intuitively through directly interacting with a possibility set. Accounts of breakthroughs in analysis often explain the process as initially confusing, as only partly conscious, and then a solution can suddenly strike the person with clarity. Typically, such breakthroughs involve a qualitative change of understanding of the very problem or situation at hand, as when detectives solve a puzzle[125] or in the face of unforeseen challenges in a military operation.[126] Information does not automatically provide situational awareness, it has to be interpreted and then one can suddenly realize that something important is going on. Furthermore, emotions have been shown to play a crucial role in

---

[124] Pina e Cunha & Chia (2007) "Using Teams to Avoid Peripheral Blindness", *Long Range Planning*, 40, pp. 559-573.

[125] Asplund (1970) *"Om Undran Inför Samhället"* (On wondering at society [in Swedish]), Uppsala, Argos.

[126] Osinga (2007) *"Science, Strategy and War – The Strategic Theory of John Boyd"* New York: Routledge.

processes like these.[127]

Intuition

In military theory it is often said that "*The human mind's intuitive process is an irreplaceable determinant of combat success.*"[128] According to Gen. Krulak[129], decision making is a central human factor in warfare; it is in fact the foremost means of lifting the "fog of war". Usually, inexperienced leaders under extreme conditions wait until they have gained as much information as possible before making a decision, which often leads to missed opportunities: "History has demonstrated that battles have been lost more often by a leader's failure to make a decision than by his making a poor one".[130]

As far as law enforcement and intelligence is concerned, this is often the case as well. Too often decisions are not made because of the belief that there is not enough information at hand. However, decisions are often made based on the situation and experience as much as the total amount of information. Marrin[131] cites Lyon "A number of assumptions and expectations (regarding how and why things happen) which lead (them) to believe that

---

[127] Johansson & Kylesten (2006) "Hur ser verkligheten ut under internationella missioner?" (What does reality look like in international missions? [in Swedish]) FOI-R-1953—SE, Swedish Defence Research Agency.
[128] Maj Reinwald, B "Tactical Intuition" Military Review September-October 2000 p.88
[129] Gen. Krulak, C. "Cultivating Intuitive Decision Making" Marine Corps Gazette May 1999 http://www.au.af.mil/au/awc/awcgate/usmc/cultivating_intuitive_d-m.htm
[130] Ibid.
[131] Marrin et al. (2009) *Intelligence Theory: Key Questions and Debates*, Routledge.

when certain things are done, certain results follow. A decision, otherwise, would never be made, an action never taken. These assumptions and expectations about decision making, even when they are only implicit, are just as much "theory" as the hypotheses of science, social or physical. It is this theory that helps a problem-solver to select from the mass of facts surrounding him those which he hopes are relevant". That is why a patrolman's or an intelligence officer's discretion is so critical to a response. The factors that Marrin refers to are critical in law enforcement and intelligence because looking for the wrong factors can lead you to the wrong decision as much as not making one or even waiting until you have all the information, which is seldom possible in most situations.

In most response forces from Fire, Police to even EOD, personnel trained to use some kind of decision tree system that relies on action and response to assess and engage in a situation. Reliance on such decision trees may not only lead to harm for the person one is trying to save or protect. It can also place the responder in a more dangerous situation. This is because such decision trees tend to reinforce beliefs that no action is the same thing as a decision and this can make an emergency situation even more dangerous.

Law enforcement officers often find themselves in situations where they must make split second decisions, whether it regards apprehending a suspect or deciding to shoot. In reference to the military, Napoleon referred to this intuitive capability to rapidly assess a situation and to make the correct decision quickly as "C*oup d'Oeil*" or "strike of the eye": he believed it was a gift of nature.[132] Behavioral psychologists have identified the creative-intuitive personality as one that is "alert, confident, foresighted, informal, spontaneous and independent. Not afraid of its experiences, accepts challenges readily, unconventional yet comfortable in its role, able to live with doubt and uncertainty, and not afraid of exposing to criticism".[133] However, the military believes that although heredity and personality certainly play a role, intuition can be *cultivated* and *developed.* Prior to WWII the Japanese called it "sixth sense" and the Germans "character"; they tried to identify this trait during recruitment and to cultivate it through stressful decision making training under extreme conditions.[134]

Intuition is often regarded as something close to a transcendental function; this is one reason why it is not seen as relevant in day to day situations. However, one definition of intuition is this: "*intuition is a developed mental faculty which involves the automatic retrieval and translation of subconsciously*

---

[132] Ibid.

[133] Col. Mrazek, J. "Intuition: an instantaneous backup system?"Air University Review January- February 1972

[134] Gen. Krulak, C. "Cultivating Intuitive Decision Making" Marine Corps Gazette May 1999.

stored information into the conscious realm to make decisions and perform actions. Organized databases of knowledge gained through education – experiences, memorization, sensations and relationships – are the building blocks for intuitive thought". [135] From the many definitions of intuition, three common traits can be identified:

- it is a phenomenon of subconscious thought
- it relies heavily on experience-based knowledge
- it is a comprehensive, unrestrained thought process [136]

There are parallels to this in the Intuitive (or Naturalistic) Theory of decision making. This model is based on the premise that people often use less formal but much faster decision making strategies in real time situations [137] According to Klein, whose Recognition Primed Decision Model is a milestone in decision making theory, the first source of power is intuition, which he defines as use of experience to recognize key patterns that indicate the dynamics of a situation. [138] This includes recognizing what is happening but also what *is not* happening, as both can provide important clues. This ability comes from experience, the ability to

---

[135] Maj. Renwald, B. R. "Tactical Intuition" Military Review September-October 2000 p. 86.
[136] Ibid. p. 80.
[137] Bryant Dr. D. J, Webb Dr. R. D.G. and McCann C. "Synthesizing two approaches to decision-making in Command and Control" Canadian Military Journal Spring 2003.
[138] Klein, G. "Sources of Power: How People Make decisions" MIT Press Cambridge MA, 1998.

see what others cannot. Because of one's experience, one is able to see the pieces of the puzzle that are not perceptible to someone with less experience or expertise.[139]

In their review of the role intuition plays in decision-making, Dane and Pratt[140] emphasize the need to understand when intuition is effective, to make sure that speed of decision is balanced against accuracy. Intuition can be seen as one side of the dual information processing mechanisms humans possess. It is in the first system that, automatic and relatively effortless processing of information takes place, making individuals learn from experience without conscious attention. This has in the research literature been called experiential, automatic, tacit, natural, associative or System 1, where non-conscious processes serve as "mental butlers". In the second system, information is processed deliberately, procedurally and has been called rational, intentional, deliberate, extensional, rule based or System 2.

Dane & Pratt (2007) argue that the intuitive processes pertain less to learning and more to how learned information is accessed and used. Consequently, **learning should be seen as an input to intuition effectiveness**. They defined intuition as "affectively charged judgments that arise through rapid, non-conscious and holistic associations". However, they remind us that effective

---

[139] Lt. Col. Wolgast, K. "Command Decision Making: Experience Counts" U.S Army War College Carlisle Barracks 2005.

[140] Dane & Pratt (2007) "Exploring Intuition and its Role in Managerial Decision Making", *Academy of Management Review*, Vol. 32. No. 1, pp 33-54.

managers often do not have the luxury of choosing between analysis and intuition, but, given the constraints they often work under, have to make use of both types of decision-making.[141] Furthermore, expert intuition may not be transferable to another field and managers need to be mindful about their environments and view problems from multiple perspectives that validate and reinforce the complexity and domain relevance of their schema. Consequently, intuition needs to be constantly challenged and fostered.

Intuition as socially constructed

If we accept Klein's definition of intuition as one based on the "experience to recognize key patterns that indicate the dynamic of a situation" a problem arises: the past experience of a Law Enforcement officer is unlikely similar to that of a terrorist who grew up in a very different context, even in the same country. Hence, the officer's intuition would be based on experiences, patterns and dynamics that generate from, and are applicable to, his own social context, but not necessarily as applicable to the context of the person he is investigating[142]. Recognizing this is the key to "understanding" and "learning" to increase Situational Awareness.

---

[141] Simon (1987) "Making management decision: the role of intuition and emotion", *Academy of Management Executive*, 1(1), 57-64.

[142] Or, even worse, they might be misleading when applied, because the *meaning* is different.

Many experienced officers depend on their years of experience to make decisions. However, in reality, experience tends to reinforce the same decision process, given the almost identical cultural considerations. The critical issue here has much to do the fact that experienced officers do not often re-evaluate their decisions taking into account the bias of past experience which, if they did, would help them make better decisions. This failure to understand the situation is often what leads in critical situations to escalation, rather than to more effective resolutions.

The way in which an individual sees the world is the product of the individual's personal history, experiences, upbringing, personality, and of his social context. The interaction between the individual and the social context has the double effect of constructing how the individual sees the world (hence the way he (or she) acts) and, in turn, constructing their social context[143].

The way we look at a situation defines (and limits) what approach we will take to that particular situation. In addition to "Cognitive Biases", Heuer[144] illustrates the typical methods of conducting analysis work in the intelligence community, and shows how the organization plays a strong role in determining such routines. These traps are socially constructed by the social context, and continue to get (re)constructed every day. Further, every-day

---

[143] See Berger, P. L. and T. Luckmann "The Social Construction of Reality: A Treatise in the Sociology of Knowledge" Garden City NY: Anchor Books, 1966.
[144] Heuer, R. "Psychology of Intelligence Analysis" Nova Science Publishers, Inc. 2006.

interaction tends to reconfirm, reinforce and perpetuate previous "***habitus***"[145].

The Role of the Organization and Organizational Culture

"People construct their worlds"[146] , and so do organizations. Organizational Culture can be defined as something like the personality of the organization. It is comprised of the assumptions, values, norms and tangible signs (artifacts) organization members possess and the sum of their behaviors. Members of an organization are influenced by their organization's culture and, in turn, they contribute to its continuous construction.[147] Furthermore, Organizational Culture influences action and interpretation within the organization. Organizational culture can be divided into three levels:

- The most superficial and visible includes facilities and disposition of the workplace, organizational charts and so forth

---

[145] Practice.

[146] Czarniawska, B. (2005) *A theory of Organizing*, Studentlitteratur, Lund.

[147] There are several definitions and schools of thought regarding Organizational Culture and Corporate Culture; see **Deal T. E. and Kennedy**, A. A. (1982) *Corporate Cultures: The Rites and Rituals of Corporate Life*, Harmondsworth, Penguin Books; **Schein, E.H**. (1985-2005) *Organizational Culture and Leadership*, 3rd Ed., Jossey-Bass; **Kotter, John** (1992) *Corporate Culture and Performance*, Free Press. Among the several models of Organizational Culture Hofstede's is one of the most famous: I will not illustrate it here as I believe our colleagues from TRADOC refer to him. **Hofstede, G**. (1980) *Culture's Consequences: International Differences in Work Related Values*, Beverly Hills, CA, Sage Publications.

- The one that is professed and communicated such as ethos, statements, official symbols.
- At the deepest level are the elements that are internalized (Schein calls them Tacit Assumptions or Unspoken Rules); these elements are not visible and often are not discussed. To understand such elements surveys and casual interviews cannot help, they require in depth interviews and ethnographically informed observation.[148]

This deepest level is often overlooked by organizational behaviorists, although it is the most crucial.[149] For instance, an organization can profess high moral standards in its mission statement while at the same time displaying rather discussable behaviors.

These differences are often referred to as ***espoused theory and theory in use***; theory in use being the more important because it is often unconscious and it actually drives behavior while the espoused theory is the one that the organization claims and *believes* guides its behavior.[150] An example can be that the leadership has a very clear mission statement and norms that portray it as a flexible organization based on empowerment and initiative taking even at the organization's lowest levels (in

[148] Schein, E.H. (1985-2005) *Organizational Culture and Leadership*, 3rd Ed., Jossey-Bass.
[149] Schein, ibidem.
[150] See Argyris, C., & Schon, D. (1978) *Organisational learning: A theory of action perspective.* Reading, Mass: Addison Wesley, Argyris, C. (1985) Strategy, Change, and Defensive Routines, Pitman Publishing Inc.

military words “Mission Command”) while in practice the organization works on principles of micro-management and *Taylorian* control.

The Importance of *seeing* what is relevant

As Heuer[151] states about most common Cognitive Biases, we tend to see what we expect to see. However, what is that we expect to see in that specific situation, what guides our attention, is *constructed:* it depends on our social context[152], organizational culture, experiences, and other such variables. Given this, how does one learn to use one’s intuition so that it is situational appropriate and yields valid apprehensible tactical signals outside one’s own experience? To understand how this can occur takes us to the idea of visual cognition and cueing.

Contextual Cueing

The contextual cuing paradigm, developed by Chun and Jang assumes that “visual context can assist localization of individual objects via an implicit learning mechanism*”.*[153] Several experiments have shown that invariant spatial context can cue the location of a target and that this happens unconsciously, leading to

---

[151] Heuer, R. “Psychology of Intelligence Analysis” Nova Science Publishers Inc 2006.
[152] Social context that is generated by interactions among people, but also among people and things; for more about this see Law, J. “Actor Network Theory and After” Blackwell and Sociological Review (co-edited with John Hassard) Oxford 1999.

[153] Chun, M and Olson, I. “Perceptual Constraints on Implicit Learning of Spatial Context” Visual Cognition 9 (3) 2002 pg. 273-302.

the conclusion that implicit memory of visual context can provide top-down guidance for attention and awareness. In other words, with repeated experience the visual system "learns" to pick up on invariant spatial relationships and uses this information to guide attention, without the need for direct conscious intervention. [154] [155]

However, "objects can be recognized without context but ***when dealing with less familiar objects, complex scenes, or degraded information, the importance of context increases***"[156] The same experiments have also shown that there are constraints at work here too. In short, ***"contextual cueing only occurs when the target was embedded within the predictive context."***[157] Visual context's function is to focus attention so as to facilitate the recognition of objects within a particular scene: we are more likely to look for a breadbox than a drum when looking at the picture of a kitchen, and this helps us to detect the breadbox much faster. [158] Once again, the predictive context is determined by what we are used to and what is obvious to us: a person who has grown up in a context where the laundry is done in the kitchen would more easily identify a clothes-washer in the kitchen rather than a person whose

---

[154] Jungs, B. Scholl, B. and Chun, M. "How is spatial context learning integrated over signal versus noise? A primacy effect in contextual cuing" Visual Cognition 15 (1) 1-11 2007.

[155] Chun, M. In press: "Scene Perception and Memory" to appear in Irwin, D. and Ross, B. *Cognitive Vision.*

[156] Ullman in Chun, M and Olson, I. "Perceptual Constraints on Implicit Learning of Spatial Context" Visual Cognition 9 (3) 2002 p. 273.

[157] Ibid. p. 284.

[158] .Chun, M. "Contextual Cueing of Visual Attention" Trends in Cognitive Sciences Vol. 4, No. 5 May 2000 pp.170-177

clothes are washed in a bathroom. In the latter case, a clothes-washer in the kitchen would not necessarily be so tied to that person's predictive and perceptual context. In short, previous ideas and personal experiences, can bias not only how we make sense of what we see, but also what we actually see, what we do not see and what conclusions we draw.

Change Blindness and Inattentional Blindness[159]

Two other phenomena that relate to visual cognition are relevant to the issues discussed here. These are Change Blindness and Inattentional Blindness. Change Blindness, what Chun calls "the dark side of visual attention"[160] , is the failure to detect changes in the presence, identity or location of objects in everyday contexts. For example over half the observers failed to note a change in the identity of a person that they were conversing with, when brief interruption occurred. Inattentional Blindness is closely related to this; in this case individuals fail to notice stimuli appearing in front of their eyes because they are focused on an *attentionally* demanding task. In other words "*what you see is what you set*".[161] Experiments have demonstrated for example that test subjects focused on observing players passing a ball to each other

---

[159] Chun, M. and Marois, R. "The dark side of visual attention" Current Opinion in Neurobiology 12. XXX 2002

[160] Ibid. p.1

[161] Most, S. and Scholl, B. (Yale University), Crifford E. (Harvard University), and Simons D.J. (University of Illinois) "What you see is what you set: Sustained Inattentional Blindness and the Capture of Awareness" Psychological Review Vol. 112, No.1, 2005, p. 217-242.

failed noticing a man in a gorilla costume who suddenly appeared on the scene. While Inattentional Blindness can be detected almost immediately, Change Blindness is often more difficult to detect even when the subject expects and actively searches for changes like these.[162]

So, research suggests that "our expectations and knowledge of a scene influence how we perceive objects associated with that scene. *Identification of objects is impaired when the given object is **incongruent** with the context of a paired scene*".[163] The contextual cuing paradigm shows how contextual information assists visual search and that implicit learning takes place. This was shown when observers in experiments learned which contexts were predictive and what markers were important through implicit learning of repeated displays.[164] Finally, the change blindness paradigm helps explain why it is so often difficult to detect change. It also demonstrates how critical attention can be when it comes to perceiving and making sense of change.

The (im)possibilities of meta-cognition and reflection-in-action

With Flavell's notion of meta-cognition (1979), consciousness was re-introduced to psychology. This also meant a

---

[162] Chun, M and Marois, R. "The dark side of visual attention" Current Opinion in Neurobiology 12.XXX 2002.
[163] Kelley, T.A, Chun, M, Chua K.P *"Effects of scene inversion on change detection of targets matched for visual salience"* Journal of Vision 2, 1-5, 2003 p.1.
[164] Kelley, T.A, Chun, M, Chua K.P *"Effects of scene inversion on change detection of targets matched for visual salience"* Journal of Vision 2, 1-5, 2003.

return to scholars who gave experience a central role in the learning process, e.g. James, Dewey, Lewin, Rogers and Freire.[165] In particular psychologists reconsidered the role that William James gave to intentional conscious experience in learning. In a similar vein, and also linked to Dewey's pragmatism, Schön (1983) emphasized the role of reflection-in-action within organization theory. [166] A review of decades' research into sense making and situated cognition shows that cognition is more fragile and less transparent than earlier assumed.[167] These findings are in line with practice theory's assumption about the conditions that inform human action: it is the outcome of what the situation *allows* for and what people *choose* to do. Hence, society, activity and individuals equally matter and different individuals may play the same hand differently according to the flow of the game.[168]

While reflection is certainly important, the conditions for it to happen have been increasingly qualified. In organization theory as in psychology, these concerns have been associated with the notion of mindfulness. Jordan et al (2009) argued that mindfulness can be seen as a prerequisite for reflection-in-action.[169] In line with

---

[165] Kolb & Kolb. (2009).

[166] Yanow & Tsoukas. (2009) "What is Reflection-in-action? A Phenomenological Account, *Journal of Management Studies*, 46:8, pp. 1339-1364.

[167] Elsbach et al (2005) "Identifying Situated Cognition in Organizations", *Organization Science*, Vol 16, No. 4, pp. 422-433.

[168] Whittington (2006).

[169] Jordan et al (2009) "Reflection and Mindfulness in Organizations: Rationales and Possibilities for Integration", *Management Learning*, 40(4), pp. 465-473.

practice theory[170], Yanow and Tsoukas (2009) also suggested the major difficulty for reflection-in-action is how it enables the practitioner to halt routine action and be mindful in the midst of social action.[171] Weick et al. borrowed the term mindfulness from Langer and applied it to organizational contexts as collective mindfulness (1999).[172] Individual mindfulness has been defined as *a receptive attention to and awareness of present events and experience*[173], while collective definitions underline the social and practical aspects of such processes. As Weick and Sutcliffe[174] put it, the critical aspect of such processes is the shift from perception to conception, i.e. when we label, name and categorize things, this can threaten rich awareness of discriminatory detail. Hence, self-reflection upon such encoding processes is necessary if actors are to benefit from the details they observe.

While mindfulness is typically associated with an outward-orientation, also own thoughts can be regarded as objects of awareness, i.e. to become aware of thoughts as thoughts rather than as reality [175], hence making the interpretive tools provided by the

---

[170] Whittington (2006).
[171] Yanow & Tsoukas (2009).
[172] Weick et al. (1999) "Organizing for high reliability: Processes of collective mindfulness", *Research in Organizational Behavior,* Vol. 21, pp. 81-123.
[173] Brown et al (2007).
[174] Weick and Sutcliffe. (2006). "Mindfulness and the quality of Organizational Attention", *Organization Science*, Vol. 17, No. 4, pp. 514-524.
[175] Brown et al (2007) "Mindfulness: Theoretical Foundations and Evidence for its Salutary Effects", *Psychological Inquiry*, Vol. 18, No. 4, 211-237.

practice context the very focus of attention.[176] This attitude forces the subject to focus on the fact that he/she looks at the world through a filter and pay attention to what that filter is made of. However, such an attitude of (self) inquiry requires openness which in turn is dependent on one's ability to make one's thinking transparent. Furthermore, surprise with its capability of triggering sense-making and reflection-in-action, should be seen not as given, but rather something that can be called into being through the attitude of the observer (Ibid.). This ability and willingness is also tied to the repertoire of both thought and action of the observer: "When people develop the capacity to act on something, then they can afford to see it. More generally, ***when people expand their repertoire, they improve their alertness***".[177]

Organization theory has been indecisive about the possibilities of mindful behavior and has mainly emphasized the less mindful, the following of rules and routines. However, while these are often being seen as opposites, these two worlds may rather be a matter of difference in theorizing than a matter of actual patterns in practice. Levinthal and Rerup[178] point at the richness of empirical findings and the nuanced interplay between cognitive processes of mindfulness and less-cognitive, less-mindful behavior

[176] Yanow and Tsoukas (2009).

[177] Weick (2006) "Faith, Evidence and Action: Better Guesses in an Unknowable World", *Organization Studies*, 27(11), pp. 1723-1736.

[178] Levinthal and Rerup (2006). "Crossing an Apparen Chasm: Bridging Mindful and Less-Mindful Perspectives on Organizational Learning", *Organization Science*, Vol. 17, No. 4, pp. 502-513.

and ask for further exploration of their interrelation. The social constellation and practices, which Kolb and Kolb call "learning spaces" cannot be ignored, and may be a matter of a design, resource and tool choice.[179]

It can be concluded that learning and training of new ways of doing and being can increase ones' ability to respond to uncertainty in new ways. As knowledge has come to be seen as a social construct, social context has also come to be acknowledged as an important resource for truth claims. The notion of knowledge as a social construct challenges our empiricist notions of the nature of reality, knowledge and our own ways of being[180]: "It is better to be aware of what theory we use, rather than deny what cannot be denied: that we are holding one".[181] Still the extent to which such self-reflection occurs is an open question: even philosophers who devote their careers to scrutinizing own and others' presuppositions frequently end up not being able to explain the provenance of their thoughts.[182] Nevertheless, in absence of any tools or methods leading to any final truth(s), the only alternative for researchers is to make their claims more transparent by

---

[179] Pina e Cunha & Chia (2007) "Using Teams to Avoid Peripheral Blindness", *Long Range Planning,* 40, pp. 559-573; March (2006) "Rationality, Foolishness, and Adaptive Intelligence", *Strategic Management Journal*, 27, pp. 201-214.
[180] Cunliffe, (2003) "Reflexive Inquiry in Organizational Research: Questions and Possibilities", *Human Relations*, 56(8), pp. 983-1003.
[181] Baert (2004). "Pragmatism as a Philosphy of the Social Sciences", *European Journal of Social Theory*, 7(3), pp. 355-369.
[182] Rorty (1991) "Introduction", in *The Linguistic Turn*, Rorty (Ed.) p. 1f.; Lovejoy (1936) "*The Great Chain of Being*", Introduction, p. 3.

identifying and making the underlying assumptions of their research explicit: "Self-reflexivity recognizes the influence of the researcher's values and assumptions on the process of inquiry. Researchers need to confront themselves and make their assumptions explicit so that the reader is aware of their impact."[183]

Implications for Education and Training

Kolb and Kolb suggest that meta-cognition may be enhanced through focusing on the "Learning Self-Identity", the "Spiral of learning", "Learning styles" and "Learning spaces". The latter two require learning strategies that take into account both the individual and context, while the first two emphasize the dynamism of individual development. Rather than seeing meta-cognition as a purely instrumental method of learning, it allows us to approach the issues of intuition or its development without falling into occultism. The emotional side of daring to learn has been acknowledged at least since Kant[184] and decision-making has been seen not only as a calculative optimization, but also as a moral enterprise depending upon character in Clausewitz's era and writing.[185] In other words, education and training should not be thought of a process of recursive progression, but one that involves

---

183 Cunliffe (2003), p. 995.

184 Kant, (1784). "What is the Enlightenment?" http://www.english.upenn.edu/~mgamer/Etexts/kant.html

185 Suminda (2008). "*Decoding Clausewitz: A New Appraoch to On War*", University Press of Kansas.

the identification and development of a person's interest, as well as the fostering of a self trusting the process of learning from experience, seeking new experience and having the ability to learn from own mistakes and others' success.[186] Such self-reflection may influence not only the deliberate information processing system, but also the experiential, automatic, natural, associative system related to notions of intuition and character. This can lead to a language of inquiry rather than one of certainty.[187] The experimental results of inattentional blindness challenge traditional training and simulation paradigms that attempt to reproduce reality (the context) as perfectly as possible, and to train for automatic "internalized and reflexive response(s)". We need to take these representations one step further; one that stimulates and develops intuitive capability rather than one that attempts to provide deterministic answers. What is often crucial in operations that involve Close Quarter Battle, Threat Assessment, or Counter Terrorism is ***to be able to see what we are not conditioned to see***. To achieve this, we need to move education and training beyond a concern with photorealism. It may be in the end more important to use technology to help individuals detect and challenge what others take to be real.

---

[186] Kolb & Kolb (2009).

[187] Yanow (2009). "Ways of Knowing: Passionate Humility and Reflective Practice in Research and Management, *The American Review of Public Administration*, Vol. 39, No. 6, pp.579-601.

The task should be to support staff capability to recognize what is salient in the reality where they are on task in place. The aim should be to teach them to move beyond what is obvious and self evident, in order to understand the context in which they are immersed, and act accordingly.

How can we train individuals and small teams to learn and respond to appropriate cues? Further, how can we embed knowledge of this kind in so that it can be available to staff without the need for direct conscious intervention? To use a metaphor, we want to teach individuals to learn from what they see out on patrol in a specific neighborhood. The task is to help individuals and small teams visually pick up as many details as possible, as well as to be receptive and observant to those details that are not part of their usual context (and hence would be overlooked). Also we want to teach them how to assemble pieces of a different puzzle and to learn how to solve it.

Training for Context Based Meta-Cognition:

First of all, individuals have to become aware of what anchors inform and drive their attention, and intuition. In particular, they have to understand how they are conditioned to approach and understand the world based on their experience, profession, social context and organizational culture. Then we must help them "unfreeze" these categories. This will help them become more receptive to signals or clues from the environments.

What have to be stressed here are those signals which are not apparent or obvious given their usual frame of reference but, because of that, are even more crucial.

We need to develop in trainees an inquisitive attitude and to train for flexibility through exercises that push them to stretch their boundaries regarding what they consider "logical, obvious, and congruent". Such exercises should be based on tasks ruled by logics that are out of the individual's frame of reference. They must make an effort to identify the relevant cues and understand what the regulating norms of the context are. Furthermore, they must be challenged with the fact that if they use their usual regulating norms the context would not make sense. According to Kolb[188], "learning is best facilitated in an environment where there is dialectic tension and conflict between immediate, concrete experience, and analytic detachment".

Students should be engaged in exercises that make them reflect upon the impact of their frames and of those provided by their organization. Furthermore they should be pushed to challenge these frames in order to foster inquiry that allows for: "the intertwining of thought and action by which we move from doubt to reason to doubt." [189] This inquiry leads to the very important experience of surprise, that mismatch of outcome to expectation,

---

[188] Kolb, B. (1984) *Experiential Learning: Experience as the source of learning & development*, Prentice Hall.
[189] In Argyris & Schön Organizational Learning II: Theory, Method & Practice.

which is essential to the process in which people come to ***see, think, and act in new ways.***[190]

Rapid Recognition Training: enhancement of visual perception skills

The exercises described above can foster the capability of seeing beyond what we are conditioned to see because of our framing. In parallel, students would engage in training that aims at increasing their capability to see, and to focus attention on objects that are not part of their visual predictive context. An example is Rapid Recognition Training (RRT), developed by Demand and Rogers.[191] This program is developed to train the neurological capability to identify as many elements as possible by looking at a scene a fraction of a second. These exercises compliment the training and education philosophy presented here; even if per absurdum, we were able to train the faculty of seeing all objects in a scene, it would be almost useless if we were not able to understand the meaning of them. We would need to make sense of what we see.

RRT rests on research done by the late Samuel Renshaw, an experiential psychologist at Ohio State, interested in the brain capability enhancement, especially in regards to reading and visual

---

[190] Ibidem.

[191] See www.observationondemand.com .

recognition. The Renshaw Recognition Systems[192] was based on the assumption that the brain has much in common with muscle and it, when trained, can dramatically increase its performance. Using a device called "tachistoschope"[193] he flashed slides containing from five to nine digits, at speeds ranging up to one-hundredth of a second, and asked the students to remember and repeat the numbers. While there was no practice in reading print, subjects that learned to recognize and remember numbers at that speed, also increased their reading time on books, magazine articles and newspapers. Students who *scored the reading speed of 1,426 words a minute were then put through a comprehension test of what they had read, and they scored almost 100% on comprehension.*[194]

The speed of the tachistoscope does not allow the eye to go from digit to digit and research subjects are forced to make one fast grab at picture as a whole. These principles have been used to develop the Rapid Recognition Training program that is used today to train Target Acquisition and results suggest the training is

---

[192] Most known is the Renshaw Training System for Aircraft and Ship Recognition, a system that saved many lives and earned Renshaw the Distinguished Public Service Award in 1955 from the U.S. Navy. An exhibit derived from the Renshaw System is on display in the Smithsonian Institution's National Air and Space Museum in Washington, D.C. Source: American Psychological Association, PsycNet http://psycnet.apa.org/index.cfm?fa=buy.optionToBuy&id=2005-08109-002&CFID=5645048&CFTOKEN=27492038 .

[193] A device that displays an image for a pre-defined amount of time, usually a fraction of a second. Benschop, R. (1998). *What Is a Tachistoscope? Historical Explorations of an Instrument*. Science in Context, 11, 23-50.

[194] There are of course critics of Dr. Renshaw's findings; a deeper research is suggested.

effective. It is suggested that the technique be used to train a wider range of skills, besides target acquisition.

"Samuel Renshaw's work was not with training objectivity, but with thresholds of perception".[195] In other words, the intent here is not to train the eye to see more of "reality"; in this way it is congruent with the epistemological and pedagogical project argued for here. If trainees could learn to perceive more details more accurately, this could help them challenge "common sense" and lead to more inquisitive and flexible thinking.

Contextual Sensitivity

In order to become skilled observers[196] trainees must develop that "sensitivity" that allows them to identify and "*feel*" the relevant elements in a given context and possible links between them. If we refer to Boyd's OODA loop which is built upon the stages Observe-Orient-Decide-Act. The education and training program suggested here would enhance not only the first three steps, but particularly it could support *learning in action*. This would provide students with richer Situational Awareness and enable them to develop and critique a broader and more creative set of alternatives.

The suggested training method rests on three principles:

---

[195] Ibidem.

[196] See literature on inductive qualitative observation for more on the concept of *sensitivity*, there used to denote "theoretical sensitivity".

1. Help the trainees identify their anchors and existing mental models; increase awareness of how such elements influence what they see and how they interpret it. This is done through self reflection and reflection in action.
2. Unfreeze existing frames ("innate" biases and capacity of knowledge) through exercises that encourage trainees to challenge these frames. The intent is to foster inquisitive thinking and to identify and use predominant frames to explore alternative ones by comparison. It is not suggested here that the identified frames can be "taken off" as if they were a dress and replaced with the ones that are thought to be more appropriate to the operational context. However reflection in action and training can increase awareness of the role such frames play in sense-making. This helps trainees to compare and contrast different frames and to recognize inherent biases. Through such comparison, the grounding and conventional aspect of other frames can be learned.
3. Increase observation capability and *the ability to recognize contextual elements that do not fit the individual's usual frame of reference.*

The first point focuses on recognizing the effect that biases have on the individual's ability to make sense of his/her, and the team's, world. This helps develop a set of internalized practices, i.e., reflection in action. The second focuses on teaching students how to learn to make sense of "foreign" contextual elements; what they can tell you about the world and how to put them into a frame of reference so they make sense. This is done by identifying and challenging one's own frame of reference and learning to use it as a point of entry to other frames of reference. The third point increases observation skills especially the capability of identifying as many elements as possible at a glance.

The three principles suggested here should be embedded equally in education and training strategies. The principles should inspire an over-all educational design, rather than being presented in a sequence. All three are necessary and reinforce each other generating synergies. The process has parallels to cracking a code. The key is usually in the encrypted document (here the context). However if one observes the whole and its parts and tries a variety of ways to approach them (make sense of this context through clues) a solution can result. In the case of law enforcement and counter terrorism, the solution or end result would be more appropriate judgment, evaluation and interpretations.

Summary

In this essay we have outlined some of the consequences bias and framing can have for the law enforcement and intelligence community. This has been supported by a review of the literature on intuitive decision making. Based on this review, the authors propose an education and training design that centers on reflection in action, fosters inquisitive thinking as common practice and that encourages the critiques of own framing so as to learn more about those of one's opponents.

Contextual Cueing, we believe, can be taught through implicit learning. Further, with proper training and stimulation, this way of thinking could become internalized, accessible and useful to novices. This kind of training and the value of its end results merit further investigation. It would provide Law Enforcement, Counter Terrorism, Intelligence, and Military personnel with a more sophisticated repertoire of capabilities and considerable competitive advantage.

References

Argyris & Schon (1978) *Organisational learning: A theory of action perspective*. Reading, Mass: Addison Wesley.

Argyris (1985) *Strategy, Change, and Defensive Routines*, Pitman Publishing Inc.

Argyris & Schön *Organizational Learning II: Theory, Method & Practice.*

Asplund (1970) *"Om Undran Inför Samhället"* (On wondering at society [in Swedish]), Uppsala, Argos.

Baert (2004) *Pragmatism as a Philosophy of the Social Sciences*, European Journal of Social Theory, 7(3), pp. 355-369.

Benschop (1998) *What Is a Tachistoscope? Historical Explorations of an Instrument* Science in Context, 11, 23-50.

Berger and Luckmann (1966) —*The Social Construction of Reality: A Treatise in the Sociology of Knowledge"* Garden City NY: Anchor Books.

Brown et al (2007). *Mindfulness: Theoretical Foundations and Evidence for its SalutaryEffects*, *Psychological Inquiry*, Vol. 18, No. 4, 211-237.

Bryant, Webb and McCann (2003). *Synthesizing two approaches to decision-making in Command and Control".* Canadian Military Journal Spring.

Chun and Olson (2002). *Perceptual Constraints on Implicit Learning of Spatial Context* Visual Cognition 9 (3) pg. 273-302.

Chun (In press). *Scene Perception and Memory* to appear in Irwin, D. and Ross, B. *"Cognitive Vision".*

Chun (2000). *Contextual Cueing of Visual Attention* Trends in Cognitive Sciences, Vol. 4, No. 5 May pp.170-177.

Chun and Marois (2002). *The dark side of visual attention.* Current Opinion in Neurobiology 12.XXX

Czarniawska (2004). —*Narratives in Social Science Research"* London, SAGE.

Czarniawska (2005). *A theory of Organizing*, Studentlitteratur, Lund.

Cunliffe (2003). *Reflexive Inquiry in Organizational Research: Questions and Possibilities*, Human Relations, 56(8), pp. 983-1003.

Dane & Pratt (2007) —*Exploring Intuition and its Role in Managerial Decision Making*, Academy of Management Review, Vol. 32. No. 1, pp 33-54.

Deal and Kennedy (1982). *Corporate Cultures: The Rites and Rituals of Corporate Life*, Harmondsworth, Penguin Books.

Elsbach et al (2005). *Identifying Situated Cognition in Organizations*, Organization Science,Vol 16, No. 4, pp. 422-433.

Johansson and Kylesten (2006). —Hur ser verkligheten ut under internationella missioner? (What does reality look like in international missions? [in Swedish]) FOI-R, 1953—SE, Swedish Defence Research Agency.

Jordan et al (2009). *Reflection and Mindfulness in Organizations: Rationales and Possibilities for Integration*, Management Learning, 40(4), pp. 465-473.

Jungs, Scholl, and Chun (2007). *How is spatial context learning integrated over signal versus noise? A primacy effect in contextual cuing.* Visual Cognition 15 (1) 1-11.

Heuer (2006). *Psychology of Intelligence Analysis.* Nova Science Publishers, Inc.

Hofstede (1980) *Culture's Consequences: International Differences in Work Related Values*, Beverly Hills, CA, Sage Publications.

Kant, (1784) *What is the Enlightenment*? http://www.english.upenn.edu/~mgamer/Etexts/kant.html.

Kelley, Chun, and Chua (2003). *Effects of scene inversion on change detection of targets matched for visual salience.* Journal of Vision 2, 1-5 p. 1.

Klein (1998). *Sources of Power: How People Make decisions.* MIT Press Cambridge MA.

Kolb (1984). *Experiential Learning: Experience as the source of learning & development*, Prentice Hall.

Kolb & Kolb (2009). The Learning Way – Meta-cognitive Aspect of Experiential Learning. *Simulation & Gaming*, Vol. 40, No. 3, pp. 297-327.

Kotter (1992). *Corporate Culture and Performance*, Free Press.

Gen. Krulak (1999) —Cultivating Intuitive Decision Making Marine Corps Gazette May http://www.au.af.mil/au/awc/awcgate/ usmc/cultivating_intuitive_d-m.htm

Levinthal and Rerup (2006) C*rossing an Apparent Chasm: Bridging Mindful and Less Mindful Perspectives on Organizational Learning*, Organization Science, Vol. 17(4), pp. 502-513.

Lounsbury (2007). *Institutional Rationality and Practice Variation: New Directions in the Institutional Analysis of Practice.* Accounting, Organizations and Society.

Col Mrazek (1972). *Intuition: an instantaneous backup system*? Air University Review January- February, 1972.

Marrin et al. (2009). *Intelligence Theory: Key Questions and Debates*, Routledge.

Most, Scholl, Crifford, and Simons (2005). *What you see is what you set: Sustained Inattentional Blindness and the Capture of Awareness Psychological Review* Vol. 112, No.1p. 217-242.

Maj Reinwald (2000). *Tactical Intuition*. Military Review September-October, p. 88.

Schatzki (2005). *The Sites of Organization*, Organization Studies, Vol. 26, No. 3, pp. 465-484.

Simon (1947). *Administrative Behavio.r* New York: Free Press. Cyert & March (1963). *A Behavioural Theory of the Firm*, Cambridge, MA, Basil Blackwell.

Pina e Cunha and Chia (2007). *Using Teams to Avoid Peripheral Blindness*, Long Range Planning, 40, pp. 559-573.

March (2006). Rationality, Foolishness, and Adaptive Intelligence. *Strategic Management Journal*, 27, pp., 201-214.

Rorty (1991). Introduction in *The Linguistic Turn*, Rorty (Ed.) p. 1f.

Lovejoy (1936). *The Great Chain of Being"*, Introduction, p. 3.

Schein (2005). *Organizational Culture and Leadership*, 3rd Ed., Jossey-Bass.

Simon (1987). *Making management decision: the role of intuition and emotion*, Academy of Management Executive, 1(1), 57-64.

Suminda (2008). *Decoding Clausewitz: A New Approach On War*, University Press of Kansas.

Osinga (2007). *Science, Strategy and War – The Strategic Theory of John Boyd* New York: Routledge.

Weick et al. (1999). *Organizing for high reliability: Processes of collective mindfulness*. Research in Organizational Behavior, Vol. 21, pp. 81-123.

Weick and Sutcliffe (2006). *Mindfulness and the quality of Organizational Attention*, Organization Science, Vol. 17, No. 4, pp. 514-524.

Weick (2006). *Faith, Evidence and Action: Better Guesses in an Unknowable World,* Organization Studies, 27(11), pp. 1723-1736.

Whittington (2006). *Completing the Practice Turn in Strategy Research.* Organization Studies, Vol. 27, No. 5, pp. 613-634.

Wolgast (2005). *Command Decision Making: Experience Counts* U.S Army War College Carlisle Barracks.

Yanow and Tsoukas (2009). *What is Reflection-in-action? A Phenomenological Account*, Journal of Management Studies, 46:8, pp. 1339-1364.

Yanow (2009). *Ways of Knowing: Passionate Humility and Reflective Practice in Research and Management.* The American Review of Public Administration, Vol. 39, No. 6, pp. 579-601.

IV. Spotting and Assessing Potential Confidential Human Sources Using the Group Analysis Protocol (GAP)

Andrew J. Bringuel, II

Federal Bureau of Investigation

Don Gemeinhardt

RTI International

Jenelle C. Janowicz

Federal Bureau of Investigation

Greg Weaver

University of Auburn

Abstract

Identifying potential confidential human sources (CHS) in criminal groups is an effective way of proactively neutralizing the criminal actions of the group. In order to spot and assess the potential source, law enforcement officers use a variety of techniques. The idea that certain individuals are more susceptible to exploitation based on personality traits is a new way of spotting and assessing potential CHSs. This essay will explore how groups recruit from all of humanity and therefore are made up of many personalities. While the group may have one singular mindset based on the group's ideology, members of the group may not all believe in the cause at the same level. If certain personalities have a propensity toward fanatic behavior others might be prone to belief levels less than that of a fanatic. If properly targeted, these individuals might be exploitable against the group. To date, there is no empirical research that looks at the levels of belief to "causes" and specifically examines how members of terrorist organizations might be exploited based on their personality traits. Thus it would be an important step in systematically documenting personality traits imbedded in typologies of believers in mass movements. This essay will outline similarities and distinctions between inclusive and exclusive mass movements, the process of personal identification, radicalization, and the resulting typologies of believers. The essay will outline the Group Analysis Protocol

(GAP) as a possible assessment tool for identifying (spotting and assessing) potential exploitable members of groups. This will be an important first step in outlining a potential field research project testing the GAP as a spotting and assessment tool in developing CHSs.

According to Eric Hoffer the distance between two fanatics of opposing causes is closer than the distance between the fanatic and the moderate of the same cause, meaning that while it might be more rare for the fanatic to convert to an opposite viewpoint, if he/she does they often embrace their new group identity (GI) with the same zeal and passion held for the old cause. Why is this? Could it be that some people are simply more prone to accepting a group's identity while relinquishing their own personal identity, therefore becoming radicalized? If some individuals are more inclined to fanaticism than others, and this zeal is based on certain personality traits, law enforcement officers should be able to spot (identify) and assess those characteristics through direct and in-direct observations. Using an analytic tool such as the Group Analysis Protocol (GAP) to assist during the spotting and assessing process should increase the efficiency and effectiveness of developing confidential human sources (CHS).

Still, it is a difficult, yet not impossible task, to change the mindset of an unwavering true believer (fanatic). One must first separate the group identity from the target so that they can reclaim their own personal identity. Using dialogue and avoiding discussion, providing the right anchors articulated into definitions that create an acceptable counter-narrative can create the right environment to introduce alternative truths. These truths maybe acceptable to the potential source if separated from the group identity (GI) they have totally accepted. Often this means creating a crisis of conscience, where the subject's trust between themselves and their accepted GI is challenged and they feel betrayed by the "cause." Given the right environment and crisis of conscience, the fanatic may reject what they have learned from the group to be untrue and perhaps embrace a new course. Otherwise religions, armies, and other groups would not have converts.

What does this possibility suggest about the exploitability of two moderates of opposing views? It could mean that moderates retain more of their personal identity (PI) from the group and therefore more willing to accept alternative truths. These individuals might respond better to a direct approach and discussion leading to personal opportunities.

It could mean that in any group, or mass movement individuals could be divided into two large categories called Radical True Believer (RTB) or Group Member (GM). From these two broad categories, the individual, based on how willing they are to accept the group's identity, will rationalize their behavior based on personal incentives or "anchors." The RTB can further be broken into sub-sets that include the violent radical true believer (VRTB), criminal violent radical true believer (CVRTB), criminal non-violent radical true believer (CNVRTB), and the suicidal criminal violent radical true believer (SCVRTB). All the true believers are radicalized and believe they own the absolute truth regarding the group's cause and are currently unwilling to accept any alternative truths. The RTB and VRTB are in fact law abiders while the rest are, by definition, criminals and perhaps terrorists. All RTBs might belong to a terrorist organization. Still one does not have to be an RTB to be a member of a group. The other category includes group members, but also includes the violent group member (VGM), criminal violent group member (CVGM), criminal non-violent group member (CNVGM), and the suicidal criminal group member (SCGM) and like the RTB, the GM and VGM are law abiders while the rest are criminals. A research question not answered in this paper is whether a criminal GM acting violently without interest in advancing a political or social claim should be defined as a terrorist or simply a criminal? This paper is more interested in exploring the member that is most exploitable as a confidential human source (CHS).

While the RTB convert may be more committed to the cause and willing to self-sacrifice for the sake of the group, the GM moderate offers the best opportunity for exploitation when offered personal incentives or personal anchors. Why is this so? It is possible that the moderate is not as "committed" to the cause as the unwavering fanatic. Alternatively, personality traits may also play a role. Furthermore, a moderate, or "affilative" [*sic*] believer may be less influenced by the situational environment or group dynamics (external factors), than personal internal drivers. All members of a group have to filter experienced events internally as they relinquish PI for GI. It is how the individual allows "anchors" to affect him/her that determines the level of acceptance the member has regarding the group's mind-set. Anchors are nothing more than biographical triggers or motivating events that draw positive or negative emotions from an individual. Anchors can be social or culturally-based, value based, or material incentives articulated into definitions that make up a narrative or ideology. A martyr maybe as effective an anchor in motivating a RTB to violence through transcendent emotions as money is in motivating a mercenary GM to act the same way.

Do transcendent emotions, or those emotions that come from faith, inspiration, or trust such as moral elevation, admiration, and compassion have as much effect as negative empirical emotions that a person experiences like fear and anger in shaping the CVRTB mindset? How does emotional intelligence affect the level of radicalization? Modern theorists agree that emotions influence what people perceive, learn, and remember, and they play an important part in personality development. All members are influenced by the way they process biographical triggers from their past, draw inspiration from the group's anchors, the situational environment they find themselves in, the level of group identity they assume, and the level of personal identity they retain, forming a complex calculus that helps shape mind-sets, attitudes, rationalizations, and behaviors. It is not so much the experience itself, but rather the way the individual interpreted the events and allowed the experience to affect his/her development of opinions, attitudes, or rationalizations affecting his/her behavior. Two people experiencing the same event may be affected in completely opposite ways. The affilative [*sic*] true believer may offer a better chance for exploitation because they are more willing to accept alternative truths, are more likely to be influenced by changing environments, have a more developed emotional intelligence, and have personality characteristics that make them more of a group member willing to use critical thinking skills that lead to less rigid mind-sets than the unwavering radicalized (fanatical) true believer. The ability to challenge one's own mind-sets is the key to avoiding cognitive bias and critical to new learning.

For the purposes of this essay, a group is defined as a collection of two or more individuals with a stable relationship between them, who share common goals and who perceive themselves as belonging to a group. They will share similar goals if they want to conduct tasks, or they may want to be together to satisfy social needs (Jenkins, 2003). Since trust is defined as predictability of behavior in a stable relationship, we will make the assumption that members of the groups we are describing share some level of trust, but the assumption includes that the level of trust varies from person to person, and from environment to environment, depending on the way the individual allows these influences to affect him/her. Is the RTB more committed to their beliefs because of internal processes? Does he/she possess certain narcissistic personality traits that allow him/her to believe they own the absolute truth (moral upper ground), and are they more inclined to become not only indoctrinated but inoculated by the cause? What role does personality play on the effects of transcendent and empirical emotions that shape the CVRTB mindset? Can law enforcement create environments that alter or exploit these affects in developing human sources combating terrorism? These important questions illustrate a number of research areas that warrant further attention.

The idea of groups acting collectively for the common good (group action), herein called mass movements, is commonly studied in social sciences. Eric Hoffer's book *True Believer* is perhaps the best study of the make up and progression of mass movements, and his thoughts are often used by other social scientists. Hoffer looked at mass movements but did not really distinguish between "good-guy" movements and "bad-guy" movements, or what in this essay are referred to as inclusive mass movements and exclusive mass movements, respectively. While Hoffer stated that all mass movements require self-sacrifice for the collective whole during the active phase of the movement, he really did not differentiate characteristics between movements, with one exception. Hoffer stated that mature mass movements could evolve into practical organizations and allow members opportunities for self-determination as opposed to self-sacrifice for the collective whole (Hoffer, 1951). While this is true with organizations that have established institutions, there are differences in characteristics between inclusive and exclusive mass movements that in part affect the behaviors of each groups' membership. In short, inclusive mass movements are those movements that promote a tolerant, peaceful, and open agenda that includes a diverse population encouraging dialogue, discussion, operates with virtue, introspection, and reform, whereas the exclusive mass movement promotes intolerance, uses violence as a means to their end state, survives on groupthink, operates without virtue, and discourages reform. Still it is true that both types of movements have much in common in terms of processing their members through the indoctrination , initiation, education, radicalization, and rationalization process. In both types of movements the goal of both groups is to have common interests and goals, allowing them to act in a unified or collective manner when necessary to achieve their mass movement's objectives (Olson, 1971).

If it is true that all mass movements draw from the same humanity, and therefore the same minds (Hoffer, 1951), then it stands to reason that all members of a group personally identify with the group's value system (ideology) in varying degrees. Certainly all FBI Agents believe in the organization's "cause" at some level, but because the FBI hires many different persons (and personalities) that come to the bureau with different motives, it stands to reason that some will become RTBs or even VRTBs while others may be GMs or possibly VGMs based on how much of their personal identity they are willing to give to the group. These members might be further defined as unwavering, affilative [*sic*], opportunistic, fledgling, or other types of true believers as defined later in this essay.

All mass movements develop RTBs who are enthusiastic unwavering true believers who hold fervent hope and an unquestioned belief that they alone own the absolute truth. Fanatic's behaviors can range from activists to extremists and even terrorists. The activist stays within the law and publicly demonstrates their position against the government or target of their protest. The extremist commits non-violent criminal actions in furtherance of their political or social objective, but since their acts are non-violent and do not target people or property, they can not be considered terrorists. The terrorist however, uses violence against people or property in order to intimidate the government of a segment of the population in furtherance of a political or social goal. The activist RTB might be as unwavering as the terrorist with the behavior the only distinguishing factor making the latter a

CVRTB. Activist movements might be inclusive mass movements but some mass movements (exclusive ones) promote hatred, intolerance, violence, and criminal violent radicalize true believers who choose terrorist tactics over peaceful ones. All mass movements demand obedience and an unquestioning faith of its members. As a result, any mass movement is capable of initiating or creating spectacular change, be it reform, redress, or revolution. Central to the purpose of the mass movement is unified action and self-sacrifice, which allows the unwavering RTB to personally identify more strongly with the group's goals and objectives (the "cause") rather than their own personal interests. In certain mass movements hatred unifies the collective whole, and Hoffer (1951) points out that a mass movement can rise without a belief in a God but not without a belief in a devil (or some personification of evil). Furthermore, that "devil" can change. For example: Osama bin Laden[1] first portrayed the Soviet Union in this fashion and following the Soviet-Afghan war, the United States assumed this role. No doubt, another target would be chosen to continue this exclusive mass movement.

According to Louise Richardson, there are three pre-requisites to become a radicalized terrorist, including "...a disaffected individual, an enabling community (group), and a

[1] Osama bin Laden was a mujahidin fighter against the Soviet Union who rose to power and later challenged the United States with a series of terrorist attacks as the leader of the Al Qaeda exclusive mass movement.

legitimizing ideology" (Richardson, 2007, p.3). The process of radicalization is merely one phase of developing the CVRTB mindset. The process begins with personal identification and the seeking of individuals who share similar beliefs or ideology. This onset often leads to the development of a group identity through indoctrination, initiation, education, radicalization, and rationalization often leading to groupthink. Furthermore each step has certain and specific processes for example indoctrination includes personal motivations for joining the group (biographical triggers, personality, and biology), introduction to group's anchors, definitions, and narratives, introducing a new social contract (group's rules or laws), repetitive use of group pledge or oath, often assigning a new personal name and often assigning a new group name. The next stage is initiation which includes isolation of the new recruit in most cases, surrendering personal identity in favor of the group's, maybe including a uniform, tattoo, other identifier, tests for standards of behavior/performance including physical and mental, tests of obedience, tests of conformity and loyalty including initiation (hazing) rites, ceremonies, or customs. The next stage is education which includes studying the group's, history, culture, as well as their narrative (ideology and social contract) and testing the recruit's knowledge regarding group's ideology and social contract. Some but not all members may become radicalized which includes acts of conformity and loyalty (can be activist (law abiding), extremist (law breaking but nonviolent), or terrorist (law breaking and violence against people or property). Finally before a behavioral decision is made the group member uses rationalization or explanations or reasoning for behaviors for law abiding or law breaking. Some believers maybe more influenced by the situational environment, personal anchors, or groupthink (affiliative GM) than a belief in the cause, while others (unwavering RTB) maybe more influenced by personal conviction to the absolute truth. This process for both inclusive and exclusive mass movements often takes place in isolation of alternative truths, which can lead to the radicalization or "inoculation" of all opposing truths for the RTBs. What often follows is an increased emotional bias which influences the motivation of the true believer and also allows for the rationalization of violence against the targeted enemy. Looking more closely, one can see that personality is a key to our identity. Personality can be defined as a dynamic and organized set of characteristics possessed by a person that uniquely influences his or her cognitions (information processing), motivations, and behaviors in various situations (Ryckman, 2007).

People generally join groups because they personally see themselves identifying with it. However, people also join groups by conscription. They are "drafted" into an army, grow up in a particular religion, or placed in a group arbitrarily because of a job assignment, etc. There is a wide variance among believers of any group because humans are motivated by different anchors and are affected by an almost unlimited number of variables. Whether it is a religion, political movement, army, police force, criminal syndicate, or terrorist group there are those members who are unwavering in their commitment and loyalty. At the same time, there are members who say they believe but do so in word rather than deed. For them the "cause" is not "the cause."

While the main determinants of human behavior include the social group environments humans find themselves in related to those associations, the individual's own cognitive processes, and his or her biology, the first step in developing an unwavering RTB is personal identification. Yet in every group there is a variance in terms of the level of commitment. If all members of an organization were unwavering RTB, there would be no informants in criminal enterprises and the FBI would have no spies like Robert Philip Hanssen, Earl Pitts, or Richard Miller[2]. In all cases there are very different motivators for joining groups but very similar processes involved during the indoctrination process.

All mass movements, whether exclusive or inclusive, require new recruits and converts to go through similar steps in order to gain membership. Exclusive groups go through phases of recruitment and at times are highly selective. For practical and

---

[2] Miller, Pitts, and Hanssen represent three FBI Agent's who were compromised by Soviet KGB and were convicted of their crimes.

realistic reasons, terrorists tend to come from smaller exclusive mass movements. There are a number of reasons why terror groups are small including the fewer people that know about a crime the better chance there is of not getting caught. In fact, it is no easy task to get larger groups to act for the benefit of the whole unless there are incentives or coercion. Even when the Klu Klux Klan had tens of thousands of members, the number of terrorists in the group were relatively small. All mass movements require the following:

* Indoctrination – Whether it is a new US Army recruit or member of a terrorist organization, recruits join for a number of different reasons and have a multitude of personalities. Most inclusive or exclusive mass movements introduced the organization's culture, history, strategy, and perhaps their tactics for achieving their strategy to the new recruit.

*New social contract – The new member is given a new set of rules to live by, and these new rules or laws include consequences if not followed. This could be the military code of conduct or a terrorist organization's manifesto. Often times the exclusive mass movement produces this document for everyone to see.

*Surrender Identity – The new military recruit often arrives to basic training with long hair, and a number of personal belongings. The terrorist recruit also brings their own identity to the organization, but they are all asked to surrender their personal identity and may in fact receive a uniform, new name, or other identifier to further blend the recruits as one cohort. Of course, this practice promotes a homogenous environment and an esprit de corps.
*Adopt new language (slang) – Very often an organization has its own language, whether it is the US Military acronyms or a street gang using slang terms, phrases, or symbols. Some religious exclusive mass movements require recruits to learn new rituals or rights.
* Repetitive use of group pledge or oath – All mass movements have an oath which could be the oath of a government office, a vow of loyalty to Al Qaeda or Osama bin Laden (called Baya) (Sageman, 2004), or Omerta in an organized crime family. Some religious mass movements require recruits to recite passages from a holy book and the same might be true from a military where the recruit has to recite regulations or code.
*Acts of conformity and loyalty – These acts include a forced relocation or transfer, including a deployment to a

war zone for a military recruit, to killing someone in the name of the exclusive mass movement.

So if both exclusive and inclusive mass movements share many of the same traits, then perhaps they are not as different as some think. However, there are significant and important differences between the two types of movements and the members' behaviors. Both movements may go through similar steps in developing trust, obedience, and loyalty among their members, so these processes are of little value in determining which believers might be more vulnerable for exploitation, or who is more likely to become a CVRTB. On the other hand, looking at the distinctions between the groups can help in understanding environments and anchors used to spot, assess, and target potential CHSs.

Hoffer wrote that all mass movements require the following:

- Self-sacrifice
- Identification with a collective whole
- Have an "active phase."
- Men of words (Leaders/Ideologies)
- Practical Men of Action (Activist Operators/Facilitators)
- Fanatics (Idealists/Soldiers) (Hoffer 1951)

Former FBI Agent William Dyson, Jr. also states that in addition all terrorists are generally:

- Committed to their "cause" but at varying degrees.
- Willing to commit violent acts in the name of their cause if they are a "violent true believer."
- Allow their cause to dictate their logic, sense of right and wrong, and drive their behavior.
- Willing to work with "like-minded" but possibly diverse people to support their cause.
- Willing to risk arrest, incarceration, and even death for their cause (violent true believer).
- It is learned behavior (Dyson, 2001)

The significant differences between the functions and goals of the exclusive and inclusive mass movement are relatively easy to identify. Since both types of movements draw from the same humanity, and therefore the same minds, it stands to reason that both types of movements have a diverse group of personalities as members. So while each mass movement might have structural similarities, a specific and professed group mindset, similar group membership requirements, and indoctrination steps, they are nonetheless different fundamentally in their ethos, morality, and tactics for accomplishing their goals. The US Army recruit is not the same as the KKK member because the group he or she personally identifies with in the former instance is fundamentally different than the latter.

Still, if members of each type of movement commit to the cause based on personality propensities, it is possible that some types of personalities might be willing to change behavior in selected environments, accept alternative truths, alter their mind-set, and modify their behavior. The differences between exclusive and inclusive mass movements and the reason the US military and terrorist groups are in fact different include:

- Exclusive mass movements are intolerant of opposing viewpoints while inclusive mass movements are tolerant and encourage dialogue and discussion including public debate.
- Because exclusive mass movements are intolerant of opposing viewpoints they are likely to polarize and fragment, whereas inclusive mass movements are tolerant and capable of reflection, introspection, and peaceful reform.
- Exclusive mass movements will use violence to achieve their end state without a just cause or as a last resort, whereas inclusive mass movements only use violence as a last resort, and only with a just cause.

- Exclusive mass movements operate without virtue. That is, they might be doing the right thing (challenging an unjust law), but they do it the wrong way (violating existing laws) whereas inclusive mass movements operate with virtue, doing the right thing the right way (maintaining the existing rule of law).
- Members of exclusive mass movements who break the existing law are considered martyrs or heroes among members of their group, whereas members of inclusive mass movements who break the existing rule of law are considered to be criminals or traitors by their group members.
- Members of exclusive mass movements that want to disengage (leave) from the movement or who violate their own social contract are often killed or severely punished, whereas members of inclusive mass movements that want to disengage from the group or who violate their own social contract are often allowed to leave or afforded due process.
- Exclusive mass movements promote hate, whereas inclusive mass movements do not.
- Exclusive mass movements have the opportunity to become inclusive mass movements, whereas

inclusive mass movements have the risk of becoming exclusive mass movements. Exclusive mass movements can never directly become a practical organization whereas an inclusive mass movement can become a practical organization.

- Exclusive mass movements often use negative coercion, oppression, and tyranny to rule their members and can do so indefinitely, but if their members gain any sense of the liberties or freedoms lost the exclusive mass movement will fail.
- Exclusive mass movements rule the will of the people, whereas the inclusive mass movements rule by the will of the people.

The effect of the group can not be underestimated. Marc Sageman, in his book *Understanding Terror Networks* wrote that the Salafi Islamists believe that since Jahili society does not allow the conditions for the Islamic way of life, they must destroy all such systems in order to realize their freedom (Sageman, 2004). This is a powerful message for followers of this exclusive mass movement that basically says, it is "us versus them." It is a hallmark of exclusive mass movements that they suffer from group paranoia through their isolation, which is not just physical in nature. Isolation is the intentional disregard for any alternative truths. In this information age, a person can find mental isolation in a New York mosque or the world's answers at a computer terminal in the middle of Montana. Sageman asserts that isolation was critical for the Salafi radicalization process, and the pull was strong, especially when there was the "group affiliation" effect. He described it as a group of trusted friends who join the Jihad or organized crime family members vouching for a new member (Sageman, 2004).

Isolation is often used as a way to develop a higher level of hatred by cutting off the member from alternative truths or through the ability of the leader to perpetuate old conflicts, promote intolerance, and stir violent passions. The leader will often use positive actions by members as examples of a good member. It is the reason movements have heroes and martyrs. This point reflects how members are willing to provide the ultimate sacrifice of self for the cause. The leader may also use negative anchors or actions by the oppressive government or targeted group to further fan the passions of emotion. Terrorists typically are not psychopathic, but will use emotion as a motivator. Donald Horowitz made the distinction between anger and hatred, saying if you are angry with someone you want them to suffer, but if you hate someone you want them to cease to exist (Horowitz, 2001).

In these isolated environments, the radicalization process can take place through interaction with other RTBs, with fledgling true believers learning the values, attitudes, techniques, and motives for criminal behavior. According to criminologist Edwin Sutherland, criminal behavior is learned behavior via social interaction with other criminals (Sutherland, 1992). If we accept that the true believer becomes a terrorist after personally identifying with like-minded individuals, then it follows that CVRTBs learn to accept the use of violence as a valid tactic from other CVRTBs. Sutherland writes about the concept of differential association and the development of self-image. This concept predicts that an individual will choose the criminal path when the balance of definitions for law-breaking exceeds those for law-abiding. In other words the criminal goes through a calculus or cost/benefit analysis which is corroborated by the group.

Investigators need to exploit the weaknesses and vulnerabilities of criminal exclusive mass movements through a strategy that identifies, infiltrates, and neutralizes their actions before members of the group can act illegally. That can be done through understanding the rationalization and radicalization process of the true believer, understanding the different believer types, spotting and assessing the most likely candidate for exploitation, and then creating the proper environment and timing to develop the human source. This is possible through intelligence base development and human factoring and can be accomplished by understanding the process of developing human sources through effective spotting, assessing, developing, recruiting, managing, and terminating techniques.

The Unwavering True Believer

This unwavering true believer is one who is less likely to accept alternative truths or to be exploitable. The unwavering violent true believer is most likely to engage in violence for the cause. In exclusive mass movements the unwavering true believer is often the group's leader, charismatic, narcissistic, and willing to use others to further his goals or ambitions even if that means their death as idealists. He/she believes they hold the absolute truth and they isolate him or herself and group members from alternative truths. He/she is very capable of appealing to the emotional elements of the issues. Any contradictory information to his/her rigidly held mind-set is discarded. In fact, critical thinking is forbidden and may be an obvious clue that the person he/she is talking to is a "nonbeliever" and should be killed. The unwavering true believer is sure he/she knows his or her destiny, and it is usually on a higher plane than earth. An example of an unwavering true believer type would be Marshall Applewhite[3] (1931-1997),

---

[3] Ironically the Heaven's Gate members were convinced by Applewhite that the earth was coming to an end and that they could survive only if they killed themselves. The group suffered from a lethal triad of a charismatic unwavering true believer as the leader, promoting a doctrine of hate, in isolation to alternative truths. The members believed that they could leave the Earth and survive if they hated this world strongly enough.

who convinced his followers to use violence against the group in a mass suicide.

They may appear to be humble or loyal to the group but they are neither. Osama Bin Laden is an example of this type. The unwavering true believer may appear to be paranoid because he/she anticipates being attacked and feels his or her aggression is justified. This paranoia acts as rationality for aggression in a defensive posture. He/she is likely to possess above average intelligence and may have an academic degree(s). He/she shuns material wealth and looks for his rewards in the next life. If he/she is the leader his or her followers become family. He/she is not likely to have a psychological disorder other than a personality disorder. He/she has learned to control his or her emotions but uses emotion to motivate others in the group. He/she often uses a cost benefit calculus in planning his attacks. There is evidence that unwavering true believers may be so inoculated by the exclusive mass movement through powerful anchors that they are unwilling to unlearn their behaviors or to be deprogrammed (Ryan, Vanderlick, and Matthews, 2007).

Applewhite often referred to his own body as a vehicle and he knew he was moving to the "next level."

There are certain believers Hoffer referred to as the fiercest fanatics, who are often the most selfish. The inordinately selfish will lose faith in themselves and attach to the greater cause. They are after self reward including money, power, or fame even in death. In this instance, suicide is a very selfish act and some of these fanatics, particularly converts, are very likely in an exclusive mass movement to be the suicide bomber. These violent unwavering true believers might also share traits with opportunistic true believers.

The Affilative True Believer

Meloy sees the affilative true believer as an anxious and dependent person who joins the group to become a part of the movement or "cause" and is primarily a follower. This person could be a facilitator or activist operator but would not likely assume the leadership role. He/she will likely respond to a strong leader and especially those who make him or her feel valued. He/she becomes agitated and depressed if separated from the group. He/she probably has average intelligence. He/she is likely easy to recruit and may in fact seek the group out him or herself (Meloy, 2001). Affilative [*sic*] true believers might "talk a good game" but their beliefs are not nearly as strongly held as the unwavering true believer's conviction, and they take second place to his personal and emotional needs. He/she is therefore exploitable if he/she feels the group has betrayed him or her or if he/she feels a stronger pull by another group. Special attention should be given in spotting and assessing this individual. If it is possible to establish rapport and trust through an emotional connection, then his or her beliefs can be easily exploited since they are secondary to his or her desires to be attached to others.

He/she may also be quite willing to join a larger, more powerful group. An example of this type of individual is Frank Ambrose, who was a member of the network-based terrorist organization known as the Earth Liberation Front. Ambrose was developed as a cooperating witness by an agent of the FBI after he left the movement. Ambrose's substantial assistance was due in part to legal considerations regarding his sentence structure but also in no small part because he developed an affilative [*sic*] relationship with the FBI Agent. The relationship was evident when Ambrose came to the FBI Academy at the request of the Behavioral Science Unit. Hoffer describes a person similar to the affilative [*sic*], that person being the frustrated believer. After WWI the German population that was frustrated with economic depression was willing to join an exclusive mass movement that offered a new future. The affilative [*sic*] that deserts his cause must find another cause to attach to, as it is not about the cause per se, but the dedication and the communion with the congregation, the group, the movement, etc.

The Opportunistic True Believer

This individual is similar in terms of narcissism as the unwavering true believer, but the major difference is this person joins to enhance his or her person. He/she is looking to increase his or her wealth, power, and control. This believer needs others to see his or her value and pay tribute to him/her with attention and admiration. He/she will likely exploit people and situations. For this individual, the cause is him or herself. He/she may seem committed but does not want to sacrifice his or her life. The beliefs which drive the mission of his or her group are secondary to his or her opportunistic desires. He/she is willing to make a deal even altering his or her values given the right opportunity. There is unlikely to be a psychiatric disorder other than a personality disorder (Meloy, 2001).

The Criminal True Believer

This person is a criminal before joining the cause and will be a criminal while a member, as well as after leaving the group. He/she might have been involved in both violent and nonviolent offenses. In severe cases, he/she will be a psychopath who takes great pleasure in violence and hurting others including other group members. He/she is likely an action seeker. It is unlikely that the criminal true believer is ever trusted by the group but he/she is needed for his or her skills brought to the group. He/she is both an asset and liability because their criminal activities bring in needed cash but could also reveal the group to law enforcement. If sociopathic [*sic*] tendencies are coupled with opportunistic traits, this believer may be exploitable if law enforcement has criminal charges against him or her. Given a choice between his or her freedom and other members of the group, this person is likely to choose to betray others. He/she is chronically angry, and is the most dangerous of all the types for both reactive, (Expressive Force) emotional violence, and more controlled, planned (Instrumental Force), unemotional violence (Meloy, 2001).

Hoffer referred to these people as "the sinners" and as persons looking for redemption. This individual could have been a criminal before finding the cause. Hoffer suggests that in some ways it seems that mass movements are custom-made to fit the needs of the criminal. Not only does it provide a catharsis for one's soul but also exercise for his inclinations and talents.

Abu Musab al-Zarqawi[4], the militant Jordanian terrorist who led the Al Qaeda of Iraq cell was a criminal true believer, who grew up in poverty and a life of petty crime only to mature into a notorious terrorist. People that remembered him as a youth said he was a simple, quick-tempered, and barely literate gangster.

---

[4] Al-Qaida of Iraq terrorist leader **Abu Musab al-Zarqawi** was killed on June 7, 2006, when the US army bombed the house he was visiting. Zarqawi was a thief, gang member, hoodlum and drunkard who found strength in religious faith and then used that faith to wage holy war in Iraq against westerner armies, unbelievers, and other Muslims.

The Betrayer True Believer

This believer simply put, is not a member for the cause but rather because he or she knows whom he or she hates and wants to betray. It is a negative belief structure, where the emotional focus is a desire to gain revenge for perceived or real threats to self or to others. This person may be driven by anger and wants to see the enemy suffer but it is more likely that he or she is driven by a pathological hatred and wants the enemy to cease to exist. This member feels victimized by past life events, and is typically quite passive, oftentimes referred to as a "passive-aggressive" personality (Meloy, 2001). An example of this type of believer would be Eric Robert Rudolph[5]. Often these individuals have a character disorder that manifests in them blaming others for their repeated failures. Lacking emotional intelligence, these types of believers often act impulsively out of emotion as a reaction to the perceived wrong. A prolonged war is likely to be followed by a period of social unrest and some veterans find it difficult to assimilate into the rhythms of their former lives (Hoffer, 1991); often the transition from war to peace is more critical than peace to war.

---

[5] Eric Robert Rudolph was a former army recruit that had failed repeatedly in school, relationships, and work. He harbored hostilities against the government for perceived injustices and after being discharged from the army because of drug possession he was interested in harming government officials who he believed betrayed him. His reasons have changed over the years and really are secondary to his hatred for the government and interest in killing police responders.

The Psychotic True Believer

Meloy included this typology which Hoffer called the permanent misfit. This individual, if seen by a psychiatrist or psychologist, would be diagnosed with a major mental disorder. Hoffer's permanent misfits are those who, due to some mental or physical defect, suffer from an inadequate personality disorder or borderline personality disorder. These people can not accomplish anything alone, so they join a group to lose themselves in the collective goals and sense of a sacrifice for the larger good. These individuals may also be victimized by the group. They might be given pharmaceuticals that alter their mood and give them the sense of invulnerability, making it difficult for the believer to make a rational decision.

The Fledgling True Believer

This new potential member of the group fits the final typology which focuses on the child or adolescent who may eventually become one of the other six types of violent true believers. The fledgling's mind-set is shaped through personal suffering and/or indoctrination. Often the fledgling has been indoctrinated by previous generations of unwavering and affilative true believers (Meloy, 2001).

The movement offers these frustrated and bored individuals a way to be part of the collective whole, and a way to preserve their identity. It gives purpose to their lives and a way to change their plight. All mass movements begin with a small group of self-chosen committed persons who share a common grievance or idea. The small size often allows for the group to make collective decisions and act in the group's best interest of the group. Soon, it is necessary for the group to reach out and attract new members. These self-chosen individuals are often joined by the bored, frustrated, dedicated, and desperate.

Thus far we have looked at two types of mass movements that have clear and distinct ideas about the utility of the existing social contract. On the one hand, the inclusive mass movement that may or may not agree with the state, or it might even be the state, but looks for orderly peaceful resolution to conflict, promotes tolerance, discourages hate, is open to alternative truths, and is seeking to mature into a practical organization. Then there is the exclusive mass movement that rejects part or all of the existing social contract, has probably published grievances (and/or?) a manifesto, operates in isolation, believes they own absolute truth, and promotes hatred, violence, and intolerance.

We can see that while both movements passively spread propaganda to influence the unconcerned, sympathizers, and advocate to their cause, they are more overt in how they proselytize and recruit from the ranks of the activists and extremists. So how does the new member in these two groups become indoctrinated and are the processes of radicalization similar between the two mass movements?

Developing a source is done through the use of empathy, understanding (minimization), and use of humor when appropriate in establishing rapport. The investigator should use active listening, mirroring, verbal and non-verbal cues while looking for common ground in an attempt to establish rapport (and then trust). Trust is usually established over a period of time with simple tasks of small but meaningful benefit. Once trust is established, the agent, gauging the appropriate timing, should engage in a dialogue providing suggestive alternative truths. Other alternatives might be reality testing or positive and negative anchoring.

It is critical to keep in mind the timing of these efforts. The person has to be willing to accept alternative truths and that means rapport and trust have to be established. Secondly the environment is critical and may change depending on the type of personality the target exhibits. Oftentimes it means the person has to be outside the influence of the group, which means no longer isolated from alternative truths. Special consideration should be given when developing sources online through computer mediated communications (CMC).

The purpose of this research is to look at the various elements in the process of establishing a true believer mind-set in different types of mass movements and determine if the development of a spotting and assessment tool for human factoring (targeting) is feasible. Understanding the structure and ideology that makes up the group's identity, how members personally identify and surrender their personal identity to that group identity, the personality traits of the target, his/her biographical triggers, the process of the group's indoctrination, initiation, and education processes will provide the analyst or investigator the intelligence needed to identify anchors, articulate them into definitions and construct environments that lead to a counter -narrative designed to encourage disengagement (assimilation) and/or exploitation. The simple equation will be to maximize the differences between the target's personal identity and the group identity they have assumed while minimizing the similarities between the target's personal identity and the group's identity at the same time maximizing the similarities between the target's personal identity and the "new" group's identity while minimizing the differences between the target's personal identity and the new group's identity. While it appears that there are a number of different typologies describing the true believer, the current typologies were developed from anecdotal rather than empirical data. The use of the GAP is intended to assist the investigator in becoming more effective and efficient in the spotting and assessing of human sources based on their personality typology. This will be done by creating various templates that are developed through more research defining personality characteristics of believers and through field research that validates the types of believers that have the greatest potential for targeting and recruiting as confidential human sources.

These templates will also act as guides for the creation of environments best suited for source development. It is also anticipated that interview suggestions would be provided through the use of these analytic tools, thereby increasing the success rate of developing human sources of information. The GAP provides an analytic tool for group analysis whereby many of the pertinent characteristics of any type of group and the individual members can be identified in order to maximize understanding, better predict behavior, and further interpersonal relationships.

References

Dyson, W. (2001). Terrorism: An Investigator's Handbook. Cincinnati, Ohio.: Anderson Publishing Company.

Hoffer, E. (1951). The True Believer. New York, New York: Harper & Brothers.

Horowitz D. (2001). The Deadly Ethnic Riot. Berkley and Los Angeles, California.: University California Press.

Jenkins, R. (2003). Social Identity. London and New York: Second Edition, Routledge Taylor & Francis Group.

Meloy J., Mohandie K, Hempel, A. and Shiva, A. (2001). The violent true believer: Homicidal and suicidal states of mind. Journal of Threat Assessment. www.informaworld.com/index/ 785037125.pdf (accessed May 15, 2009).

Olson, M. (1971). The Logic of Collective Action, Public Goods and The Theory of Groups. Cambridge, Mass.: Harvard University Press.

Ryan, C. Vanderlick, J. and Matthews, W. (2007). A Paradoxical Analysis of Social Learning Theory as Applied to the Potential Reform of Terrorist Offenders. Professional Issues in Criminal Justice, Vol. 2, Number 1, January 2007.

Sageman M. (2004). Understanding Terror Networks. Philadelphia, Pennsylvania.: University Pennsylvania Press.

Sutherland, E. and Cressey, D. (1992). Principles of Criminology. 11th ed. Lanham, Md.: AltaMira Press.

V. Terrorism and Counterfeiting: A Synopsis of Critical Issues and Research Opportunities

Steven M. Chermak

Michigan State University

Andrew J. Bringuel II

Federal Bureau of Investigation

Joshua D. Freilich

John Jay College of Criminal Justice

James K. Shearer

Federal Bureau of Investigation

Abstract

Although terrorism has become a top concern among policymakers, business executives, and law enforcement officials since the terrorist attacks of September 11th, and a growing body of empirical research has been produced to understand and address the threat of terrorism, scholars have virtually ignored how terrorist organizations are funded. Moreover, there is almost no empirical research that specifically examines how terrorist organizations finance their operations using counterfeited goods. Thus it is important to systematically document what is known about the nature and use of counterfeiting products by terrorist organizations, what strategies have been used to respond, and what interventions appear to be particularly promising. Indeed, there has been considerable effort and resources by private companies to respond to the counterfeiting of products generally, and some specific and successful government interventions, but there has yet to be a synthesis of what is known about the effectiveness of response strategies.

This essay will be an important first step for addressing these issues. There are two elements to the essay. The first is the presentation of a comprehensive literature review on research related to the nexus between counterfeit products and terrorist organization funding. It will describe what is known about the funding of terrorist organizations, synthesizing scholarly, government, and journalist accounts on this issue; and, it will critique the evaluations that have been done on strategies to disrupt the flow of funding to terrorist organizations and general research related to responding to the trafficking of counterfeited products. Second, the literature review will focus on highlighting research gaps and proposing a long-term research agenda for future collaborative work in this area.

Introduction

It was not surprising that policy and academic interest in terrorism grew significantly after September 11th, 2001, but terrorism has a long history and the response following other attacks, such as the bombings of Pan Am Flight 103 over Lockerbie, Scotland, the World Trade Center in, 1993, and the Murrah Federal Building in Oklahoma City, also resulted in significant changes. The 9/11 attacks, however, highlighted an even greater need to think creatively and urgently about issues such as the prevalence of terrorism, its etiology, how to respond, and the key obstacles for protecting the homeland. Thus, the political, social, and cultural changes that occurred following 9/11 were significantly different. This coordinated mass casualty attack was stunning, resulting in widespread fear and panic.

Policymakers wasted little time formulating policy responses, and considerable resources were spent to overhaul the government in order to be better prepared for another attack. For example, the priorities of law enforcement agencies shifted, with resources devoted to hiring new agents, reconfiguring organizations, and implementing new programs and strategies to respond to terrorism. Scholarly attention to this topic has increased dramatically evidenced by the amount of funding, number of degree programs, new journals, and publications related to the study of terrorism. The result has been a better understanding of many issues related to terrorism, but an appreciation that many questions remain unexplored and/or unanswered.

Intellectual property crimes, like terrorism, should be understood and responded to as a global problem. The counterfeiting of products, such as automobile parts, purses, and perfumes, and the illegal duplication of software, movies, music and other products, have had widespread impact on business, governments, and consumers. The costs associated with the trafficking of counterfeited goods are incredible, affecting jobs, product production, and tax revenue. Although the costs are significant, there is little political concern about intellectual property crimes and the public appears to be quite ambivalent about such crimes (Australian Institute of Criminology, 2008). Research by Harbaugh and Khemka (2002: 6) found that 14 percent of respondents thought copying software was a serious crime, compared to 30 percent who thought that it was a serious crime to drive 40 miles per hour in a 25 speeding zone. Music downloading is not viewed as stealing by 53 percent of US internet users (King, 2000). It is important to note that counterfeited products must be developed, processed, and then distributed often through international networks. Moreover, counterfeiting is often linked to many other serious crimes, including extortion, human trafficking, kidnapping, credit card fraud, identity theft, and arms trading (Amendolara, 2005; Canadian Centre for Intelligence and Security Studies, 2006; Noble, 2003; Ehrenfeld, 2003; Shelley and Picarelli, 2002; Shetterly, 2005; GAO, 2003). When one considers the extent of the problem, how products are distributed, and the profits earned, it would seem logical for terrorist groups to be substantially involved in intellectual property crimes.

Although terrorism has become a top concern among policymakers, business executives, and law enforcement officials since the terrorist attacks of September 11th, and a growing body of empirical research has been produced to understand and address the threat of terrorism, scholars have virtually ignored how terrorist organizations are funded. Moreover, there is almost no empirical research that specifically examines how terrorist organizations finance their operations using counterfeited goods. Thus it is important to systematically document what is known about the nature and use of counterfeiting products by terrorist organizations. This essay provides a first step in filling this gap by providing a comprehensive literature review on research related to the nexus between counterfeit products and terrorist organization funding. It will describe what is known about the funding of terrorist organizations, synthesizing scholarly, government, and journalist accounts on this issue. It will conclude with a discussion of a research agenda for future work in this area.

Understanding the Significance of the Problem

There are several reasons why increasing our understanding of the use of counterfeited goods is an important topic to examine. First, the costs of counterfeiting and other intellectual property crimes are alarming (Amendolara, 2005; Interpol, 2003; Noble, 2003; Union des Fabricants, 2004). It is difficult to pinpoint exact costs, but estimates put losses in a range between, 200 (OECD, 2007; Noble, 2003) and 500 or 600 billion dollars per year (Amendolara, 2005; IACC, 2005). Although the counterfeiting of products is not a new phenomenon, research indicates that there has been a significant expansion and a shift from luxury items to much more common products (OECD, 2007, p. 11; see also Amendolara, 2005; Nasheri, 2005). In, 1982, for example, the International Trade Commission estimated that losses due to counterfeiting were about 5.5 billion. Losses were estimated at 60 billion in the late, 1980s and at, 200 billion by the mid-1990s (IACC, 2005). More recent reports estimate that losses are over 500 billion dollars (Amendolara, 2005), representing between 5 and 7 percent of world trade (IACC, 2005). Other indicators of the growth of counterfeiting products can be found in reports of product seizures. Amendolara (2005: 807; see also Australian Institute of Criminology, 2008) reported that "by the middle of, 2003, the Department of Homeland Security reported 3117 seizures of counterfeit goods, a forty-two percent jump in seizures from the previous year. By the middle of, 2004, 3693 seizures of counterfeit goods were reported, and by end of September, 2004, counterfeit goods valued at $138 million were seized at the country's borders."

It is reasonable to expect that the amount and types of products counterfeited will continue to grow. Counterfeiting of luxury items is substantial, but counterfeiters have expanded to duplicate almost any product bearing a name that consumers recognize, including food, computer, automobile, pharmaceutical, chemical, electronic, household, and toy products (Australian Institute of Criminology, 2008; Nasheri, 2005). According to Nasheri (2005: 88), "due to today's sophisticated global economy—with its easy and widespread access to technological advances such as computers, copiers, and scanners—there are virtually no product lines, corporations, or consumers that can escape the reach of counterfeiters and/or pirates" (see also, OECD, 2006;, 2007; Bryce and Ritter, 2005; Luckenbill and Miller, 1998; Union des Fabricants, 2004; Piquero, 2005; Treverton et al., 2009). Technological advances, outsourcing, globalization, the global war on terror, and information sharing have provided opportunities for individuals and groups to become involved in counterfeiting, increased the quality of the duplicates, and enhanced the efficiency of product manufacturing. Profit margins for most products are great, and there is a general acceptance that there is little risk of apprehension, and if arrested, the penalties are low (Treverton et al., 2009).

Second, the companies that manufacture products are significantly impacted by the distribution of counterfeited products. Companies not only lose the profits from the sales of their goods, but they must incur additional costs to protect their brand and investigate counterfeiters. Consumers purchase a brand because it is known for its performance, and thus the reputation of specific product brands suffer as counterfeiting products fail or are not satisfactory to the consumer (Allen Consulting Group, 2003; Australian Institute of Criminology, 2008; OECD, 2007; IACC, 2005; Nasheri, 2005). When a brand's reputation is damaged, sales go down. Companies may be unwilling to invest in certain economies because of the risk of counterfeiting is too great and the investments made to protect their brand impacts their ability to hire staff. "For example, the software industry has argued that a 10-point drop in piracy globally could create 2.4 million jobs, $400 billion in economic growth and $67 billion in additional taxes" (Australian Institute of Criminology, 2008, p. xiii). Counterfeiting also impacts foreign investment and trade, impacting the types of goods imported and exported (OECD, 2007).

Third, consumers are impacted in various ways. Although the consumption of pirated/counterfeited goods "is a common, widespread, and normalized practice," (Bryce and Rutter, 2005), consumers are harmed because they receive inferior products, have less diversity of product choice, and incur health and safety risks (Allen Consulting Group, 2003, p. 8; see also Australian Institute of Criminology, 2008; IACC, 2005; Nasheri, 2005). Concerns about health and safety risks are particularly acute for some industries frequently victimized by counterfeiters, including electrical component, automotive, consumer good, and pharmaceutical companies (IACC, 2005). Counterfeited pharmaceuticals are dangerous as they typically do not contain the correct active ingredients. Pollinger (2008: 87) concludes that "the costs of counterfeit medications amount to $17 billion worth of losses for the legitimate pharmaceutical industry and an incalculable loss of life." Others estimate that counterfeit drugs might account for 10 percent of all pharmaceuticals, with this percentage increasing significantly in some countries (IACC, 2005: 10). For example, eighty percent of drugs found in pharmacy stores in Lagos, Nigeria were counterfeit (IACC, 2005).

Fourth, counterfeiting products have many additional direct and indirect effects that are difficult to measure, but important to note. Such unfair practices impact governments in significant ways -- as tax revenues are adversely impacted, jobs are lost, and resources and personnel are used in enforcement activities (FBI, 2003; IACC, 2005; OECD, 2007; Union des Fabricants, 2004; Nasheri, 2005). One estimate is that China loses 3 billion dollars in tax revenues every year (Union des Fabricants, 2004: 4). Such revenue deficits in the United States affect public works, schools, roads, the military, police departments, and other government services (Amendolara, 2005: 805; see also Gallant, 2007). Individuals who create products might also be deterred from producing new products by the threat of copyright infringement (Luckenbill and Miller, 1998: 97). Although creativity is key to economic development, "the absence of laws and regulations governing the rights of individuals to freely create and develop innovations may stymie technology, cultural, and intellectual advancements" (Piquero, 2005: 40). Finally, the manufacturing of counterfeited products is completely unregulated, and producers will do anything to minimize costs, including polluting the environment, forcing workers to work in deplorable conditions, and bribing government officials (OECD, 2007; see also IACC, 2005).

According to the IACC (2005: 3), "present day counterfeiting and piracy levels threaten to undermine the national economic security of the United States and other nations whose intellectual property and product brands also contribute to the American economy. The currently available statistics and data detailing the total economic impact of intellectual property theft are staggering." Although clearly a global problem that is growing, there is very little understanding within the research literature of the perpetrators of IP crimes. Who is a typical counterfeiter? How do offenders manufacture, distribute and sell counterfeited products? How are unique offenders or groups connected in order to profit from counterfeiting products? Have established organized crime groups ventured into the business of counterfeiting products? Have new organized crime syndicates emerged to focus efforts on counterfeiting products? Have terrorist networks and/or groups attempted to profit from counterfeiting products? This review focuses primarily on the links between terrorism and counterfeiting, although it is difficult to fully engage this topic without considering issues related to general offending patterns and organized crime involvement in moving counterfeiting products.

Funding Terrorism

Most terrorist organizations do not have very long life spans. Although there is very little research examining the birth and death of terrorist organizations, most scholars estimate that the majority of groups "die" within about one year as most are ephemeral-sporadic groups (Canadian Centre for Intelligence and Security Studies, 2006: 5; see also, Jones and Libicki, 2008; LaFree and Dugan, 2008; Rapoport, 1992). For example, Joshua Freilich and Steve Chermak identified nearly 6,000 white supremacist organizations that existed in the United States after, 1990. Only 279 of these groups were able to maintain a presence for at least three years (Freilich, Chermak, and Caspi, 2010). There are many variables that impact the survival rate of terrorist organizations, but it is clear that funding is a critical issue. The importance of funding is also made clear in the acknowledgement by the FBI's Terrorist Financing Operations Section that all terrorism cases involve some financial component (General Accounting Office, 2003), although the funding of terrorist organizations is a complex phenomenon to understand. According to Raphaeli (2003: 59), "the financing of terrorism is a subterranean universe governed by secrecy, subterfuge, and criminal endeavors; but also a good measure of sophistication and an understanding of the global financial system. It is best described as octopus with tentacles spreading across vast territories."

Terrorist organizations need funds for various reasons. Specific terrorist actions are not necessarily expensive. For example, the 9/11 commission estimated that the, 1998 East African Embassy attacks cost $10,000, the, 2002 Bali bombings cost Al Qaeda $20,000, and the costs for the 9/11 attacks have been estimated between $400,000-500,000 (National Commission on Terrorist Attacks Upon the United States, 2004). It is however costly to build and maintain an organizational capacity—and this issue is critical as terrorist groups choose their targets and forms of criminal activity that corresponds to their capacity level (Canadian

Centre for Intelligence and Security Studies, 2006: 5). Complex terrorist networks must finance security, operations, support, intelligence, propaganda, material, recruitment, training, housing and food, communications, bribery, weapons, travel, forged documents, and living expenses. Groups also must use funds to pay individuals to demonstrate in support of their cause and must compensate families for family members killed (Ehrenfeld, 2003: 2; General Accounting Office, 2003; Kane and Wall, 2005; O'Neil, 2007). Donahue (2006: 305) notes that the Provisional Irish Republican Army's (PIRA) organization costs are about £1.5 million per year, and the Ulster Defense Association requires about £500,000. Al Qaeda's operating budget is significantly higher, estimated to be between, 20 and 30 million dollars per year (Noble, 2003) with ten percent being used for specific operations and ninety percent for infrastructure. Al Qaeda also uses funds to pay other groups to support them and to enhance their presence and influence in key regions (Noble, 2003).

There appears to be a relationship between funding and operational effectiveness. Specifically, terrorist organizations that are effective fund raisers increase their capacity to commit serious criminal actions, including mass casualty events (O'Neil, 2007). In the last twenty years, however, funding has become increasing challenging as state sponsorship of terrorism has declined after the end of the cold war (Sanderson, 2004). Once state sponsored support declined, and globalization opened up new markets and opportunities (Treverton et al., 2009), groups had to innovate in search of new revenue streams to survive—some building an internal funding capacity of legitimate and illegitimate sources, others partnering with various crime syndicates, and others simply relying on criminal activities. O'Neil (2007: 2), for example, discusses that there has been an increase in the number of groups committing precursor crimes for fundraising. These increases were attributed to the decline in state sponsorship of terrorism, but also the amateurization and decentralization of terrorism, enhanced counterterrorism measures, and a changing terrorist demographic.

It is reasonable to assume that the number and types of legitimate and illegitimate funding sources for a terrorist organization increases with the sophistication of the organization. Terrorist groups rely on some 'legitimate' sources for funding, such as receiving money from charitable organizations, profits from the manufacturing and sale of extremist literature, and business ventures like taxi companies, banks, construction companies, and restaurants. In addition, terrorist organizations are involved in many different types of illegitimate funding enterprises, including fraud, forgery, identity theft, smuggling, human trafficking, money laundering, extortion, burglary, robbery, kidnapping and drug smuggling (Raphaeli, 2003: 61; see also O'Neil, 2007). Drug trafficking, for example, is a particularly important source of funding for terrorist organizations (Bibes, 2001). In fact, some scholars argue that drug trafficking probably provides the largest source of profits for terrorist groups (Shelley and Picarelli, 2002, p. 312; see also Canadian Centre for Intelligence and Security Studies, 2006; General Accounting Office, 2003; O'Neil, 2007). Sanderson (2004) reports that 14 of the 36 State Department-designated foreign terrorist organizations traffic in narcotics. A few of the groups known to traffic drugs are Al Qaeda, Hezbollah, the Kosovo Liberation Army (KLA), Islamic Movement of Uzbekistan (IMU), FARC, the Tamil Tigers, and Sendero Luminoso.

Understanding funding is complicated because most terrorist organizations have multiple sources of overlapping funds used to support various objectives. In fact, the greatest potential for profit with these products occurs for those organizations that have multiple sources of funding because networks have been established that can be used as assets to develop, move, and hide such products. That is, in order to traffic drugs, humans, jewels, weapons, or any product for a profit, a network of processes must be established for production, sales, distribution, and protection. These networks are then available to traffic other products, such as counterfeited goods. Stohl (2005: 61), for example, examined illicit trafficking in small arms, concluding that the market for small arms is about four billion per year and the illegal market is close to one billion. In discussing how illicit markets are used, she concludes (p. 63): "Once brokers acquire the small arms and light weapons, they enter the shadowy world of the black market and become difficult for law enforcement to recover or track. There is no separate market for each commodity. Rather, weapons become one part of an illicit network that deals in drugs, guns, jewels, art, humans, and anything else worth trading through unofficial channels. While some dealers may specialize in weapons, most are plugged into the general international underground economy. These networks operate across borders with an international cast of characters, staying one step ahead of the law." In the next section, it is discussed whether and how terrorist organizations might use such networks to traffic and profit from counterfeited products.

Counterfeiting Products as a Source of Funding

Research indicates that some terrorist groups have profited from counterfeiting products, that the problem is growing, and that intellectual property crimes might be fast becoming the preferred method of financing for several terrorist groups (IACC, 2005; General Accounting Office, 2003; Noble, 2003; OECD, 2007: 15; O'Neil, 2007; Union des Frabicants, 2004). Terrorist groups appear to be directly involved in the counterfeiting business in that they will identify market niches, acquire the necessary production materials, produce, and then sell goods. In addition, sympathizers, supporters, and militants may be involved in counterfeiting in a variety of different ways, from small to large-scale operations, and then remit a portion of their profits to a terrorist organization (Noble, 2003; Treverton et al., 2009). Whether a terrorist group is directly involved or benefits indirectly from counterfeiting products, the profits are used to fund groups in ways that allows them to accomplish their ideological objectives.

Money from counterfeiting goods is critical to the survival, legitimacy, and growth of terrorist organizations. These funds might also be used to support specific terrorist actions. For example, there is evidence that the, 1993 World Trade Center attackers were funded in part by counterfeit textile sales (Facts on Fakes). Another example can be observed from the multiple federal indictments of terrorist cell members in North Carolina and Michigan who sold contraband cigarettes and other goods, producing counterfeit cigarette tax stamps, and money laundering. Some of the profits from these operations were given to the terrorist organization Hezbollah's "orphans of martyrs" program (see Kouri, 2006). The funding was thus used to train terrorists, house them in safe houses, travel to targets, and purchase material used in terrorist actions, among other things.

Terrorists, like other individuals, groups, and organized crime syndicates, rely on counterfeiting products for several reasons. First, there is general realization that entry into the counterfeiting product business is relatively easy and straightforward as there are minimum financial and technical barriers for counterfeiting most products. Second, such groups are well aware of the demand for such products and thus the potential profits that can be achieved (Noble, 2003; Pollinger, 2008; Raphaeli, 2003; Treverton et al., 2009). In fact, some argue that "the high profitability of many counterfeiting and piracy activities … exceeds the profitability of illegal drug trades" (OECD, 2007: 15). Third, terrorists know that it is not likely that they will be detected as it is a low priority offense for law enforcement, and if caught and prosecuted, the sanctions are minimal. Fourth, being involved in these businesses is consistent with their desire of these groups to maintain some degree of anonymity. Counterfeiting is generally a cash-only business, and any equipment needed is purchased from companies or parties that do not keep reliable business records (IACC, 2005: 24).

Criminal Linkages

It is impossible to understand the involvement of terrorists within the counterfeiting product industry without considering their involvement in other criminal activities. Counterfeiting products often is only one of many different types of criminal enterprises that a terrorist group is involved in, and their involvement in the counterfeiting business may be dependent upon their successes in other criminal enterprises. In addition, it is important to explore whether the potential profits that can be achieved from counterfeiting products has resulted in collaborative arrangements between terrorist and organized crime syndicates. These issues are discussed below.

Criminal enterprises

The terrorist organizations that are significantly involved in the manufacture, sale and distribution of counterfeited products are involved in a network of criminal enterprises, mimicking organized criminal groups (Dishman, 2005). The funds generated can be used to support the organization, including financing other criminal activities (Australian Institute of Criminology, 2008, p. 4). Counterfeiting products is thus one type of precursor crime that some terrorist groups use to accomplish their objectives. Most terrorist groups are involved in various types of criminal activities, and their involvement is opportunistic, choosing activities that are consistent with their organizational capacity. Similar to how violent street gangs or groups of individuals may be involved in counterfeiting specific products, small terrorist groups may produce and sell specific products as one strategy to finance their activities. The most organized terrorist groups, however, require consistent streams of income and thus become involved in different types of criminal enterprises, and may be more significantly involved in counterfeiting products (Canadian Centre for Intelligence and Security Studies, 2006: 3). For example, intelligence analysts have indicated that Middle Eastern Jihadist Groups, especially Hezbollah and Al Qaeda, appear to have shown "a marked propensity" to use counterfeiting (see Lowe, 2006: 256).

Hezbollah, for example, appears to be significantly involved in counterfeiting products both in the United States and abroad. One successful federal investigation of this group showed how they were making several million dollars smuggling pseudoephidrine from Canada to the United States and converting it to methamphetamine for sale (Lowe, 2006: 256). In addition, according to William Bratton (2007), the former police chief of the Los Angeles Police Department, individuals involved in counterfeiting activities and the illegal sale of cigarettes raise funds for Hezbollah, and they have specific cases where literature and flags supportive of the group were discovered in the homes of counterfeiters (Union des Fabricants, 2004: 13). Several scholars have written about the successful investigation called "Operation Smoke Screen" (Ehrenfeld, 2003; Raphaeli, 2003; Treverton et al., 2009), which resulted in over twenty arrests. Individuals indicated in the case would purchase large amounts of cigarettes in North Carolina, and then transport and sell them in Michigan. The tax for cigarettes is small (5 cents) in North Carolina, but it is large in

Michigan (75 cents). It is estimated that each carload of cigarettes resulted in a $3,000 to $10,000 profit. In just two years, the smuggling ring generated almost eight million dollars and the profits were funneled to Hezbollah (Ehrenfeld, 2003: 137), and to be successful, the cell had to commit numerous other crimes, including "fictitious marriages, visa fraud, and fraud against the Small Business Administration" (Shelley and Melzer, 2008: 3). Hezbollah have also been connected to smuggling automobile brake pads (Union des Fabricants, 2004, 13). Noble (2003), in testimony before Congress on the growing threat of intellectual property crime, also concluded that Hezbollah's international involvement in counterfeiting products is substantial. He argued that that "funds generated from IPC may be remitted to Hezbollah using the following modus operandi. Counterfeit goods produced in Europe are sent to a free-trade zone in South America by a group of Lebanese criminals sympathetic to Hezbollah. The goods are then smuggled into a third country, to avoid import duties, where they are sold via a network of sympathizers and militants originating in the Middle East. An unknown amount of money generated through this activity is suspected to be remitted to Hezbollah."

The Irish Republican Army (IRA) may have been the first terrorist group to recognize the potential profit from counterfeiting products (Lowe, 2006). Lowe (2006: 256) discusses an operation where two IRA members provided set-up money to produce a fake livestock anti-parasite drug manufactured by Merck. Bottles for the fake drug were obtained from an Atlanta firm and the labels were produced in Northern Ireland. The drug, although only containing water, was distributed and profits were "put to further criminal use in purchasing banned growth hormones for cattle from the US which were then smuggled into Northern Ireland" (Lowe, 2006: 256). The IRA appears to use their established criminal enterprises, such as smuggling, racketeering, black taxis, drinking clubs, and drug smuggling, to carry out and enhance the profitability of counterfeiting such products as DVDs, game consoles, video cassettes, and designer clothes (Union des Fabricants, 2004: 17). Profits from counterfeiting may be several millions of dollars with at least 1.5 million in profits from film piracy (Treverton et al., 2009: 84).

Similarly, Treverton et al. (2009) examined the linkages between film piracy, organized crime, and terrorism. Their report includes fourteen case studies, and "three of the documented cases provide clear evidence that terrorist groups have used the proceeds of film piracy to finance their activities" (p. xii). They conclude that terrorists become involved in film piracy in three ways: they adopt the methods of organized crime, a criminal group transforms itself into a terrorist organization, and in some cases a terrorist group may transition to a criminal group abandoning its ideological agenda for one in favor of profit (p. 74). They argue the best case for establishing a direct link between terrorism and counterfeiting is their analysis of the Irish Republican Army (IRA), concluding that the IRA case study provides evidence of a terrorist group transitioning away from its ideological objective to focus solely on making profits: "Both republican and loyalist groups in Northern Ireland made the transition from terrorism to the enterprise of full-time crime. The 'commercialization' of these groups began years before the hostilities stopped, but both were able to use their piracy infrastructure to maintain some sort of political legacy" (p. 96).

Organized Crime

Organized crime syndicates are actively involved in many illicit trade markets, including narcotics, untaxed cigarettes, human trafficking, and counterfeiting products (Canadian Centre for Intelligence and Security Studies, 2006; Nasheri, 2005). Such groups are attracted by the potential profits in these products, thus "exacerbating the scale and scope of the problem" (Allen Consulting Group, 2003: 8). According to an important overview of the counterfeiting issue presented by the Australian Institute of Criminology (2008, p. xii), "there is a substantial quantity of international literature (including Organization for Economic Cooperation and Development, United States Department of

Justice, Federal Bureau of Investigation and Interpol Reports) asserting links between IP crime and organized criminal networks, and a recent Australian Crime Commission (ACC) intelligence assessment on the Australian situation found evidence of network members engaging in IP-related crime, along with other illicit activity, as a relatively low-risk means of generating income." Although terrorist and organized crime groups imitate each other's successful practices (Shelley & Picarelli, 2005; Sverclick, 2005), and that reports indicate that groups such as Al Qaeda, Hezbollah, the IRA, Hamas, Armenian, Russian, Italian, Japanese, and Chinese Mafia are involved in counterfeiting (Corrs, 2006: 3), an important question is whether they actually work collaboratively.

There is considerable analysis that explores that possibility that terrorist organizations might partner with organized crime groups to conduct counterfeiting and other types of illicit activities. Several scholars note that there are significant obstacles that should be considered in exploring these linkages. The obvious obstacle is a lacked of shared motivation in that a terrorist's primary effort is focused on pursuing a political objective and an organized crime group is driven by financial interests (Schmid, 1996). Treverton et al.'s (2009: 15) recent analysis of counterfeiting in the film industry summarized this divide effectively: "Terrorist organizations engage in criminal activity to advance their agendas—ideological, social, or political—whereas criminal organizations engage in violence to protect their criminal agendas. Terrorist groups seek to destroy the status quo, while criminal syndicates seek stable shadow business environments." There are other obstacles that reduce the likelihood of collaborative arrangements between terrorist groups and organized crime syndicates. Terrorist groups prefer to operate as a closed network and partnering with other individuals or other organizations may increase law enforcement scrutiny. Any collaboration would require trust to build a working relationship which may be a substantial obstacle to overcome. In addition, there must be some mechanism for an introduction between groups to occur. Members of both types of organization prefer to be anonymous and thus even making contact would take considerable effort (see Treverton et al., 2009). Finally, either group might decide that it would be to their advantage to enhance their own capacity in specific areas in order to maximize their own profits rather than collaborate.

Although significant obstacles exist, there is certainly evidence that such collaboration between terrorist and organized crime groups have occurred (Belov & Putintsev, 2005; Shelley, 2005; Shelley & Picarelli, 2005) and a recent analysis of film piracy concluded that the links may be stronger than previously thought (Treverton et al., 2009). Ehrenfeld (2003: 3), in her book Funding Evil, discusses that the "nexus of terrorist groups and international criminal organizations is complex, linking money, geography, politics, arms, and tactics to create a mutually beneficial relationship" (Ehrenfeld, 2003: 3). Sanderson (2004: 53) discusses how "both organized crime and terrorist groups run in the same circles—they already operate outside of the law and they often need the same resources, including: false identification, shipping documents, operators, transportation networks, and counter-surveillance techniques." Shelley (2005: 9) argued that such linkages existed in the Balkans, the Caucasus, and in Central Asia, that Middle Eastern terrorist groups, especially Hezbollah, Hamas, and Al Qaeda, are linked with crime groups in the Tri-Border/Triple Frontier Region of Argentina, Brazil, and Paraguay, and Al Qaeda collaborates with crime groups in West Africa.

The collaboration of terrorist and organized groups results from overlapping activities and potential benefits from a relationship. Both groups are most effective in states with weak government and law enforcement controls, both have troubles collecting and laundering money, and both must have the means to communicate secretly (Sverdlick, 2005: 86; Shelley & Picarelli, 2002: 309). Organized crime groups seek opportunities to enhance their own capacity and profit by seeking out collaborations with international terrorist groups. Terrorist groups benefit because organized crime can provide financial, logistical, and technical support (Shelley, 2005). Terrorists might hide themselves within international organized crime organizations, or such groups might agree to traffic a terrorist to a specific destination. Unfortunately, little attention has been paid to exploring these linkages more closely and developing strategies that could be used to disrupt the linkages between organized crime and terrorist groups (Shelley, 2005).

Research Needs

In sum, counterfeiting is a significant global problem that harms governments, businesses, and consumers in several different ways, but not much is known about the types of individuals and offenders involved in counterfeiting products. Although there is some research that examines the involvement of terrorist and organized crime groups in intellectual property crime violations, the scholarly literature lacks a strong empirical foundation. In fact, both practitioners and scholars who have engaged this topic conclude that a particularly challenging issue for the better understanding of counterfeiting is the lack of data availability and systematic research on the topic. Below are some excerpts that highlight these concerns:

1. "Few sources exist that report comprehensive and seemingly reliable data on the extent of the problem" (Nasheri, 2005: 83).

2. "There is a limited amount of information available from IPSG criminal files and INTERPOL Member States on IPC and terrorist financing" (Noble, 2003).
3. "Data on IPR violations are limited (i.e., incomplete and unreliable), like data on many White Collar Crimes. No source provides data that reflects the full scope of IPR violations, and comparisons among data sources are difficult because of different methodologies and biases" (National White Collar Crime Center, 2004: 25-26).
4. "The true extent of terrorist use of alternative financing mechanisms is unknown, owing to the criminal nature of the activity and the lack of systematic data collection and analyses. ....The limited and sometimes conflicting information available on alternative financing mechanisms adversely affects the ability of U.S. government agencies to assess risk and prioritize efforts on terrorist financing mechanisms." (GAO, 2003: 23).
5. "Researchers should develop comprehensive data sets on enforcement and use them to determine how vigorously officials have acted against offenders." (Luckenbill and Miller, 1998: 115).
6. "Efforts must be developed to initiate a nationwide data collection effort that targets information regarding the prevalence of intellectual property theft with special

attention made to include all varieties of intellectual property violations." (Picquero, 2005: 57).

7. "There is very little information known about the causes and correlates of intellectual property theft and what little information is known seems to raise more questions than it answers." (Picquero, 2005: 57).
8. "To create a stronger model with which to analyze the effect of any policy changes, obtaining more accurate, in-depth data is obviously of greatest importance." (Pollinger, 2008: 98).
9. "The clandestine nature of counterfeiting and piracy means that statistics, if they exist, are often of poor quality, or based largely on custom seizures which are hard to relate to actual market figures." (Olsten, 2005: 7).
10. "No published details on the representativeness of samples, or of research instruments and measures." (Australian Institute of Criminology, 2008: xiii).

The rest of this essay provides an overview of several research areas as well as specific projects that could be undertaken that address several of the gaps in the research literature. The focus of the discussion is on furthering understanding the behaviors of counterfeiting offenders generally, and the links between terrorist organizations and counterfeiting specifically. General ideas for future research and potential methodologies are also presented.

As discussed above, there has been some research and many anecdotal claims exploring the involvement of terrorist groups in raising funds through counterfeiting, the links between terrorist groups and organized crime and other criminal networks to enhance profit potential in this particular area, and the relationship between counterfeiting profits and others sources of terrorist funding. Most of this research is qualitative or anecdotal (Pollinger, 2008). It is clear that we know very little about the nature of counterfeiting offending and the types of individuals and groups involved in counterfeiting products. Moreover, although it is important to continue to explore the linkages between terrorist groups and other criminal enterprises, it is as important to document general patterns of counterfeiters and the offending capacities of organized group counterfeiters (e.g., terrorists, organized crime, and criminal gangs), criminal networks, groups whose sole source of illegal funding is counterfeiting, and chronic offenders and other individuals.

There would be great value in understanding the similarities and differences between the various types of counterfeiters in terms of product selection, nature of criminal involvement (does a group manufacture, sell and distribute the goods?), organizational structure and skills, past offending histories, how the criminal justice system and private industry have responded to their counterfeiting, and the group's motivation for becoming involved. It would be critical to collect information at both the group and individual level. What groups are involved in counterfeiting? How frequently are they involved? What other criminal activities, if any, are they involved? Are they more or less successful in counterfeiting compared to their criminal enterprises? How are their counterfeiting operations separate or connected to other criminal enterprises? Why did the group decide to become involved in offending? How long have they done it? How did they gain the operational and technical capacities to counterfeit products? Do the individuals have prior offending histories in counterfeiting and/or other types of criminal activities? What is the background of counterfeiters? How are chronic offenders similar and different from episodic counterfeiters? What are the patterns of legal processing of these offenders? Who are the typical street dealers, and what indicators exist that might link these individuals to terrorist groups?

Developing a research plan that would answer questions such as these would have significant scholarly and practical implications. We know very little about counterfeiting patterns and the offending behaviors of counterfeiters and thus it is difficult to develop innovative law enforcement practices. Moreover, understanding how counterfeiters might be similar (or different) compared to other types of offenders might help identify other potential strategies that might be valuable for deterring counterfeiting. Finally, enhancing our understanding of the links between various types of offending groups will help in determining how resources might be best distributed to respond more effectively to counterfeiters.

There are several research methodologies that might be used to begin to understand the offending patterns of counterfeiters, but it seems that it would make sense to first conduct multiple case studies and interview key informants. It would be valuable to do a series of case studies of counterfeiting cases to better understand these issues. The primary focus of the case studies would be on the nature of offending and the groups/individuals involved in counterfeiting products. The case studies could be used as a vehicle to compare and contrast the involvement of different types of individuals and groups in counterfeiting products. For example, we might examine two/three successful FBI investigations and one/two state/local investigations. The data collection strategy for the case studies could include a compilation and analysis of case-specific and open source documents, as well as detailed interviews with personnel from law enforcement and business, and potentially convicted counterfeiters as well.

Conclusion

The counterfeiting of products is a serious global problem that significantly impacts governments, businesses, and consumers. Although the scope of harm is substantial, there is little research that explores the etiology of counterfeited products and a limited empirical understanding of how terrorist groups and/or organized crime networks are involved in these types of crimes. This essay explored the harm caused by these crimes, and highlighted some potential areas of collaboration between these different groups. The next steps that need to be taken to further develop these issues would be to conduct a series of systematic case studies to better understand the offending behaviors of counterfeiters. The results would have significant implications for law enforcement practice.

References

The Allen Consulting Group. 2003. Counterfeiting of Toys, Business Software, and Computer and Video Games. Report to the Australian Toy Association, the Business Software Association of Australia and the Interactive Entertainment Association of Australia, Sydney.

Amendolara, Lauren D. 2005. "Knocking Out Knock-Offs: Effectuating the Criminalization of Trafficking in Counterfeit Goods." Fordham Intellectual Property Media & Entertainment, 789-836.

Australian Institute of Criminology. 2008. Intellectual Property Crime and Enforcement in Australia. Canberra, Aus: Australian Institute of Criminology.

Below, Ye and O. Putintsev. 2005. CIS: Countering Threats to Security and Stability. International Affairs, 51 (1): 95-105.

Bibes, Patricia. 2001. Transnational Organized Crime and Terrorism: Columbia, A Case Study. Journal of Contemporary Criminal Justice, 17 (3): 243-258.

Bratton, William F. 2007. The Mutation of the Illicit Trade Market. The Police Chief, 74 (5).

Bryce, J and J. Rutter. 2005. Fake Nation: A Study into an Everyday Crime. A Report for the Organized Task Force, Northern Ireland Office.

Canadian Centre for Intelligence and Security Studies. , 2006. "Actual and Potential Links Between Terrorism and Criminality." In Trends in Terrorism Series sponsored by the Integrated Threat Assessment Centre. URL: http://www.itacciem.gc.ca/pblctns/tc_prsnts/index-eng.asp

Corrs, Chambers. , 2006. Strengthening anti-counterfeiting law enforcement in Australia.

Dishman, Chris. , 2005. The Leaderless Nexus: When Crime and Terror Converge. Studies in Conflict and Terrorism. 28 (3): 237-252.

Donohue, Laura K. , 2006. "Anti-Terrorist Finance in the United Kingdom and United States." Michigan Journal of International Law, 27 (2): 303-435.

Ehrenfeld, Rachel. , 2003. Funding Evil: How Terrorism is Financed — and How to Stop It. Los Angeles, CA: Bonus Books.

Freilich, J., Chermak, S., and Caspi, D. (2009). "Critical events in the life trajectories of domestic extremist groups: A case study analysis of four violent white supremacist groups." *Criminology and Public Policy*. 8 (3): 497-530 .

Gallant, M. Michelle. , 2007. "Tax and Terrorism: A New Partnership?" Journal of Financial Crime, 14 (4): 453-459.

General Accounting Office, 2003. "Terrorist Financing: U.S. Agencies Should Systemically Assess Terrorists' Use of Alternative Financing Mechanisms." Washington DC: United States Government Accountability Office.

General Accounting Office., 2005. "Better Strategic Planning Needed to Coordinate U.S. Efforts to Deliver Counter-Terrorism Financing Training and Technical Assistance Abroad." Washington DC: United States Government Accountability Office.

Harbaugh, R and R. Klemka. , 2002. "Does Copyright Enforcement Encourage Piracy? In: Australian Institute of Criminology. , 2008. Intellectual Property Crime and Enforcement in Australia. Canberra, Aus: Australian Institute of Criminology.

The International Anticounterfeiting Coalition. "Facts on Fakes." Downloaded from www.iacc.org.

Interpol. 2003. Intellectual Property Crime. Available from: www.interpol.int/Public/FinancialCrime/IntellectualProperty/Default.asp.

Kane, John and April Wall. , 2005. "Identifying the Links between White-Collar Crime and Terrorism." Washington DC: National Institute of Justice.

King, B. , 2000. "Study: Napster Use Isn't Stealing." Published in WIRED News, 9/30.

Kouri, Jim. , 2006. "Two men plead guilty in US to funding terrorist group Hezbollah." Downloaded from the WWW: RenewAmerica.com.

Jones, Seth G. and Martin C. Libicki., 2008. *How terrorist groups end: Lessons for countering Al Qaeda*. Santa Monica: Rand Corporation.

LaFree, Gary and Lauro Dugan. (2008). Tracking global terrorism trends, 1970-, 2004. In Thomas Feucht and David Weisburd (Eds.), *To protect and to serve: Dilemmas in* policing and terrorism and serving the public.

Lowe, Peter. , 2006. "Counterfeiting: Links to Organized Crime and Terrorist Funding." Journal of Financial Crime, 13 (2): 255-257.

Luckenbill, David F. and Susan L. Miller. , 1998. "Defending Intellectual Property: State Efforts to Protect Creative Works." Justice Quarterly, 15 (1): 93-120.

Nasheri, Hedieh., 2005. Addressing the Global Scope of Intellectual Property Crimes and Policy Initiatives." Trends in Organized Crimes, 8 (4): 79-108.

National Commission on Terrorist Attacks Upon the United States, 2004. The 9/11 Commission Report. Available from the WWW at: http://www.9-11commission.gov/

National White Collar Crime Center. , 2004. "Intellectual Property and White-Collar Crime: Report of Issues, Trends, and Problems of Future Research." Washington DC: US Department of Justice.

Nobel, Ronald K. , 2003. "The Links Between Intellectual Property Crime and Terrorist Financing." Testimony before the United States House Committee on International Relations, July 16, 2003.

Olsten, Karsten. , 2005. "Counterfeiting and Piracy: Measurement Issues." Background Report for the WIPO/OECD Expert Meeting on Measurement and Statistical Issues.

O'Neil, Sioban. , 2007. "Terrorist Precursor Crimes: Issues and Options for Congress." Washington DC: Congressional Research Service.

Organization for Economic Co-operation and Development. , 2007. "The Economic Impact of Counterfeiting and Piracy."

Piquero, Nicole Leeper. , 2005. "Causes and Prevention of Intellectual Property Crime." Trends in Organized Crime, 8 (4): 40-61.

Pollinger, Zachary A. , 2008. "Counterfeit Goods and Their Potential Financing of International Terrorism. Michigan Journal of Business. Available online at: http://michiganjb.org/issues.shtml

Raphaeli, Nimrod. , 2003. "Financing of Terrorism: Sources, Methods, and Channels." Terrorism and Political Violence, 15 (4): 59-82.

Rapoport, David., 1992. Terrorism. In Mary Hawkesworth and Maurice Kogan (Eds.), *Encyclopedia of Government and Politics*, Volume II. New York: Routledge.

Sanderson, Thomas M. , 2004. "Transnational Terror and Organized Crime: Blurring the Lines." SAIS Review, 24 (1): 49-61.

Schmid, Alex P. , 1996. "The Links between Transnational Organized Crime and Terrorist Crimes." Transnational Organized Crime, 2 (4): 40-82.

Shelley, Louise. , 2005. "Unraveling the New Criminal Nexus. Georgetown Journal of International Affairs. 6 (1): 5-13.

Shelley, Louise I. and Sharon A. Melzer. , 2008. "The Nexus of Organized Crime and Terrorism: Two Case Studies in Cigarette Smuggling." International Journal of Comparative and Applied Criminal Justice. 32 (1): 1-21.

Shelley, Louise I. and John T. Picarelli. , 2002. "Methods not Motives: Implications of the Convergence of International Organized Crime and Terrorism." 3 (4): 305-318.

Shelley, Louise I. and John T. Picarelli. , 2005. "Methods and Motives: Exploring Links Between Transnational Organized Crime and International Terrorism." Trends in Organized Crime, 9(2): 52-67.

Shetterly, Daryl. 2005. "Starving the Terrorists of Funding: How the United States Treasury is Fighting the War on Terror." Regent University Law Review, 327-348.

Stohl, Rachel. 2005. "Fighting the Illicit Trafficking of Small Arms." SAIS Review, 25 (1): 59-68.

Sverdlick, Ana R. 2005. "Terrorists and Organized Crime Entrepreneurs in the 'Triple Frontier' among Argentina, Brazil, and Paraguay." Trends in Organized Crime, 9 (2): 84-92.

Treverton, Gregory F., Matties, Carl, Cunninghmam, Karla J., Jeremiah Goulka, Greg Ridgeway, and Anny Wong. 2009. Film Piracy, Organized Crime, and Terrorism. Santa Monica, CA: RAND Corporation.

Union des Fabricants. 2004. "Counterfeiting and Organized Crime." Paris. Available from the WWW: http://counterfeiting.

VI. Behavioral clues to deception in counter-terrorism situations: Critique and prospectus

Mark G. Frank

University at Buffalo

Don Gemeinhardt

RTI International

Carl J. Maccario

Transportation Security Administration

David Matsumoto

San Francisco State University

Abstract

One of the most important tasks that a counter-terrorism officer has is to ascertain information and vet it for accuracy. In the post 9/11 world, a large portion of this information will come from individual assets/sources/informants. There are many obstacles to obtaining accurate information from these individuals, including faulty recall or hearsay. The most prevalent obstacle is interpersonal deception – where a source lies to a checkpoint, intelligence, or other law enforcement official. General reviews of the research literature are not so optimistic about the ability to spot deception from unaided perceptible sources – faces, bodies, voices. It is more optimistic about the unaided non-perceptible sources – e.g., heart rate, blood pressure, galvanic skin response, pupil dilation, facial heat.

However, general reviews of the literature do not take into account the types of scenarios faced by law enforcement officers, and how those scenarios may affect clue patterns observed. Moreover, not all techniques – particularly the non-perceptible ones – are robust to all scenarios, especially naturalistic human interaction, and require strict protocols that in many instances can be readily counter-measured.

This paper will outline some of the most important variables to consider when trying to spot deception, including aspects of scenarios, types of behaviors and their measurements, optimal ways to deploy those behaviors, and the limits of different techniques. It will incorporate these sorts of analyses into a better understanding of the research literature and to cull out those studies that do not have relevance to counter-terrorism. We will consider some concrete pros and cons of different techniques, when they may be useful, cautions and pitfalls, to arrive at a prospectus on what might be more or less helpful to the real world counter terrorism issues faced by the security, intelligence, and law enforcement officer. Specifically, our applied research orientation will ideally lead to better ways to utilize and deploy the knowledge and observation/measurement methods we use now so that we can turn our knowledge into action.

Introduction

A terrorist act originates within the mind of a human being. In fact, the only linking thread through all stages of a terrorist attack is the presence of a human being, who develops hatred, plans, gathers materials and information, co-opts others, and executes the attack. This renders the problem of detecting and preventing terrorism at any stage of the process, from plan to attack, to becoming a human intelligence problem. It is true regardless whether the terrorism takes the form of a physical assault, a Weapon of Mass Destruction (WMD) attack, an Improvised Explosive Device (IED) attack, and even a cyber attack. A security/intelligence officer cannot effectively detect and prevent such attacks without possessing the skills to develop a deep understanding of what motivates people and how they act when engaged in terrorism. Essential to developing these skills is the ability to 'read' the true intentions of any human being. This allows the security/intelligence officer to weight any information they receive for veracity – regardless whether the security/intelligence officer is interacting with suspected terrorists, those harboring them, informants/assets, or witnesses. It is an indispensable tool in their toolbox.

Weighing this information gathered from individuals is replete with obstacles that affect its accuracy. These include the well documented shortcomings of human memory, honest differences of opinion, and even outright deception (Hauggard & Repucci, 1992). Although most of these factors are inadvertent, outright deception – i.e., telling a lie – is the only one that involves an *intentional* effort to mislead another by generating false information or concealing the truth (Ekman, 2001). Because a lie is a deliberate, conscious behavior, we can speculate that it will leave some trace, sign, or signal that would at least suggest that it is happening. It is these signs or signals that, if and when they occur, security/intelligence officers' hope to recognize so as to allow them to weigh accurately the information they have gathered to defeat the terrorist.

Research has shown that there is no one sign, signal, or behavior that occurs only when people tell lies – that is, there is no human equivalent of the mythical Pinocchio's nose. Yet researchers agree that there are some behavioral clues to deceit, perceptible to the naked eye or ear, that on the aggregate predict that a lie is being told at rates better than simply guessing (e.g., DePaulo et al., 2003). Similarly, researchers agree that there are some physiological clues to deceit, mostly imperceptible to the naked eye or ear but made accessible through technology, that also predict that a lie is being told at rates greater than chance (often stronger than the aforementioned behavioral clues). However, these physiological clues require specialized equipment, whereas the behavioral clues can be detected by observers with the naked eye or ear. This makes them robust to detection in any observational or interactive information gathering encounter, and thus they are our focus.

Our goals in this chapter are to summarize briefly the existing research on behavioral clues to deceit in a way to make it applicable to improving counter-terrorism efforts. This means that although it won't be a comprehensive review, we will cast a critical eye toward the ecological validity of the existing research literature behind these behavioral clues. We hope this will correct what we believe to be a recurring error in the application of any laboratory based deception research study to real world counter terrorism. We will critically examine the ways in which behaviors are measured, the utility of various behavioral channels for detecting lies, and then describe a prospectus for future research that may produce more pertinent science regarding detecting lies in counter-terrorism situations.

Definition

Ekman (2001) describes a number of ways one can lie – one can fabricate, distort, or conceal information, (i.e., not uttering a falsehood), as well as a telling-the-truth-falsely lie (i.e., telling a factual truth in a sarcastic or other way so as to make a target disbelieve the fact). The vast majority of the lies studied in the nonverbal deception literature have been the fabrication lies; that is, the subject says something that is contradicted by reality. The concealment type lies have been more popular in some of the physiological measurement deception studies such as the P300 brain response work (Farwell & Donchin, 1991) - but those studies have not focused on the nonverbal correlates of deception. It appears to us that terrorism situations require studying all types of lies, not just fabrication/distortions as per the current behavioral literature. We really don't know what effect different sorts of lies have on perceptible behaviors.

Processes that generate behavioral markers of deception

The general consensus in the behavioral literature is that although there is no unique signature for deception (no Pinocchio response), there are clues that can predict deception greater than chance. The assumption is that telling a lie raises the cognitive load, elicits emotions, and brings forth efforts to control one's behaviors (Zuckerman, et al., 1981). Telling a lie also generates fewer markers in the words of an individual that indicates he or she truly experienced the event they have claimed (Johnson-Laird, 1980; Undeutsch, 1967). We note that these four sources of behavioral clues are general trends and are influenced by the context under which the individual is observed or the way in which they are interviewed.

The first category of behavioral clue that can betray a lie are clues to the emotional state of the individual. Liars tend to feel more detection apprehension (tension or fear), guilt, and on occasion even joy, sadness disgust, or other emotions that are inconsistent with the line taken by the individual (Ekman, 2001). Context is important to determining whether these emotions are clues to deception; for example, a facial sign of disgust would betray the person who claims they enjoyed what they just ate. But a similar facial sign of disgust would support the person who claims what they just ate tasted awful. Moreover, other events can trigger these emotions independent of truth or lie. An individual being tortured may show signs of fear when they utter statements regardless of their veracity – and the interrogator would not know whether they observed the fear of a liar who is afraid of getting caught, or the fear of a truth teller who is afraid he or she will be harmed further. The nature of human emotion is such that emotions do not telegraph what has triggered them; they only inform the observer that the emotion has happened (Ekman, 2003). Emotions are very interesting emotion clues because they are hard wired, universal to all people on the planet, and are involuntary reactions, and leave perceptible signals that they have been activated (Ekman, 2003; Matsumoto, et al., 2008). When emotions are aroused other subsidiary clues may appear such as changes in pupil dilation, foot movements, higher voice pitch, and so forth;

these clues are elicited because the act of lying can generate guilt, fear of getting caught, pleasure at 'pulling the wool' over someone's eyes, (Ekman, 2001). These reactions occur with lying for most people because they have been raised with strong prohibitions against lying, and fear of the consequences for getting caught, or the guilt at violating the trust essential in all relationships.

The second category of behavioral clue that can betray a lie are clues to the raised cognitive load of the liar, manifested in signs of increased mental effort. These are manifested in the verbal style and body. The arise because telling a lie is typically harder to do than telling the truth; a liar has to remember what he or she has said, and to whom and when; a liar has to weigh each statement for consistency and plausibility, and a liar has to spin his or her story to match the details as they understand the lie catcher to know them (i.e., deliver a plausible alibi; Ekman & Frank, 1993). All this requires more mental effort than just recalling information to the best of one's ability. Context matters here too, as one would often expect an individual to engage in higher mental effort to answer a complicated question about personal philosophy, whereas one would not expect such mental effort when an individual is asked his or her name (Frank & Ekman, 2004). These sorts of clues include longer responses, longer response latencies, greater speech errors, changes in patterns of pauses and speech rate (DePaulo et al., 2003).

The third category of behavioral clue that can betray a lie are clues to increased behavioral control. These are manifested in the body, face, and voice, through reduced illustrators (hand/arm/ head movements that illustrate, amplify, or qualify speech), increased smiling, changes in eye contact, and so forth (reviewed by Vrij, 2008). The process is deliberate and strategic - a liar knows that liars should not fidget, thus they control their body, limb, and finger movements to reduce those movement (e.g., Ekman & Friesen, 1972; Vrij et al., 1997). However, the liar often over-controls these movements, and thus the strong reduction in these behaviors can be diagnostic. This strategic decision on the part of the liar is attempted to manage the impression they create in others (DePaulo et al., 2003).

The fourth category of behavioral clue that can betray a lie are clues in the narrative account generated by the person that suggests the person truly experienced the event in the account. These clues are in the word choices made by individuals, and reflect processes known in natural human memory (Johnson-Laird, 1980; Undeutsch, 1967). Natural memories involve accounts that are physically possible to happen, have details appropriate to the significance of the event to the person, contain clues to context tied into the life of the narrative speaker, contains temporal and spatial information and relationships, fewer self references and more hedging of statements (DePaulo et al., 2003).

Channel clues in deception

The security/intelligence officer has at his or her disposal only those behaviors that are perceptible with the naked eye or ear. This means they have access to the speech and voice of the individual, the face, and the body, and must rely upon these channels to ascertain the presence of emotions, mental effort, behavioral control, and unedited memory. In fact, all channels are capable of revealing each of the four categories of behavioral clues.

Voice clues

Vocal clues to deceit are generated by emotions, mental effort, memory processes, and behavioral control. Moreover, these vocal clues can be accessed where the facial and body clues cannot, e.g., over the phone, or even in a written correspondence. One essential aspect of trying to detect clues in the voice is that these clues are person specific. This means some baseline reading of the person's normal pauses and pitch must be known beforehand in order to calibrate the deviation. To this end, it may be a very useful pursuit to look at an operationally applied baseline test that can be gleaned through some initial process or engagement protocol. This baseline should be ideally similar in gravitas to the critical questions asked (Vrij, 2004). For example, a rise in voice pitch usually indicates anger, fear or excitement; a reduction in pitch coincides with sadness, and research suggest that these too may be universal (Scherer & Walbott, 1994). However, one cannot know whether it is a rise or fall without the baseline. Pauses in speech are normal, but if they are too long or too frequent they indicate an increase in probability of deceit. Also, change in speaking rate, speech error rate, indirect or confusing speech are typically signs of extra cognitive activity which accompanies a lie (reviewed by DePaulo et al., 2003).

Facial clues

Although the voice has information about memory, emotion, and behavioral control, the face has specific information about the emotional state of the individual that is considerably clearer than the body. The reason is that the face is directly connected to the emotional system, and a facial expression is part of an emotional reaction (Darwin, 1872; Ekman, 2003; Rinn, 1984). Research supports this idea that these facial expressions of emotion are universal across cultures. However, the face is also connected to the volitional movement system (via cortical motor strip), which means it can also pose expressions that the individual does not feel. Research suggests that culture is an important part of human facial expressions; culture affects the interpretation of social information (e.g., whether cooked chicken feet elicit happiness or disgust), but also affects the management of the facial expression once an individual experiences it (Matsumoto & Willingham, 2006). This dual control of the face can result in the display of micro facial expressions, as a 'tug of war' (Frank, Matsumoto, Ekman, Kang, & Kurylo, 2010) over control of the face results in very quick, fragmentary displays of emotion that last less than ½ a second. These clues are usually missed by observers, although recent data suggest individuals can be trained within 30 minutes to recognize them (Frank et al., 2010). Finally, the face can communicate emotional information in the change in pupil size (DePaulo et al., 2003); however this is more apparent in individuals with lighter colored irises.

The face can also display symbolic messages (a wink, an eyebrow flash), signs of mental effort (pursed lips, lowered brows) and even signs of behavioral control (tightened lips; Ekman, 2003). The face may also show behavioral control clues through changes in eye contact or gaze during the course of the interview (DePaulo, et al., 2003).

Body clues

The body can serve as an amplifier for emotional behavior, sends its own symbolic gestures, and manifests behavioral control signals. For example, a highly nervous individual may shake, sweat, change their breathing patterns, and so forth (DePaulo et al., 2003). The body can also communicate phrases and words (head shakes for 'no', nods for 'yes', raised middle finger as an insult). The body can also communicate mental effort through arm movements or postural shifts. Finally, the body can exhibit signs of behavioral control by engaging in comforting gestures (known as manipulators, e.g., like a hand rubbing the back of the head, rubbing the chin, thighs, or arms (Ekman, 2001). These have been erroneously labeled as "red flag indicators" of deception in the past (e.g., Inbau, Reid, & Buckley, 1986), but research shows they tend to have a weak relationship to deception (DePaulo et al., 2003). The body can also exhibit behavioral control by squelching as much extraneous body behavior as possible by reducing the gestures that accompany speech (illustrators) and reducing finger and head movements (Ekman & Friesen, 1972; Vrij et al., 1997).

Measurement issues

The most recent and comprehensive meta-analysis of the research literature on behavioral clues to deceit has concluded that at a general level, motivated liars are betrayed because they appear to be less forthcoming, their accounts are less compelling, they appear to be more tense, and their accounts are a bit too polished (DePaulo et al., 2003). Translating impressions such as less compelling into hard judgments – from which one may make predictions about veracity - may be difficult because they are subjective and in fact can be interpreted at a number of different levels of specificity (Frank, 2005). How do we measure forthcoming? How do we measure tense? We can choose to measure these variables at the most elemental *physical* units level, such as logging the movements in the hands, feet, arms, legs, torso, head, eyebrows, lips, eyelids, or counting eye-blinks, measuring pupil dilation, fundamental frequency, amplitude, jitter in the voice, or counting words, number of pauses, response latency, or time spent talking in the speech. Or we choose to measure these variables at the most elemental *psychological meaning* level, which although are composites of the physical units described above, have their own types and patterns of movements to which researchers have identified empirical or conceptual reasons for examining them as distinct units. Some of these variables include manipulators (also called adaptors, which involve touching, rubbing, etc., of various body parts), illustrators (which accompany speech to help keep the rhythm of the speech, emphasize a word, show direction of thought, etc.), or emblems (gestures that have a clear speech equivalent, such as a head nod meaning "yes"). Note that an arm movement downward to keep the rhythm of speech (illustrator), or an arm movement downward but with a down turned thumb (emblem), or an arm movement downward that has fingers rubbing the thigh (manipulator) all have the same physical movement for the arm – but the psychological meaning, derived from associated actions, is vastly different. In this case the illustrator would convey engagement, which we see more often in truth telling (Ekman & Friesen, 1972); the emblem (thumbs down with arm movement) would convey a highly negative 'this is no good', which we could possibly see either when telling the truth or lying (Ekman et al., 1980); and the manipulator (rubbing the thigh) would convey tension/discomfort, which we see more often when lying (reviewed by DePaulo et al., 2003). Other examples of psychological meaning derived from basic physical measurements include emotions from facial expressions through particular facial movements, e.g., brow movements, lip movements (Ekman, 2003), emotions and mental effort from voice, e.g., fundamental frequency, speech rate, response latency (Scherer, 1984). Finally, we can choose to measure these variables at the more global *a*level, such as rating subjects as to how immediate, cognitively complex, or plausible their account is (DePaulo et al., 2003). This level – which is a more gut level, abstract level type judgment – may be the hardest to judge reliably.

The general problem with all these levels is that at times the variables may be perfectly understood, but at other times conceptually confused. For example, researchers studying deception and the smile have never defined in their reports what they meant by a smile, and yet coders have always showed extremely high inter-rater reliability (above 0.90) when scoring the number of smiles (Frank, 2003). In contrast, researchers have often proposed a role for "arousal" in detecting deception, yet in different reports arousal has meant things as variable as an orienting response (deTurck & Miller, 1985), to a full blown emotional expression of fear (Frank, 1989) along with some apparently indeterminate points in between (Buller & Burgoon, 1994; Waid & Orne, 1982). Arousal in the physiological detection of deception literature has also been used to describe physiological states as different as stress, anxiety, embarrassment and even anger (Steinbrook, 1992).

The prognosis for behavioral clues predicting deception is likely best at the psychological level of measurement because this is where the action is in the mind of a deceptive person. The liar knows what they saw, heard, or did. Their task is to conceal this by staying quiet or fabricating an alibi, all the while concealing his or her emotions. That means their reactions to topics, their descriptions of events, contain clues to this fabrication, feigned clues to credibility, or signs these are being squelched. Thus the liar is managing his or her emotions, signs of mental effort, and signs he or she has invented the account of the event in question. These are all psychologically meaningful behaviors that will be at odds with what the liar is saying. A side benefit of focusing analyses at the psychologically meaningful level is that these clues may be easier to transition these results to security/intelligence officers in the field – in particular with regards to training them. It is likely much harder to train security/intelligence officers to count various body movements, or instructing them to make general impressions as the looseness of the definitions may make it harder for operational personnel to grasp these concepts. Researchers have tried this indirect route by instructing judges to rate liars and truth tellers as to 'who is thinking hard' rather than who is lying, but the results showed the average difference in ratings between liars and truth tellers was lower when judges made these indirect judgments compared to direct truth/lie judgments (in contrast to the authors' conclusions; Vrij et al., 2001). However, a meta analysis of the research on training individuals to improve their abilities to detect deception suggests strongly that even poor training methods results in small, but significant improvements in accuracy – and speculated that more precise measurements and training would improve accuracy even further (Frank & Feeley, 2003).

Paradigm issues

A lie told to foster a terrorist attack would be assumed to be a high stake lie. High stakes lies are those that have strong incentives for successful deception, and strong punishments for unsuccessful deception. In contrast, a 'white' lie about some offhand compliment told to a friend would be considered low stake, as there are weak incentives and punishments, and these lies may be expected as the price of smooth social discourse. These low stake lies are the most common in our daily lives, but also the most common in the research literature (DePaulo et al., 2003). This means that the majority of the research literature may not be directly relevant to detecting deception in high stake counter-terrorism scenarios, or may even generate misleading results by underestimating the emotional clues to deception, and how they interact with the cognitive clues. We can observe this in the research literature that examines peoples' abilities to judge deception from behavior. A recent meta-analytic study showed that law enforcement was no better at detecting lies than laypeople, and neither group was accurate at rates much better than guessing (e.g., Bond & DePaulo, 2006). Yet when the studies featuring law enforcement were reanalyzed, and law enforcement's accuracy at detecting high stake lies was compared to their accuracy detecting low stake lies, they were significantly more accurate judging high stake lies (O'Sullivan, Frank, Hurley, & Tiwana, 2009). This was likely due to the high stakes generating the types of clues more often seen in real life high stakes law enforcement situations. Thus we should exercise caution when relying upon the meta-analytic studies, which are tilted quite strongly in favor of low stakes lies.

This is apparent in the internal analyses done in the most recent comprehensive meta analytic review; when the authors separated out the data by those studies featuring high and low motivation (analogous to, but not exactly the same as stakes), they found stronger effects for emotion based clues in the high motivation studies (DePaulo et al., 2003).

Relationship to terrorism

It is clear to us that terrorism situations will feature a number of presses that will push for more of some of these 'lie clues', but not others. Terrorism is truly high stake, freely chosen behaviors, with motivation to assist the group foremost, with individual achievement secondary. Therefore, any scientific research scenario must contain those essential elements. A lie scenario that is low stake will likely underestimate the importance of the face and voice tone. A lie scenario with close ended, yes or no questions will likely underestimate the role of memory based clues, and likely mental effort clues as well. A lie scenario in which the individual is surreptitiously observed may underestimate the presence of behavioral control clues.

Therefore, we need to cast a more critical eye on the existing literature and predict what sorts of behaviors might exist in the context of counter terrorism. This critical look should also concentrate on aspects of detection of behaviors that are most readily identified by the vast majority of operations or field personnel or aspects of behavior that can be trained in a manner that can be explicit to the trainee. Eventually we have to determine how well our counter-terrorism professionals can make these judgments accurately, as well as whether they can do this in real time, and without technological assistance. But we first need to pin down which behaviors may be most diagnostic. Second we need to understand the best way to utilize these clues. It may not be productive to allow security/intelligence officers to render a judgment of 'deceptive' based upon the presence or absence of these clues. It may be more productive to think of these as 'hot spots' in behavior that need additional examination (Frank, Yarbrough, & Ekman, 2006). Thus they become a means to an end, and not an end in of themselves. The information gathered in this process can then generate the level of detail that allows the security/intelligence officer to compare those details with other information to produce evidence that corroborates or fails to corroborate the account of the individual. And given the lack of guaranteed signs of lying, this might be the most productive way to catch a lie based upon perceptible behavior.

Future questions and prospectus

In order to effectively leverage deception detection research to defeat terrorism, we must alter our current approaches to the study of deception, and address a number of important research questions along the way.

1. Scientists must facilitate close cooperation with security/ intelligence officers on all behavioral research.

We believe that this approach is the most productive given the historical mistrust between academics and practitioners when it comes to behavioral science. The academics seemed predisposed toward the counter-intuitive findings that appeared to law enforcement/security personnel to be biased against them (It is easier to get published a paper on "cops are dumb" than "cops do well"), and the practitioners seemed predisposed toward discounting all academic research because the designs and paradigms were not grounded in the real world, thus irrelevant to their concerns and needs. We also warn that we cannot simply put together any academic with any practitioner. They must be the right folks at both ends – those who understand, appreciate, and respect the work of the other. Not having the right people may instead exacerbate tensions, produce more defensiveness, and kill the disclosure needed to advance both the science and the utility of the work.

It is important then to do two things: to open up the real world to academics, and to open up the labs to practitioners. This is one of the main goals of the TRAP program. The goal of a grounded, visually clear program that is user or outreach driven is to insure that whatever is developed is operationally applicable, which will insure that the concept is used – and the more it is used the more useful it becomes on many levels.

When we allow academics into the practitioner's real world setting, we must let them sit in on a practitioner's actual work to witness what really happens, so that they can design their research paradigms to more adequately address the issues faced by the practitioner. This may involve efforts to get various security clearances for academics, but we feel this is worthwhile. Moreover, the academics can add research value to the materials used by the practitioners; for example, academics can teach the practitioners techniques for recording audio, video, or physiology that will allow much more detailed behavioral analysis by either humans or machines. This is certainly a two way effort; however, what needs to be driven home is that this is operationally applied approach, just the same as any applied medical research would be in the solution to a disease.

When we allow practitioners into the academics' laboratories, we must let them have input into the design phase of empirical work, so that they "buy in" to the results that emerge; i.e., we must have the "customer" in on the planning. Moreover, the practitioners may suggest questions that may not be apparent to the academics but which are very important to day to day security situations. And, what both groups need is to get a third partner involved – the public. We should not lose site of essential legal issues like probable cause or reasonable suspicion, as public rights needs to be considered in any of these endeavors. We must keep an eye toward the issues of public perception and the procedures the public is asked to endure - that while not always legally a concern, are always a concern when hoping to sustain a successful program. The public would need to consent to any new security procedures, and would need to allow researchers access to that information to perform analyses.

The practical experience of our group suggested that the most effective way to start this cross-communication is to identify a cadre of academics who respect and appreciate the practitioners, and practitioners who respect and appreciate the academics. This cadre can become the nucleus of a safe and trusted forum for the frank exchange of ideas. As this group builds credibility with each other and with their larger communities, they can then begin to attract other academics and practitioners into dialogue about their various concerns that will ultimately benefit both. Thus, this critical initial cadre can then serve as some sort of rudimentary germ around which the rest of the pearl can coalesce, thus insuring clear trusted pathways that allow the direct communication between the controlled world of science and the less constrained real world.

2. Because behavior is a constituent of people in situations, we must better understand those situations in which the behavior is analyzed.

After all, people plan and commit terrorist acts, not their underwear, shoes, or the suitcases they carry. Thus, we feel it is important to flesh out the particular situations that pose the relevance to a security screening, such as a checkpoint, a sit down interview, informal conversations, and surveillance. For example, the checkpoint can be a stand up checkpoint, as in an airport pre-board, customs/immigration post board, a non-immigrant visa interview, or military or other secure facility entry. These checkpoints can also be sit down, as when a border crossing or security checkpoint involves a car, train, boat, or other vehicle The sit down can be in service to investigating a suspect, witness, informant/asset, or potential employee, and in situations ranging from an immigration Customs and Border Protection secondary interview to an embassy walk-in. Conversations may be planned but appear to occur informally, or by accident to someone who is under suspicion of espionage, or is otherwise of interest. Surveillancc involves observing those outside your embassy, military establishment, public transport hub, or elsewhere for clues to intended malfeasant acts. We felt that it was very important to mirror carefully these real life situations to fully understand the patterns and pressures involved in each human interaction (or observation in the instance of surveillance) – in other words, to identify their structural features - so that we can test them under more controlled conditions, or to actually manipulate these conditions to try to create an environment that produces the maximum differential pressure on deceptive and non deceptive people - or hostile/non hostile - so that the behavior that is observed can more clearly delineate these groups.

In terms of mirroring the contexts, we recognize that more research energy and effort must be spent on understanding the interpersonal context between the two people in the interview – do they share world-views? Is it confrontational or simply informational interview? Does the interviewer build rapport, or do they act impenetrably serious? What if the interview is conducted standing up versus sitting down? For example, thermographic technology has shown promise as a means to detect deception in a sit down interview (Tsiamyrtzis et al., 2007) – but can this technology work in a checkpoint situation, where the act of walking up to the checkpoint and lugging baggage may create so much body heat "noise" as to bury to the body heat "signal" that serves to accurately classify liars and truth tellers? What are the patterns of rewards and punishments associated with the interviewer's judgment? How much time is allotted for questioning? What is the pattern of questioning? What form do the questions take?

In terms of manipulations, how do we *create* the contexts upon which behavior emerges that most clearly separates liars and truth tellers? For example, what sort of questions will generate the clue patterns that most likely separate the malfeasant from the rest? Is it simply a function of open versus closed ended, or are there patterns of questioning more effective than the rest? We know the polygraph has studied forms/patterns/types of questions, but the behavioral area has not done nearly so much. Of course, how these manipulations play out in different cultural contexts are also critically important to understand as well. The particular phrasing of a question to appear sympathetic in one culture may appear insulting in a different culture. These different reactions may be mistaken for different clue patterns, which also is of gigantic important. We don't know the answer as the majority of the research on deception has been done on American subjects. However, we can start the process of understanding these interactions by having the practitioners describe the details of the situations they faced in their work and their observations of other cultures.

In this same vein, we recognize how the context affects the behaviors one might interpret. In other words, the environment in which you gather the data affects what you see, and how you interpret it. If you physically threaten someone in an interview, and you see signs of fear, what does that mean? What if instead you have built a good rapport with this person – now what is likely to be the cause of a manifestation of fear? Thus we recognize that we need to spend more time identifying best practices in interview techniques, proxemic set up (the use of space, chairs, tables, etc. in the an interview setting), and so forth, so that one can create an environment that the security personnel can get the most accurate information possible. In intelligence work, or even in the hiring process, it is the *accuracy* of the information that is paramount to the investigator. One cannot make good decisions with inaccurate information. Thus, with more accurate data, he or she can make better decisions, be it in conducting a raid or hiring a person for a sensitive government position. Moreover, are there other clever ways to facilitate the human judgment process to take maximal advantage of the information available? For example, we find independent judges do better at spotting deception than dependent judges. So, why not have people who interpret these clues observe them independently? What about simply identifying the best judges and place them in the high value target interviews? How do you screen for these people? What is the best way to train people to recognize these behaviors?

This idea also means there must be room to fund replications of experimental studies. We have seen various models where people toss 80 variables based upon 25 subjects into a regression equation and come up with 3 predictors; then they run the same 80 on a different sample of 30 and get 3 different predictors, and yet publish both. It is unclear how or why these situations differ, how their structural features may account for these differences, or whether these results are just noise. Thus, replication will allow more precise understanding of the structural features, and also cut down on the amount of noise published in the field. Moreover, the idea of constructing a basic, high stake paradigm as a control paradigm that enables clear comparisons amongst findings may serve to facilitate the accumulation of information in a more systematic way. This points out that we should be wary of our own ignorance of operational settings. We may end up deciding that the only relevant studies are those that look at real life situations, despite the problems in establishing ground truth.

3. We need to examine clues beyond just deception.

In fact, it might be more productive to think of clues to reality, rather than clues to deceit. Thus, clues that indicate a potential attack are important. Also important are clues to the actual identity of a person (e.g., culturally specific emblems, speech patterns, terms/colloquialisms, etc) so that one has a basis for judging deception (e.g., a person claims they are a Shi'a

Muslim, yet they use the characteristic emblem gestures/word usage patterns of a Sunni Muslim). Also important is the ability to identify 'hot spots' in behavior -- ie, when the nonverbal behavior contradicts the verbal, there are verbal clues to unusual cognitive activity, or more generally, any change in behavior patterns for a specific topic. Hot spots are very important to recognize the subjective reality of the person in question. These clues are often micro-momentary, and can be missed with the untrained naked eye. They represent fleeting glimpses of the actual emotional or cognitive state of the person. However, it is important though to realize exactly what those clues are – clues to people thinking on their feet or that they have recognized something, or clues to emotion. Thus, one is still left to interpret why someone may feel this way, or are thinking on their feet. Developing techniques to identify these hot spots – which we now have evidence can be done, but we are still uncertain as to what is the optimal way to teach it – and then learning the limits of what one can infer from them is important because the ability to identify emotions – which signal behavioral intentions – can expand our understanding of others in security settings to optimize decision making, be in on a border of a job application.

There is evidence that some of these emotions are cross-culturally universal, whereas emblems and other gestures tend to be more culturally specific. Identifying dictionaries of the characteristic behaviors/styles/tones for different cultural groups would thus provide a more relevant comparison for behavioral pattern analysis in the future.

What this also means is that we should examine the residue of behavior – travel patterns, phone usage, or other patterns that identify those in need of more security scrutiny. In screening contexts, the key is to get that potential terrorist into the next level of scrutiny, and that information (as found in CAPPS, but now we know more and should update that) might be extraordinarily useful because that allows us to learn patterns related to malfeasance, as well as to develop a ground truth baseline to compare with a subject's response to other unknown pieces of information.

4. We need to examine these behavioral clues more cleverly.

The behavioral literature has identified around 100 different measures, and a meta-analysis by DePaulo et al (2003) concluded that there do seem to be some clues that on the more abstract level predict deception at statistically significant levels, particularly when liars are motivated, such as liars appear to be less forthcoming, their accounts are less compelling, they appear to be more tense, and their accounts are a bit too polished. However, we note that in order to apply findings derived from meta-analyses to security settings - which typically involve many studies featuring low stake lies, which are not usually found or even important in security settings - we must redouble our efforts to examine only those behavior patterns that occur in high stake settings. Otherwise excellent meta-analyses may not be as useful to security settings as they have been applied in the past, and future work should focus more directly on the high stake lies.

Given that untrained individuals do best at the *impressionistic* level, it is seems likely then that there are variables – or patterns and relationships amongst variables – that researchers haven't measured adequately yet. That is, there are behaviors associated with a judgment of "less compelling", and maybe our typical approach fails to capture them. One possibility is that we are simply missing some measure – that would be very possible. For example, Darwin was given photos of a man who was genuinely happy, and the same man posing a smile, and he noted that people could tell which was which, but he didn't know what the difference was. We noted in our studies (Frank, Ekman, & Friesen, 1993) that laypeople could sort out these smiles. A close examination showed differences in the muscles used to make the smile (i.e., the orbicularis oculi in conjunction with the zygomatic major), and in the symmetry of the smile. But the second possibility is that we are not measuring their patterns effectively, for example, the dynamic flow pattern of the variables themselves. For example, in this same study we also noted that the dynamic flow patterns of the smile muscle differed depending upon whether the smile was caused by genuine happiness, or was posed for politeness sake and without emotion present. The reason we might miss a variable like this is that we historically in behavioral analysis count things. We count the number of smiles. We count the number of leg movements. We count the length of the speech latency. But we don't examine nearly as well the flow of the muscle movement, the flow relationship between the gestures and the speech (we know when you separate in time gestures and speech it hurts people's comprehension of that same speech). In our smiling research, we found that there were 3 dynamic variables that distinguished these smiles – their onset patterns (smooth v. irregular), duration, and synchrony with other muscles. Thus time based coding of behaviors in relation to each other is a potentially fruitful direction. Luckily, many machine based tools do this very well.

5. We should find a role for technology in the behavioral analysis process.

Technology can be a powerful augmentation to detecting those with hostile intent. Given no Pinocchio response, at this point the technology may be only able to give us probabilistic information on behavior – but that might be enormously useful to the human decision maker. But also, technology may help identify the physical clues that are contributing to the interpretive level analysis, for example, The Computer Expression Recognition Tool (CERT; Bartlett, Movellan, Frank, & Littlewort, 2006) and other cutting-edge automated facial movement software. Maybe these technical solutions could reveal meaningful and useful behavioral information in other behavioral channels, or even in a more general behavioral array that are missed by human judges Thus, technology can facilitate observation and possible detect patterns that humans have a great deal more difficulty articulating. We do not know yet exactly how to integrate these into the decision making process, but it is clear it can play an important role, and efforts to create these systems in real-time are instrumental to this process. Modeling, in the area of intent can certainly aid in the development of a readily usable tool in a real world environment that could aid the investigator. There is a possibility that a handheld application could be devised to even drive the information search needed to continue an interview to obtain the behaviors needed for an even more conclusive decision. This type of tool is essential for resource allocation in an era of more often less resources to combat more threat.

6. We must obtain more real world data.

We know that more and more of the interactions between law enforcement, counter-intelligence/terrorism personnel, screening personnel and the subjects of those interviews are being recorded. As we mentioned earlier, academics can provide tips on how to record (e.g., we have experience with multiple government agencies advising them on the optimal way to record interviews to make them most useful to researchers). We also know there are locations where they are videotaping every interview. Certainly this should be made available to academics, and procedures can be drawn up to insure the confidentiality of these analyses. We recognize that we must obtain a satisfactory level of ground truth – i.e., what is the actual truth – in these instances, which is not as easy a task as it sounds. One can certainly agree that a bomb found in a suitcase is ground truth, but a subject's actual intentions may be a bit harder to determine with confidence. Videos of failed suicide bombers are another potential rich source of such information.

Gathering these data, and obtaining a satisfactory ground truth, is essential to allowing us to pursue other means of gathering knowledge. For example, obtaining real world data, or allowing us academics to help guide some efforts to collect it, may provide us with a more accurate understanding of the base rates for these malfeasant behaviors. These base rates allow decision makers to do their jobs more effectively/accurately, and to devise and develop techniques that will eliminate that single deadly false negative. Specifically, obtaining accurate base rates will also allow us a better perspective when analyzing in much more detail the false positives and false negatives of earlier security screening attempts. We feel that an in-depth analysis of these false positives/negatives is an important and untapped source of information that would be hugely important to creating better security screening techniques. Thus, to understand why this person falsely raised suspicion, or how this malfeasant person escaped additional scrutiny, will help patch unapparent holes in the screening process, and to develop adequate counter-techniques, and to be able to assess the relative cost-benefit balance of these techniques if and/or when they are implemented. In other words, what can we learn from these errors that can enable us to screen more efficiently and effectively to reduce those events in the future?

There are at least 5 general constraints to these real world data. These include the *legal* (what the subject says, whether subjects have right to not respond, or the use of surreptitious recording), *political* (will law makers have the public support to put these changes into practice), *social* (will these procedures affect the public's perceptions of security and ultimately be accepted) *practical* (where to put the camera, the 90 seconds allotted to do the interview), and the *financial* (are there funds to pay for the technology or the training) for doing this work. These can be overcome with a solid partnership between the academic and practitioner communities. This is why we must bring the public along, to inform them that we will experiment with new techniques from time to time, and to obtain their forbearance for the inevitable inconvenience that will engender. This means the public must be fully informed that these events will happen so that they can be convinced to be a willing partner to facilitating their own security, and that their occasional inconvenience is their contribution to national security.

Conclusion

We hope we have been sufficiently critical to correct what we've felt has been a recurring error in the application of research on detecting deception to real world contexts, such as terrorism. Scientists have not always combined studies with an eye toward their ecological validity. So if we can extend a research agenda beyond improvement in the measuring and weighting of clues – to the context in which they emerge – we could facilitate our ability to distinguish the terrorist from the human being whom simply wants to pursue a good productive life.

References

Bartlett, M. S., Littlewort, G., Frank, M. G., Lainscsek, C., Fasel, I., & Movellan, J. (2006). Fully automatic facial action recognition in spontaneous behavior. *Journal of Multimedia, 6,* 22-35.

Bond, C. F., & DePaulo, B. M. (2006). Accuracy of deception judgments. *Personality and Psychology Review*, 10, 214-234.

Buller, D. B., & Burgoon, J. K. (1994). Another look at information management: A rejoinder to McCornack, Levine, Morrison, and Lapinski. *Communication Monographs, 63,* 92-98.

Darwin, C. (1872/1998). *The expression of the emotions in man and animals.* New York Philosophical Library.

Darwin, C. (1998). 3rd ed. with Introduction, Afterword and Commentary by Paul Ekman: London: Harper Collins; New York: Oxford University Press.

DePaulo, B. M., Kashy, D. A., Kirkendol, S.E., Wyer, M. M., & Epstein, J.A. (1996). Lying in everyday life. Journal of Personality and Social Psychology, 70, 979-995.

DePaulo, B. M., Lindsay, J. J., Malone, B. E., Muhlenbruck, L., Charlton, K., & Cooper, H. (2003). Cues to deception. P*sychological Bulletin, 129,* 74-112.

deTurck, M.A., & Miller, G.R. (1985). Deception and arousal: Isolating the behavioral correlates of deception. *Human Communication Research, 12,* 181 -201.

Ekman, P. (1985/2001). *Telling lies: Clues to deceit in the marketplace, politics, and marriage.* New York: W. W. Norton & Co.

Ekman, P. (2003). *Emotions revealed: Recognizing faces and feelings to improve emotional life.* New York: Times Books/Henry Holt & Co.

Ekman, P., & Frank, M. G. (1993). Lies that fail. In M. Lewis & C. Saarni (Eds.) *Lying and deception in everyday life.* (pp 184-200). New York: Guilford Press.

Ekman, P. & Friesen W. V. (1972). Hand movements. *Journal of Communication, 22*, 353-374.

Ekman, P., Friesen, W. V., & Ancoli, S. (1980). Facial signs of emotional experience. *Journal of Personality and Social Psychology, 39,* 1125-1134.

Farwell, L. A., & Donchin, E. (1991). The truth will out: Interrogative polygraphy ("lie detection") with event-related brain potentials. *Psychophysiology, 28*, 531-547.

Frank, M. G. (2005). Research methods in detecting deception research. In J. A. Harrigan, R. Rosenthal, & K. R. Scherer (Eds.), *The new handbook of methods in nonverbal behavior research* (pp. 341-368). New York: Oxford University Press.

Frank, M. G., & Ekman, P. (2004). Nonverbal detection of deception in forensic contexts. In W.O'Donohue & E. Levensky (Eds.), *Handbook of Forensic Psychology* (pp. 635-653). New York: Elsevier.

Frank, M. G., Ekman, P., & Friesen, W.V. (1993). Behavioral markers and recognizability of the smile of enjoyment. *Journal of Personality and Social Psychology, 64,* 83-93.

Frank, M. G. (1989). *Human lie detection ability as a function of the liar's motivation.* Unpublished doctoral dissertation, Cornell University, Ithaca, NY.

Frank, M. G., & Feeley, T. H. (2003). To catch a liar: Challenges for research in lie detection training. *Journal of Applied Communication Research, 31,* 58-75.

Frank, M.G., Matsumoto, D. M., Ekman, P., Kang, S. & Kurylo, A. (2010). *Improving the Ability to Recognize Micro-Expressions of Emotion.* Manuscript under review.

Frank, M. G., Yarbrough, J. D., & Ekman, P. (2006). Improving Interpersonal Evaluations: Combining Science and Practical Experience. In T. Williamson (Ed.) *Investigative Interviewing: Rights, research, regulation.* (pp 229-255). Portland, Oregon: Willan Publishing.

Haugaard, J. J. & Repucci, N. D. (1992). Children and the truth. In S. J. Ceci, M. DeSimone-Leichtman, and M.E. Putnick (Eds) *Cognitive and social factors in early deception.* Hillsdale, NJ: Erlbaum

Hazlett, G. (2006). Research on detection of deception: What we know versus what we think we know. *Educing Information: Interrogation – Science and Art* (National Defense Intelligence College). pp 45-62.

Inbau, F. E., Reid, J. E., & Buckley, J. P. (1986). *Criminal interrogation and confessions*. Baltimore: Williams and Wilkins.

Johnson-Laird, P. N. (1980). Mental models in cognitive science. *Cognitive Science, 4,* 71-115.

Matsumoto, D., Keltner, D., O'Sullivan, M., & Frank, M.G. (2008). Facial expressions of emotion. In M. Lewis, J. Haviland-Jones, and L. Barrett (Eds). *Handbook of Emotions* (3rd edition). New York: Guilford Publications.

Matsumoto, D., & Willingham, B. (2006). The thrill of victory and the agony of defeat: Spontaneous expressions of medal winners of the, 2004 Athens Olympic games. *Journal of Personality and Social Psychology, 91*, 568-581.

O'Sullivan, M., Frank, M.G., Hurley, C.M., & Tiwana, J. (2009). Police lie detection accuracy: The effect of lie scenario. *Law and Human Behavior, 33,* 530-538.

Rinn, W. E. (1984). The neuropsychology of facial expression: A review of the neurological and psychological mechanisms for producing facial expressions. *Psychological Bulletin, 95*, 52-77.

Scherer, K. (1984). On the nature and function of emotions: A component process approach. In K. Scherer & P. Ekman (Eds.) *Approaches to emotion.* (293-317). Erlbaum: Hillsdale, NJ.

Scherer, K. R., Wallbott, H. G., & Summerfield, A. B. (Eds.). (1986). *Experiencing Emotion: A cross-cultural study.* Cambridge: Cambridge University Press.

Steinbrook, R.(1992). The polygraph test: A flawed diagnostic method. *New England Journal of Medicine, 327,* 122-123.

Tsiamyrtzis, P., Dowdall, J., Shastri, D., Pavlidis, I., Frank, M.G., & Ekman, P. (2007). Imaging Facial Physiology for the Detection of Deceit. *International Journal of Computer Vision, 71*, 123-253.

Undeutsch, U. (1982). Statement reality analysis. In Trankell, A, (Ed). Reconstructing the past: The role of psychologists in criminal trials (pp. 27-56). Kluwer, Deventer, The Netherlands.

Vrij, A., Akehurst, L., & Morris, P. (1997). Individual differences in hand movements during deception. *Journal of Nonverbal Behavior 21, 87-102.*

Vrij, A. (2004). Invited article: Why professionals fail to catch liars and how they can improve. *Legal and Criminological Psychology*, *9*, 159-181.

Vrij, A., Edward, K., & Bull, R. (2001). Police officers' ability to detect deceit: The benefit of indirect deception detection measures. *Legal and Criminological Psychology*, *6,* 185–196.

Vrij, A. (2008). *Detecting lies and deceit: The psychology of lying and the implications for professional practice*. Chichester: John Wiley.

Waid, W. M., & Orne, M. T. (1982). The physiological detection of deception. *American Scientist, 70*, 402-409.

Zuckerman, M., DePaulo, B. M., & Rosenthal, R. (1981). Verbal and nonverbal communication of deception. In L. Berkowitz (Ed.), *Advances in experimental social psychology* (pp. 1-59). San Diego, CA: Academic Press.

VII. The Role of Emotion in Predicting Violence

David Matsumoto, Ph.D.

San Francisco State University

Mark G. Frank, Ph.D.

University at Buffalo

Abstract

Human emotion is a crucial aspect of behavior that is often overlooked by researchers, operators, and policy makers. We believe that understanding emotions as discrete entities provides an important source of the motivation for behavior, and allows for analysis and prediction of how or when individuals or groups – particularly terrorist or politically active extremist groups – engage in violence. In this paper we describe our research in two areas, one examining the role of emotion in predicting violence by terrorist and other ideologically motivated groups, the other examining facial signs of imminent aggression. We describe some of our own novel thinking in these areas, the findings obtained to-date, and possible research questions that can be addressed in the near future. We consider how best to tailor these ideas and approaches to active security, law enforcement, and intelligence officers.

Introduction

One crucial aspect of human behavior that is often overlooked by researchers, operators, and policy makers is that of human emotion. Although emotion is often viewed as too soft for serious consideration or research, an understanding of emotion is central to an understanding of any individual or group behavior. On the individual level, emotions are evolutionarily evolved information processing systems that aid in survival (Cosmides & Tooby, 2000; Darwin, 1872/1998). They are transient, fleeting reactions to events that have implications for our welfare, and require immediate response (Ekman, 2003; Lazarus, 1991). They prime behaviors by initiating unique physiological signatures and mental structures (Levenson, 1999, 2003). They aid in bonding memories and cognitions (Bower, 1981; Forgas & Bower, 1987). And most importantly, they are a major source of motivation for behavior (Tomkins, 1962, 1963).

Emotions also exist on the group level, and serve similar functions. Group emotions are *emotions shared by individual members of groups, often about their own groups or other groups*. Group emotions occur when a sufficient proportion of individual members of a group have similar emotions about their group (the 'ingroup') or about other groups (the 'outgroup'), although there is no definition or consensus in the field about what that proportion may be. Like individual-level emotions, groups have emotional reactions to events that have consequences to their perceived welfare and survival. Group level emotions serve as motivations for group behaviors. They are woven into the group's overarching narratives of life, and thus provide guidelines and bases for making attributions about ingroups and outgroups. And they aid in regulating social behavior and preventing social chaos (Matsumoto et al., 2008). Thus, a complete understanding of behavior starts with the recognition of the importance of emotion, because emotion *is* motivation (Tomkins, 1962, 1963). This is true on the level of individuals as well as groups. Importantly for this article, it is true for the understanding of the behavior of individuals and groups in predicting acts of hostility.

Theoretical Framework

Understanding Emotions as Discrete Constructs

There are many ways to understand and categorize emotions. A simple way, for instance, is to classify emotions simply by their valence (positive or negative) or intensity (strong v. weak). Indeed, this way of understanding emotions is very popular not only among laypersons but also in academic psychology (Feldman Barrett, 2004; Russell & Feldman Barrett, 1999), and its simplicity merits attention. But there is a large body of literature that demonstrates convincingly that not all emotions are the same, nor should they be reduced to simple dimensions such as valence or intensity (Ekman, 1999; Izard, 2007; Panksepp, 2007). This framework is known as a *discrete emotions* perspective, and in this perspective, different categories of emotion are qualitatively and uniquely distinct from each other; that is, emotions are discrete entities.

Take the emotions of anger and fear. Most law enforcement groups have heard the terms ‘fight or flight’ to describe these emotions, respectively. These emotions activate different areas of the brain, produce very different patterns of body reactions (sweat, surface vasoconstriction vs. dilation, etc.) and nonverbal expressions, and laypeople simply do not confuse the subjective sensations associated with them. Whether one expresses fear versus anger has major implications for a person’s well being; inmates who express fear are assaulted, those who express anger are not. Yet a valence/intensity model would label both anger and fear similarly as ‘negative’ and ‘intense’.

Now compare anger, contempt, and disgust, all of which can be considered negative emotions in the simplistic valenced view above. There are important differences among these emotions that make it clear that they are not alike, and these have major practical implications. Anger, contempt, and disgust are very different emotions, with different physiological reactions, different associated mental states, and different nonverbal expressions

(Ekman, 1999), all of which prepare us for different behaviors. When we are angry, for instance, our heart rate increases, and the blood flows differentially to our arms and hands, preparing us to fight (Levenson, 2003); the function of anger, therefore, is to remove obstacles. The function of disgust, however, is to eliminate or repulse contaminated objects, while a primary function of contempt is to make a statement about one's evaluations of another's actions vis-à-vis status and hierarchy. Anger, therefore, is an emotion about what someone or a group did. Contempt and disgust, however, are emotions about who the person or group is.

Although laypersons often do not make such distinctions among emotions, those distinctions are important. In particular, there is a special place for disgust in understanding terrorism and violence, for several reasons. First, studies of emotions in interpersonal conflicts indicate that it is disgust (and contempt), not anger, that is associated with the breakdown of a relationship (which could be seen as a component of hostile acts between groups; see Gottman & Levenson, 2002; Gottman, Levenson, & Woodin, 2001). Second, as mentioned above, disgust is a basic, primary emotion, elicited by perceptions of agents of contamination or disease. It is universal, not only in its signal properties (Ekman, 1993), but also in terms of its elicitors (Rozin, Haidt, & McCauley, 1999; Rozin, Lowery, Imada, & Haidt, 1999). Third, disgust is a moral emotion, and it is often used to sanction our moral beliefs and behaviors (Chapman, Kim, Susskind, & Anderson, 2009). Fourth, our anecdotal observations of the videos of terrorists such as Osama Bin Laden or the Virginia Tech University shooter Cho Seung Hyi, as well as the speeches and writing of world leaders who incited wars (e.g., Hitler, Milosevic, etc.) indicated an escalation of disgust (in facial expressions) leading up to violent acts. Disgust leads individuals to kill cockroaches, and it doesn't matter whether the cockroaches are male, female, or infants; they are cockroaches and must be eliminated. Likewise, terrorist acts do not differentiate between men, women, or children; they must be eliminated because they are vermin (or infidel dogs).

Thus, although much research on aggression has focused on anger, in today's context of terrorism as a global phenomenon, disgust must be considered a central emotion to study on the group level, as there it represents a shift toward making an assessment of the inherent characteristics of the other group, rather than a temporary judgment about an act committed by that group. Disgust transforms aggression, which sometimes can be constructive, into hostility, which is almost always not, and anger into hatred. The transformation of anger to contempt and then disgust is akin to a transformation of a situational attribution about an act to a dispositional attribution about the person. Consequently, if a person or group does something bad, anger is focused on the act, but the person or group may or may not be bad, and in fact may be rehabilitated in some way in the future. Evaluations resulting in contempt and disgust, however, mean that the person or group is inherently bad and there is no chance for rehabilitation; thus the logical recourse is to eliminate them. Elimination can occur in various manners: from the extreme form of violently eliminating them, to shunning, to avoidance, to simply dissociating them from one's consciousness.

Intergroup Emotions

Although the scientific study of emotion has traditionally focused on the individual, in recent years group level emotions have increasingly become an object of scientific research. Most studies have examined the types of emotions felt by members of groups toward outgroups. Studies of intergroup anxiety, for instance, suggest that anxiety toward outgroups may occur because of fear of embarrassment about not knowing what to do with the outgroup, fear of negative behavioral consequence, fear of negative evaluations, a history of negative intergroup relations and minimal previous contact with the outgroup, large status differences between the ingroup and outgroup, or higher ratios of outgroup members compared to ingroup (i.e., more of "them" than "us") (Niedenthal, Krauth-Gruber, & Ric, 2006; Stephan & Stephan, 1985). Studies on the Cho Seung Hyi *Content Model* suggest that group members have different emotions toward outgroups based on the dimensions of perceived warmth and competence (Cuddy, Fiske, & Glick, 2007). *Intergroup Emotions Theory* suggests that group members feel anger toward outgroups when the ingroup is in conflict with the outgroup and the ingroup view is the majority; this anger will lead groups to confront, oppose, or attack the outgroup (Mackie, Devos, & Smith, 2000).

Some studies have also examined the emotions that are attributed to ingroup and outgroup members. *Infrahumanization Theory*, for instance, suggests that ingroup favoritism and outgroup derogation leads to the attribution of more human characteristics, including emotions, toward ingroup members compared to outgroups (Cortes, Demoulin, Rodriguez, Rodrigues, & Leyens, 2005; Demoulin et al., 2004; Rodriguez Torres et al., 2005). Thus ingroups are more likely to attribute the more "human" emotions of compassion, shame, serenity, bitterness, or contempt to ingroups. At the same times, ingroups attribute more "basic" or "primary" emotions such as surprise, anger, pleasure, fear, attraction, or disgust to outgroups. Interestingly, these emotions are those considered to be shared between humans and non-human primates (LeDoux & Phelps, 2008).

Thus, the dehumanization of outgroups involves emotional attributions about those outgroups associated with animals, not humans, and intergroup emotions are the glue that keep such attitudes about outgroups connected. Without their emotional bases, these attitudes would have little meaning or practical consequence. But intergroup relations are complex and potentially deadly, especially among ideologically based groups, precisely because outgroup cognitions are associated with strong emotions.

The Role of Emotions in Predicting the Escalation of Terrorist Groups to Violence

Cultures of Hatred based on Emotion

Not only are emotions important to the creation and maintenance of intergroup attitudes and relations, but *changes* in those emotions across time may be associated with different intergroup behaviors (because the primary function of emotion is to motivate behavior, on both the individual and group levels). In our view, violence and hostility are the direct result of the planned inculcation and careful, methodical nurturing of hatred in terrorist groups. As mentioned above, this theoretical framework is based on a view of discrete emotions (Ekman, 1999), most notably those having to do with morality (Rozin & Fallon, 1987; Rozin, Lowery et al., 1999; Tangney & Fischer, 1995). Although emotions such as shame and guilt have received considerable attention as moral emotions in the past (Shweder & Haidt, 2000; Tangney & Fischer, 1995), more recent work has focused on anger, contempt, and disgust and their relationship to autonomy, community, and divinity (Rozin, Lowery et al., 1999). More specifically, Rozin and colleagues (1999) proposed that anger, contempt, and disgust are often elicited in response to violations of autonomy, community, and divinity, respectively, known as the CAD (community, autonomy, divinity) Triad hypothesis.

Sternberg (2003) has proposed a triarchic theory of hatred that is based on these three emotions, and fear. He proposes that hatred is based on a negation of intimacy (based on disgust), passion (based on anger and fear) and decision-commitment based on devaluation and diminution of others (based on contempt). According to his model, different kinds of hatred can exist based on different combinations of these three components. Because there are three components, they can yield seven different combinations of hatred: cold, cool, hot, simmering, boiling, seething, and burning hatred.

An interesting aspect of Sternberg's (2003) theory is that hatred is propagated via stories or narratives. Stories serve an important and interesting purpose, bringing to life the various components of hatred in a concise, easy-to-understand and easy-to-communicate method. It provides group leaders with a platform by which group emotions can be developed, fostered, maintained, or extinguished, and for those same emotions to be propagated within groups by its members who communicate the stories to others.

According to Sternberg (2003), there are many different types of hate stories that achieve this purpose:

- the stranger
- impure other (v. pure ingroup)
- controller (v. controlled)
- faceless foe (v. individuated ingroup)
- enemy of God (v. servant of God)
- morally bankrupt (v. morally sound)
- death (v. life)
- barbarian (v. civilized ingroup)
- greedy enemy (v. financially responsible ingroup)
- criminal (v. innocent party)
- torturer (v. victim)
- murderer (v. victim)
- seducer-rapist (v. victim)
- animal pest (v. human)
- power crazed (v. mentally balanced)
- subtle infiltrator (v. infiltrated)
- comic character (v. sensible ingroup)
- thwarter-destroyer of destiny (v. seeker of destiny

Stories also serve the important function of providing members with a way to communicate attitudes, values, beliefs, and opinions across generations, a central component of culture, which refers to a shared meaning and information system transmitted across generations (Matsumoto & Juang, 2007). Terrorist groups, like many groups, are uniquely characterized by their own cultures.

Collectively, this system provides guidelines for normative behavior, the basis for the nature and function of attributions, communication systems, and intergroup relations. Terrorist organizations are often characterized by sacred values and beliefs (Atran & Axelrod, 2007; Ginges, Atran, Medin, & Shikaki, 2007), but then again so are many ideologically-based organizations (e.g., pro- or anti-abortion groups, gun groups, death penalty groups, etc.). Research on terrorists and other ideologically-based groups suggests that they are comparable to each other in their social psychological dynamics (Stahelski, 2005). Hatred and disdain of others is facilitated by a culture of hatred and disdain that is permeated throughout the group, and future generations are similarly enculturated. Moreover, these narratives or stories color the perception of all new information; information that confirms the narrative is accepted at face value, information that disconfirms the narrative is dismissed through accusations of bias, conspiracies, or even flat out logical fallacies (Nisbett & Ross, 1980). Thus once established, narratives are self-perpetuating.

Emotions Associated with a Ramping up toward Violence

Work on the CAD Triad hypothesis (Rozin, Lowery et al., 1999) is important because it highlights the importance of specific, discrete emotions in moral systems. Sternberg's (2003) work is important because it uses the CAD Triad hypothesis as a basis to understand the various components of hatred. Building on this previous work, we propose that these emotions are transformed over time, often via stories, to inculcate cultures with hatred and violence. Specifically, we suggest three phases in this emotion transformation:

Phase 1 – Outrage based on Anger.

Phase 1 involves the group identifying events that obstruct goals or are based on perceptions of injustice. Phase 1 may also involve the group identifying threats to well-being, physical safety, or ways of life. These interpretations and attributions lead to, or are fueled by, feelings of anger toward the outgroup.

Phase 2 – Moral Superiority based on Contempt.

In Phase 2, groups begin to reinterpret anger-eliciting situations and events identified in Phase 1, and take the high road; that is, they reappraise the events from a position of moral superiority, identify links between similar behaviors or events, no matter how tenuous, thus making the attribution that the outgroup is morally inferior. These reappraisals and attributions lead to, or are fueled by, the emotion of contempt.

Phase 3 – Elimination based on Disgust.

In Phase 3, there is a further reappraisal of events and situations that lead to the conclusion that distance needs to be placed between the ingroup and outgroup (the mild form of elimination), or that the outgroup needs to be eliminated (the extreme form). These ideas are promulgated by the emotion of disgust.

This perspective allows us to understand how groups can hate, but not all hatred leads to violence or hostility. Hatred based primarily on anger and/or contempt will not be associated with violence or hostility, but hatred that involves disgust does, because disgust is the emotion of repulsion and elimination. Groups can be angry or contemptuous, but when they are also disgusted, they may become dangerous. Further, it is interesting to note that many definitions of hatred involve concepts of intense aversion, which is related to the emotion of disgust, or intense animosity, which has its roots in animals (and therefore not human), also related to disgust.

How do these appraisals and reappraisals occur, and group emotions get created or transformed? Powerful leaders set the tone for groups to interpret or reinterpret events in certain ways that then lead to group emotions. Leaders do this by creating stories based on their appraisals or reappraisals of critical events and situations, and by communicating the emotions associated with their reappraised stories to their followers and subordinates. The communication occurs through the specific types of emotion-laden and emotion-related words, metaphors, images, and analogies used, as well as nonverbally through their faces, voices, gestures, and body language. That is, it is not the case that emotions are communicated directly to groups (e.g., we perceived an obstacle, so we must be angry); instead, emotions are communicated indirectly via the associations made to groups with emotion-laden words, metaphors, analogies, and nonverbal behavior. Through the careful use of language and nonverbal behaviors, leaders are in a position to motivation, escalate, or defuse situations, and incite action or not, through emotion.

A Possible Research Agenda

This perspective leads to several research questions that can be addressed in the future, all focusing on the following basic claim: Specific and discrete emotions involving anger, contempt, and disgust, are transformed in careful, methodical ways across time in terrorist groups to produce a ramping up and escalation of violence toward outgroups. Further, we believe that disgust is the crucial emotion that turns cold hatred into hot hatred, leading to violence and hostility.

Based on this main research question, we would like to test the following hypotheses, all of which have important theoretical implications for basic science and understanding of group emotions, and practical ramifications for national security:

1. Discrete emotions of anger, contempt, and disgust toward outgroups are communicated by leaders verbally and nonverbally;
2. The development of hatred corresponds to the amounts and types of these emotions communicated by leaders toward outgroups across time;
3. The ramping up toward violence by Terrorists and Other Ideologically Based Groups (TOIBG) occurs across phases that can be identified according to the appraisal, reappraisals, attributions, and emotions portrayed by leaders across time;
4. Violence and aggression only occur when disgust becomes part of the story portrayed by leaders.

Potential Research Possibilities

There are many ways in which the ideas set forth above can be tested. We describe two that may be readily doable given FBI resources: (1) the study and analysis of the emotion-based content of justifications of violence from the written records and statements, and (2) the analysis of the emotional content in video records of terrorist group leaders speaking about other groups. Both projects would involve the compilation of written statements and/or video records of leaders of terrorist groups as they speak about groups to which they are opposed. Written statements would be analyzed for their emotional content using either readily available analytic tools (such as LIWC, SCAN, etc.). We have are also in the process of developing proprietary tools to do so from written record. Nonverbal expressions of emotion in videos could be captured by measuring facial expressions, a methodology that both authors of this report are world leaders in. In both cases, analyses would provide indices of the discrete emotions expressed by the terrorist group leaders as they talked about the outgroups they despise, and changes in the expressed emotion over time can be correlated with whether or not the group ramped up to violence or not.

Facial Expressions of Emotion as Indicators of Imminent Aggression

Identifying Facial Signs of Imminent Aggression

Emotions evolved as rapid, information processing systems that enable humans to adapt to changes in their environment with minimal conscious intervention (Ekman, 1999; Lazarus, 1991; Tooby & Cosmides, 2008). When elicited, emotions recruit a host of physiological, cognitive, and expressive behaviors that are organized and coordinated with each other (Levenson, 1999). Facial expressions are part of this coordinated response package. Darwin (1872/1998) claimed, in his principle of serviceable habits, that facial expressions are the residual actions of more complete, whole body responses that prepared individuals for action by priming the body to act. Thus, anger is expressed by furrowing the brow and tightening the lips with teeth displayed because these actions are part of an attack response; disgust is expressed with an open mouth, nose wrinkle, and tongue protrusion as part of a vomiting response. Recent research has suggested that different facial expressions – e.g., fear and disgust - do facilitate the acquisition or rejection of sensory information (Susskind et al., 2008).

This important theoretical perspective suggests a link between specific facial expressions of emotion and subsequent behavior. Although disgust may energize the narrative to produce violence at a distal level, anger energizes the physical action of assault at the proximal level. Recently, we examined the possibility that variants of the facial expression of anger are reliably associated with acts of immediate, subsequent violent behavior. It makes sense that signs of anger may be seen prior to acts of aggression or assault, if anger primes the body to aggress and facial expressions are part of the anger response package. Given that assassinations, shootings, and physical violence often occur in a matter of seconds, the existence of such facial signs is a distinct possibility, and has important practical ramifications.

In our studies, law enforcement officers (LEOs) in five countries were shown an array of faces posed by a single

Caucasian male – a professional actor. Each expression depicted a variant of the full-face, prototypic version of anger found in stimulus sets such as the Pictures of Facial Affect (Ekman & Friesen, 1976) or the Japanese and Caucasian Facial Expressions of Emotion stimulus sets (Matsumoto & Ekman, 1988). That is, all expressions included at least some of the muscles identified by the Facial Action Coding System (FACS; Ekman & Friesen, 1978) that are involved in the full face prototype; the expressions differed in the amount and intensity of those muscles, and in the presence or absence of zygomatic major (the smiling muscle). The expressions were generated by first asking the actor to produce the face that had seen in previous videos involving assaults, attacks, and assassination attempts. Additional expressions were then generated by asking the actor to portray as many different kinds of anger as he knew. This resulted in a preliminary selection of 16 expressions. Pilot testing with a separate group of American LEOs indicated that some of the expressions were almost never selected in the procedures; four expressions were thus dropped, resulting in the final stimulus set involving 12 expressions, which were placed in a random array and numbered.

LEOs in each of the countries were simply asked to select a face, from the 12 provided, they saw moments before either a premeditated physical assault, or an assault due to a momentary loss of impulse control. (Prior to doing this task, the LEOs were asked if they were ever involved in such attacks, if they remembered the face of the attacker, and if they could recall the face if they saw it again.) The LEOs identified two faces – one for premeditated assaults and one for loss of impulse control – at high agreement rates. Moreover, the same faces were identified by LEOs in different countries, two of which were not English speaking (Israel and South Korea).

Moreover, university students who were shown the same set of faces and engaged in the same experimental procedures did *not* select the same faces at above chance rates, suggesting that our previous findings were not due to a process of elimination among the 12 available faces. We are currently in the process of replicating the same findings using different arrays of faces.

Potential Research Possibilities

We are keen to replicate the studies conducted to date with FBI personnel and other LEOs. The study methodologies are entirely online and can be done remotely in about 15 minutes. Additional data would go a long way in ensuring that the faces that have been identified to date are indeed the faces of these two different types of violence.

We would also like to expand the notion of violence from the spontaneous and planned to that special category of suicide bomber – particularly one who believes they have divine dispensation to conduct their attack. We have no data concerning the facial signs of this type of imminent aggression, but we have no reason to believe that the face of the suicide bomber is the same as the face of the person carrying out a premeditated attack or who loses control and attacks. There are data bases within the government with video footage prior to attack that our team would be uniquely qualified to analyze for signs of impending attack through both facial expression and bodily movements such as gait or tension.

Moreover, there are additional research questions that can follow on this line of research. For example, we have developed tools to help train individuals to identify what we call the two types of dangerous faces; as of this date, however, we have no data concerning its efficacy, either as a training tool or in the field. Such data is a must. We have developed the experimental protocols to do so, and these can be done within a relatively short period of time.

Conclusion

The findings to date have significant potential implications for national defense and security, intelligence, and law enforcement operations. For example, the elucidation of the role of emotion in leading to acts of aggression by members of ideologically-motivated groups suggests the existence of signs that can be used as markers of escalation toward hostility. This, combined with the creation of sensor technologies that can recognize those markers – either through the analysis of the emotional content of verbal statements, nonverbal behavior, or the emotional profiles of groups – leads to the interesting potential for these markers to predict hostile acts before they are enacted, allowing for evasive action that may save lives. Technologies that analyze the verbal content of speeches can identify emotions associated with this escalation, allowing for the production of automated detectors of aggression potential based on ramp ups of disgust across time. The same potential exists for automated detectors of aggression ramp ups based on video analyses of faces, or voices. These technological advances are all predicated on the establishment of empirically validated signs of aggression escalation based on emotion, which has been found preliminarily, but require further validation. The identification of facial signs of premeditated assault leads to the interesting possibility that automated expression recognition technologies can be developed to scan crowds for such faces to identify individuals of interest; this capability would surely be useful for those in protective services. And the identification of the face of loss of impulse control is important for anyone – including FBI agents – who interact with individuals who may have the potential to explode to violence at any time. Knowing what signs to look for is important for anyone in harm's way.

References

Atran, S., & Axelrod, R. (2007). Sacred barriers to conflict resolution. *Science, 317*, 1039-1040.

Bower, G. H. (1981). Mood and memory. *American Psychologist, 36*(2), 129-148.

Chapman, H. A., Kim, D. A., Susskind, J. M., & Anderson, A. K. (2009). In bad taste: Evidence for the oral origins of moral disgust. *Science, 323*, 1222-1226.

Cortes, B. P., Demoulin, S., Rodriguez, R. T., Rodrigues, A. P., & Leyens, J.-P. (2005). Infrahumanization or familiarity? Attribution of uniquely human emotions to the self, the ingroup, and the outgroup. *Personality and Social Psychology Bulletin, 31*(2), 243-253.

Cosmides, L., & Tooby, J. (2000). Evolutionary psychology and the emotions. In M. Lewis & J. M. Haviland-Jones (Eds.), *Handbook of emotions* (2nd ed., pp. 91-115). New York: Guilford Press.

Cuddy, A. J. C., Fiske, S. T., & Glick, P. (2007). The BIAS map: Behaviors from intergroup affect and stereotypes. *Journal of Personality and Social Psychology, 92*(4), 631-648.

Darwin, C. (1872/1998). *The expression of emotion in man and animals*. New York: Oxford University Press.

Demoulin, S., Leyens, J.-P., Paladino, M. P., Rodriguez Torres, R., Rodriguez Perez, A., & Dovidio, J. F. (2004). Dimensions of "uniquely" and "nonuniquely" human emotions. *Cognition and Emotion, 18*, 71-96.

Ekman, P. (1993). Facial expression and emotion. *American Psychologist, 48*(4), 384-392.

Ekman, P. (1999). Basic emotions. In T. Dalgleish & T. Power (Eds.), *The handbook of cognition and emotion* (pp. 45-60). Sussex, United Kingdom: John Wiley and Sons, Ltd.

Ekman, P. (2003). *Emotions revealed* (2nd ed.). New York: Times Books.

Ekman, P., & Friesen, W. V. (1976). *Pictures of facial affect*. Palo Alto, CA: Consulting Psychologists Press.

Ekman, P., & Friesen, W. V. (1978). *Facial action coding system: Investigator's guide*. Palo Alto, Calif.: Consulting Psychologists Press.

Feldman Barrett, L. (2004). Feelings or words? Understanding the content in self-report ratings of experienced emotion. *Journal of Personality and Social Psychology, 87*(2), 266-281.

Forgas, J. P., & Bower, H. G. (1987). Mood effects on person-perception judgments. *Journal of Personality and Social Psychology, 53*(1), 53-60.

Ginges, J., Atran, S., Medin, D., & Shikaki, K. (2007). Sacred bounds on rational resolution of violent political conflict. *Proceedings from the National Academy of Sciences, 104*, 7357-7360.

Gottman, J. M., & Levenson, R. W. (2002). A two-factor model for predicting when a couple will divorce: Exploratory analyses using 14-year longitudinal data. *Family Process, 41*(1), 83-96.

Gottman, J. M., Levenson, R. W., & Woodin, E. (2001). Facial expressions during marital conflict. *Journal of Family Communication, 1*, 37-57.

Izard, C. E. (2007). Basic emotions, natural kinds, emotion schemas, and a new paradigm. *Perspectives on Psychological Science, 2*(3), 260-280.

Lazarus, R. (1991). *Emotion and adaptation*. New York: Oxford University Press.

LeDoux, J. E., & Phelps, E. A. (2008). Emotional networks in the brain. In M. Lewis, J. M. Haviland-Jones & L. Feldman

Barrett (Eds.), *Handbook of Emotions* (3rd ed., pp. 159-179). New York: The Guilford Press.

Levenson, R. W. (1999). The intrapersonal functions of emotion. *Cognition and Emotion, 13*(5), 481-504.

Levenson, R. W. (2003). Autonomic specificity and emotion. In R. J. Davidson, K. Scherer & H. H. Goldsmith (Eds.), *Handbook of affective sciences* (pp. 212-224). New York: Oxford University Press.

Mackie, D. M., Devos, T., & Smith, E. R. (2000). Intergroup emotions: Explaining offensive action tendencies in an intergroup context. *Journal of Personality and Social Psychology, 79*(4), 602-616.

Matsumoto, D., & Ekman, P. (1988). Japanese and Caucasian Facial Expressions of Emotion and Neutral Faces (JACFEE and JACNeuF). Available from www.humintell.com.

Matsumoto, D., & Juang, L. (2007). *Culture and Psychology* (4th ed.). Belmont, CA: Wadsworth.

Matsumoto, D., Yoo, S. H., Nakagawa, S., Alexandre, J., Altarriba, J., Anguas-Wong, A. M., et al. (2008). Culture, emotion regulation, and adjustment. *Journal of Personality and Social Psychology, 94*(6), 925-937.

Niedenthal, P. M., Krauth-Gruber, S., & Ric, F. (2006). *Psychology of emotion: Interpersonal, experiential, and cognitive approaches*. New York: Psychology Press.

Nisbett, R. E., & Ross, L. (1980). *Human inference: Strategies and shortcomings of social judgment*. Englewood Cliffs, NJ: Prentice Hall.

Panksepp, J. (2007). Neurologizing the psychology of affects: How appraisal-based constructivism and basic emotion theory can coexist. *Perspectives on Psychological Science, 2*(3), 281-296.

Rodriguez Torres, R., Leyens, J.-P., Rodriguez Perez, A., Betancour Rodriguez, V., Quiles del Castillo, M. N., Demoulin, S., et al. (2005). The lay distinction between primary and secondary emotions: A spontaneous categorization? *International Journal of Psychology, 40*(2), 100-107.

Rozin, P., & Fallon, A. E. (1987). A perspective on disgust. *Psychological Review, 94*(1), 23-41.

Rozin, P., Haidt, J., & McCauley, C. R. (1999). Disgust: The body and soul emotion. In T. Dalgleish & M. J. Power (Eds.), *Handbook of cognition and emotion* (pp. 429-445). New York: John Wiley and Sons Ltd.

Rozin, P., Lowery, L., Imada, S., & Haidt, J. (1999). The CAD triad hypothesis: A mapping between three moral emotions (contempt, anger, disgust) and three moral codes (community, autonomy, divinity). *Journal of Personality and Social Psychology, 75*(4), 574-585.

Russell, J. A., & Feldman Barrett, L. (1999). Core affect, prototypical emotional episodes, and other things called *emotion*: Dissecting the elephant. *Journal of Personality and Social Psychology, 76*(5), 805-819.

Shweder, R. A., & Haidt, J. (2000). The cultural psychology of the emotions: Ancient and new. . In M. Lewis & J. M. Haviland (Eds.), *The handbook of emotions* (pp. 397-414). New York: Guilford Press.

Stahelski, A. (2005). Terrorists are made, not born: Creating terrorists using social psychological conditioning. *Cultic Studies Review, 4*(1).

Stephan, W. G., & Stephan, C. W. (1985). Intergroup anxiety. *Journal of Social Issues, 41*, 157-175.

Sternberg, R. J. (2003). A duplex theory of hate: Development and application to terrorism, massacres, and genocide. *Review of General Psychology, 7*(3), 299-328.

Susskind, J. M., Lee, D. H., Cusi, A., Feiman, R., Grabski, W., & Anderson, A. K. (2008). Expressing fear enhances sensory acquisition. *Nature Neuroscience, 11*, 843-850.

Tangney, J., & Fischer, K. W. (Eds.). (1995). *Self-conscious emotions: The psychology of shame, guilt, embarrassment, and pride*. New York: Guilford Press.

Tomkins, S. S. (1962). *Affect, imagery, and consciousness* (Vol. 1: The positive affects). New York: Springer.

Tomkins, S. S. (1963). *Affect, imagery, and consciousness* (Vol. 2: The negative affects). New York: Springer.

Tooby, J., & Cosmides, L. (2008). The evolutionary psychology of the emotions and their relationship to internal regulatory variables. In M. Lewis, J. M. Haviland-Jones & L. Feldman Barrett (Eds.), *Handbook of Emotions* (3rd ed., pp. 114-137). New York: The Guilford Press.

VIII. Animal and environmental rights extremists and crime: Setting forth a research agenda

Joshua D. Freilich

John Jay College of Criminal Justice

Andrew J. Bringuel II

Federal Bureau of Investigation

Steven M. Chermak

Michigan State University

James K. Shearer

Federal Bureau of Investigation

Abstract

Environmental and animal rights extremists pose a significant threat to public safety. Domestic terrorism attacks generally outnumber international ones 7 to 1 in the United States, and among domestic movements, environmental/animal rights extremists are especially dangerous. The criminal activities of these extremists, however, are a neglected research topic. Most terrorism research focuses on international terrorism. Studies on environmental and animal rights extremists usually rely on anecdotal or case study data. The few empirical works restrict their examinations to "terrorist" acts prosecuted on the federal level. Our project extends previous efforts and sets forth a research agenda that will first build a database on the suspects, victims, event, and group characteristics of all known homicides, attempted homicides, bombings, and arsons committed by extremist environmental and animal rights supporters from, 1995-to the present. Information will be extracted from open-source materials. We then discuss how these unique data can be used to examine pressing theoretical and empirical questions related to terrorism and extremist criminal activity. The results of this research will benefit law enforcement and other agencies and significantly enhance understanding of the number and types of crime committed by these extremists.

Introduction

Animal and environmental rights extremists[1] pose a threat to American public safety. Domestic terrorism attacks usually outnumber international ones 7 to 1 in the United States (LaFree, Dugan, Fogg and Scott, 2006) and animal/environmental rights extremists compose a dangerous segment of homegrown extremist movements (Smith, 1994). The criminal activities of these extremists, however, are a neglected research topic. Most terrorism research focuses on international terrorism (Lum, Kennedy and Sherley, 2006). After 9/11 the infusion of monetary resources from the United States government increased research on understanding the etiology and activities of Al Qaeda and other foreign groups. For example, scholars have used the Global Terrorism Database (GTD)—a Department of Homeland Security and National Institute of Justice supported product--to investigate the distribution of terrorist acts across nations, the life course of terrorist groups, the relationship between state failure and the number of terrorist attacks, and the impact of British counterterrorism measures (see for e.g., LaFree & Dugan, 2007; LaFree, Dugan & Fahey, 2007; LaFree, Dugan & Korte, 2009).

Research on domestic political extremists has focused mostly on far-right extremists. Gruenewald, Freilich & Chermak (2009) identified over 320 studies on far-right wing extremism and political crimes in the fields of criminology, political science, sociology and terrorism. Conversely, our review of the literatures on animal/environmental rights extremists in these disciplines found less than 70 studies. Most research on domestic terrorism is non-systematic and the majority of works on animal/environmental rights extremists' crimes rely on anecdotal or case study data. The few empirical domestic terrorism studies have focused on prosecution strategies in trying terrorists (see for e.g., Smith & Damphousse, 1996; 1998; Smith, Damphousse, Jackson & Sellers, 2002) and restricted their examinations to acts labeled as "terrorist" by the FBI. Such studies exclude prosecutions on the state level, many lone wolf acts, non-ideological crimes and nonviolent offenses (Hewitt, 2003; Smith, 1994).

There is a need to systematically collect incident, suspect, victim, and group data about the crimes committed by animal/environmental rights extremists to empirically investigate for the first time a series of policy-relevant and theoretically important questions. This chapter summarizes the research on eco-terrorism and animal/environmentalism extremism, highlighting gaps in our knowledge base. It will document important research questions, and describe research strategies to begin filling these gaps. Our goal is to enhance scholarly, law enforcement, and policy makers understanding of the criminal activities of these extremists.

Understanding the Significance of the Problem

There is considerable evidence that animal/environmental rights extremists pose a danger to the public order and there is a need for scholarly investigation of this problem. Smith's (1994: 200) seminal domestic terrorism study in the early, 1990s concluded that animal/environmental rights extremists "show distinct promise of increasing in number and activity before the close of the twentieth century." Indeed, one of the FBI's leading domestic terrorism agents subsequently reported to Congress that environmental and animal rights extremists had committed over 600 criminal acts causing more than $40 million in damages in the United States between, 1996 and, 2002 (Jarboe, 2002). Young's (2004) doctoral dissertation that examined a longer period (1993-2003) identified over 1,400 incidents of eco-terrorism, while Varriale-Carson's (2009) doctoral dissertation proposal documented 1,025 criminal incidents committed by extremist eco-groups between, 1970 and 2007.

Leader & Probst (2003) identified 100 criminal incidents conducted by supporters of the Earth Liberation Front (ELF) between 1996 and 2001, including over 30 arson attacks and over 55 acts of sabotage or vandalism. These crimes were identified from acts listed on ELF's website, the ELF/ALF annual report and media accounts. Leader and Probst limited themselves to ELF actions and omitted acts committed solely by supporters of animal rights. Animal rights extremists are also active. The watch-group the Anti-Defamation League (ADL, 2006: 2-3) noted that the Department of Justice and Agriculture "reported more than 313 incidents of break-ins, vandalism, arson and thefts in the name of animal rights between, 1979 and 1993." The varying numbers reported by these studies are due to different time periods and inclusion criteria.

Lee (1995) reported that forestry executives in Washington State stated that monkey-wrenching crimes- acts of sabotage- committed by environmental rights extremists caused more than $2 million dollars in damage every year just in Washington State. Obviously, the amount of financial loss to the nation as a whole each year would be considerably higher. Smith and Damphousse's (2009) American Terrorism Study documents the large-scale financial losses the attacks by these extremists have caused in the United States. The terrorist group "The Family," for instance, committed twenty-one arson and "ecotage" incidents between, 1995 and, 2001. Their most spectacular crime was an arson attack at the Vail ski resort in, 1998 that caused close to $25 million dollars in damage. Other case-specific examples include arson attacks at an over, 200 unit apartment complex in San Diego in August, 2003 that caused almost $50 million in damage (Ackerman, 2003a; Joosse, 2007).

Law enforcement agencies have also concluded that animal and environmental rights extremists pose a major threat. In, 2005, the Deputy Assistant Director of the FBI, John Lewis, stated that animal and environmental rights extremist groups like ALF and ELF were the most serious domestic terrorist threat. Freilich, Chermak and Simone (2009) recently surveyed the 50 American state police agencies about their perceptions of a number of terrorism issues and received a response rate of 74%. They asked the state police to rate the threat posed by 17 extremist movements (including far-right, far-left, jihadi, environmental, and animal rights extremists) to public safety both nationally and to their specific state. While almost all respondents strongly agreed that jihadists were a threat to national security and state security, most agencies were also significantly concerned about environmental and animal rights extremists. In fact, these groups were the second and third highest rank national threat and the fourth and fifth highest ranked threat at the state level. The state police respondents also reported that extreme animal rights supporters were among the most active in both legal and criminal activities. Finally, 80% of the agencies reported that animal rights extremists were present in their state and over 70% reported the presence of environmental rights extremists.

Despite the threat posed by animal/environmental rights extremists, there is a void in our understanding of their criminal activities. Again, most research on these extremists does not rely on systematic data and many frequently cited works have been produced by journalists or watch-groups. The studies which rely on empirical data have narrowed their scope of inquiry (e.g., Smith & Damphousse focus on individuals indicted federally for domestic security and terrorism crimes), and exclude many incidents, such as non-violent crimes, non-ideological crimes, or crimes falling under state jurisdiction. There is a need for scholars to systematically collect data on the incidents, suspects, victims and groups associated with the crimes committed by animal/environmental rights extremists. This will allow scholars, crime analysts and law enforcement agents to empirically examine these theoretically important and policy significant issues for the first time.

Setting Forth a Research Agenda

A necessary first step to setting forth a research agenda on these extremist movements is for academics, law enforcement and others to reach a consensus about how to operationalize "animal rights extremists" and "environmental rights extremists." This is important because, as we discussed, one reason for the varying estimates of the number of terrorist and criminal incidents committed by these extremists are different definitions, inclusion criteria and coding protocols. To begin this discussion, we offer the following description we developed (see also Freilich and Chermak, 2010) based upon a review of academic, law enforcement and watch-group studies published on these movements in general and its association with political crimes in particular (see for e.g., Abbey, 1975; Ackerman, 2003; ADL, 2006; Amster, 2006; Arnold, 1997; Beck, 2007; Eagan, 2006; Einwohner, 2002; Foreman, 1991; Jarboe, 2002; Joosse, 2007; Leader and Probst, 2003; Lee, 1995; 1997; Liddick, 2006; Manes, 1990; Monoghan, 2000; Rosebraugh, 2004; Scarce, 1990; Smith, 1994; Smith & Damphousse, 2009; Schwartz, 1998; Taylor, 1995; 1998; 2003; Trujillo, 2005; Varriale-Carson, 2005; Zakin, 1993):

Environmental and animal rights extremists are individuals or groups that subscribe to aspects of the following ideals: Support for biodiversity and bio-centric equality (i.e., that humans are no greater than any other form of life and have no legitimate claim to dominate earth); the earth and/or animals are in imminent danger; the government and /or parts of society such as corporations are responsible for this danger; this danger will ultimately result in the destruction of the modern environment and/or whole species; the political system is incapable and/or unwilling to fix the crisis by taking actions to preserve American wilderness, protect the environment and support biological diversity; there is a need to defend the environment and/or animals. *Environmental rights extremists* (primarily) are most focused on the environment while *animal rights extremists* (primarily) are most concerned with the rights of animals.

In the next sections, based upon our systematic review of the social science literature on animal/environmental rights extremists and crime, we list important issues that could be empirically investigated using these descriptions.

1. *Disaggregating the terrorist threat; and the need for dynamic analyses*

Our literature review demonstrates that scholars, law enforcement officers, crime analysts and policy makers must "disaggregate' the threat posed by animal/environmental rights terrorists from other terrorists. Terrorist and extremist movements vary from each other. Prior research indicates that American animal/environmental rights (and left-wing) terrorists differ from right-wing terrorists in important ways—they are younger, better educated, have better occupations, are less religious, and are more likely to operate in urban areas (Handler, 1990; Hewitt, 2003; Smith, 1994, Smith & Morgan, 1994; Stenz, 1990). These movements also vary temporally and spatially in the preparatory activities undertaken prior to the commission of their terrorist attacks. Environmental terrorists- like other single-issue terrorists- engaged in the shortest amount of preparation for their subsequent terrorist attacks, while far-rightists and jihadists appeared to engage in longer planning and preparation (Cothren, Smith, Roberts & Damphousse, 2008). Similarly, Hamm (2007; see also Smith & Damphousse, 2009) found that jihadist terrorists differed from far-rightists in the crime types they tended to commit in the United States. Freilich and Chermak (2009) found that in the last, 20 years far-right extremists have been involved in more fatal encounters with law enforcement personnel than either animal/environmental rights extremists, far-left or jihadist extremists. Different crime types will result in different prevention strategies (Clarke, 1995).

Importantly, terrorist threats are not static (Chermak, Freilich, & Caspi, 2009; Freilich, Chermak & Caspi, 2009). As discussed, Freilich, Chermak, & Simone's (2009) survey of state-police agencies demonstrated that animal/environmental rights extremists were seen as posing a greater threat to both national and state security than other extremist and terrorist movements. However, Carlson's (1995) survey of police chiefs in large-sized American cities (>100,000) in the early, 1990s found different results. He asked the chiefs to rank the top four groups that, in their opinion, were most likely to commit a terrorist act within the next two years. Despite the celebrated nature of the, 1993 Trade Center bombing, police chiefs did not think that Middle-Eastern terrorists posed the greatest threat. Interestingly, neither animal nor environmental extremists were seen as posing threats to public safety. Instead, anti-abortion perpetrators and white supremacists were rated the two greatest threats.

Relatedly, Damphousse (2009) points out that terrorist groups and/or movements must adapt to their environment and the measures taken against them to endure. He discusses how segments of the far-right moved from hierarchal structures that resulted in the easy dismantling of their organizations by law enforcement agencies to lone wolf and small decentralized structures that are harder to combat (we discuss lone wolf tactics below, and see Simi et al., this volume). These results demonstrate that terrorism threats are dynamic and change over time.

Our understanding of these extremist movements would also be enhanced if attention was paid to the subtle and not so subtle similarities and differences in the ideology, structure, and criminal activities of the various segments and supporters within the animal rights, environmental and anarchist movements. Such appreciation might make the difference between a successful and unsuccessful investigation. Presently, these segments are often treated as a single, cohesive entity. Observers have linked animal rights and environmental extremists to each other, to anarchists, the anti-global movement, and far-leftists (Ackerman, 2003; Chermak, Freilich, & Simone, 2010; Leader & Probst, 2003; Smith, 2004; Smith & Damphousse, 2009). Such linkages are important and may provide greater understanding to both law enforcement and scholars, but it is also important though, to realize that while certain segments may agree on most matters and imitate strategies and tactics, differences may remain over fundamental issues. In short, nuance is important (Joosse, 200; see also Chermak, Freilich, & Shemtob, 2009). Taylor (2003: 176) criticized Ackerman's (2003) threat assessment of ELF, for instance, because he "conflate[ed] the radical environmental, animal liberationist and green anarchist movements." Taylor states that activists from each sub-movement differ over the issues they prioritize and the tactics they endorse. Similarly, as we next discuss, while some academics note the potential for parts of the environmental movement to target humans, the majority of this movement opposes this strategy for both moral and pragmatic grounds. Chermak, Freilich, and Simone's (2010; see also Freilich, Chermak and Simone, 2009) survey of state police agencies also revealed that respondents perceived animal and environmental rights extremists differently in certain instances.

2. Investigating the likelihood of violent attacks against people

Another critical question to study is whether all animal rights, environmental rights extremists avoid attacking human targets. Many scholars conclude that such extremists differ from other radical movements, like far-rightists and jihadists, because they purposefully *avoid* targeting people for harm. Instead, their attacks are only directed against property targets. Amster (2006: 288) argues that the threat of eco-terrorism is exaggerated "and in fact, no human or animal was injured in the acts attributed to the recent eco-arrestees;" Taylor (1995: 9) contends that the "most radical environmentalists refuse to deploy sabotage to risk injuries to humans;" and the ADL (2006: 9) notes that "no one has yet been injured in a domestic [eco] attack." Cothren, Smith, Roberts and Damphousse (2008) speculate that this may be why environmentalists are more likely to attack at night when most offices or buildings are unoccupied.

Other researchers are more cautious and argue that the possibility that humans will be intentionally targeted cannot be dismissed (Ackerman, 2003; Trujilo, 2005). Recent communiqués and other propaganda and direct actions bolster this claim. Trujilo (2005: 164) reports, for example, that a communiqué received following a, 2002 fire at a research station in Pennsylvania threatened that: "In pursuance of justice, freedom, and equal consideration for all innocent life across the board, segments of this global revolutionary movement are no longer limiting their revolutionary potential by adhering to a flawed, inconsistent, 'non-violent' ideology. While innocent life will never be harmed in any action we undertake, where it is necessary, we will no longer hesitate to pick up the gun to implement justice."

Ackerman (2003) discusses a series of additional statements by animal/environmental rights extremists that endorse violent personal attacks. Other examples of direct actions that demonstrate a willingness to attack human targets include the planting of jars of cyanide in Minneapolis to protest genetic engineering of animals (see Trujilo, 2005). Moreover, Freilich and Chermak's (2010) Extremist Crime Database (ECDB) study is currently investigating over 15 violent acts committed by possible supporters of extremist animal and environmental rights movements that targeted persons. These incidents include, the Unabomber's letter bomb attacks (see also Ackerman, 2003; Eagan, 1996; Lee, 1997; but see Amster, 2006; Taylor, 1998); two attacks- one fatal- by the gang "Straight Edge" which embraces vegan lifestyles free of alcohol and drugs; the murder of a Red Bluff Police officer by a self proclaimed anarchist who also criticized corporate malfeasance including their harmful actions against the environment (see also Ackerman, 2003); a car bomb attempted murder of a veterinary officer (see also Eagan, 1996); and the firebombing of a car belonging to a University of California Santa Cruz scientist that resulted in injuries to both of his feet.

In short, scholars and others disagree about the threat posed to people by animal/environmental rights extremists. It is important for scholars to collect as much of the "true universe" of crimes committed by these extremists to investigate this issue. Engaging this issue will also fill gaps in the overall terrorism literature as most terrorism databases *do not* collect information on victims, and most scholars have not empirically studied victimization or target issues. It is usually claimed that such incidents are less worthy of academic investigation because they occur "randomly." Thus, a systematic investigation of both the personal victimization characteristics as well as attributes of locations, dwellings and other places of terrorist attacks promises to make significant conceptual contributions as well.

3. Studying the lone wolf threat

The threat of lone wolf terrorism is a significant concern generally (see Simi et al., this volume), and it is logical to consider the possibility that a lone environmental supporter could attack human targets and engage in mass casualty tactics. Scholars commonly claim that animal/environmental rights extremists embrace lone wolf tactics[2], and do so more so than other movements (Eagan, 1996: 1; Joosse, 2007; Leader & Probst, 2003: 37- 38; Smith & Damphousse, 2009). Leader and Probst (2003) note that ELF's website supports lone wolf tactics and allows individuals to access the site to list any crimes they commit to support the movement. Joosse (2007) concludes that lone wolf tactics protect against police infiltration and make it less likely for ideological disputes to hamper the movement. This tactic allows movement supporters to act independently and record their actions on ELF's website (see also Freilich, Pichardo-Almanzar & Rivera, 1999). This decentralization allows the movement to increase its mobilization potential and avoid ideological disputes.

Conversely, our discussions with key informants in federal law-enforcement charged with investigating domestic terrorism uncovered an interesting disconnect. While, our informants recognized that ELF/ALF activists openly supported the use of lone wolf tactics, in their experience, the picture on the ground was different. They indicated that since the mid-1990s, most crimes committed by animal/environmental extremists were not perpetrated by lone wolves, but small groups (i.e., between two and five) of like minded people. These individuals shared a common belief system and usually coalesced together through their involvement with an above ground organization.

Chermak, Freilich, and Simone's (2010) survey of state-police agencies similarly found that far-leftists in general and supporters of ALF and ELF specifically were not seen as usually committing their crimes alone. They asked the agencies whether supporters specified extremist movements tended to commit crimes as lone wolves, with others, or both alone and with others. Only 4.5% of the respondents said that ALF and 9.5% for ELF usually commit their crimes as lone wolves. In contrast, 50% of responding agencies said that anti-tax protestors, 28% that freemen/sovereign citizens and 21.4% said that both extreme anti-abortion and Christian Identity usually commit crimes as lone wolves.

This disconnect between academic conclusions and law enforcement perceptions of the lone wolf threat from far-left and ALF/ELF extremists is interesting and should be looked into further. There are many questions that need to be examined. First, how frequently are environmental, animal rights, and anarchist criminal acts carried out by lone individuals compared to group crimes? It would also be interesting to examine variations in lone wolf crimes by comparing activities by environmental, animal rights, and anarchists. Second, is there variation in terms of tactics, seriousness, and response of incidents committed by individuals compared to groups? Researchers discuss how terrorist groups imitate and learn from the tactics of other terrorist organizations (see Trujillo, 2005), but it would be significant if such imitation extended to individuals loosely affiliated with a movement. Third, it would be important to document which investigative tactics have been used to successfully identify, investigate, arrest, and prosecute individuals involved in these movements when acting alone as compared to those acting in groups. Finally, while it is difficult to successfully investigate these groups, lone wolves pose additional unique challenges. It would be helpful to law enforcement, after identifying a sample of lone wolves, to examine their criminal histories, extremist involvement history, and other background characteristics to better understand their escalation towards political violence and highlight potential opportunities for the investigation and arrest of these extremists.

4. Investigating whether animal/environmental rights extremists "specialize" in their criminal activity

It is important for scholars and law enforcement agents to examine a universe of criminal incidents that include "all" violent crimes committed by these extremists, including (1) ideologically motivated crimes that are defined as terrorist (e.g., ELF bombing attacks) (2) ideologically motivated crimes that are not defined as terrorist (e.g., vandalism, defacement of property or sabotage), and (3) non-ideological 'routine' crimes (e.g., an animal rights activist is arrested for domestic violence murder). Limiting data collection to "terrorist" incidents systematically excludes an important part of the picture—lone wolf strikes; state-level crimes and non-ideological crimes (Dishman, 2005).

Incorporating this broader universe of cases allows a greater number of theoretical questions to be investigated such as whether ideological offenders- both terrorist and non-terrorist- tend to also commit non-ideological 'routine' crimes. Hirschi and Gottfredson (2001) argue that routine offenders have low levels of self control, while ideologically motivated perpetrators, especially terrorists, have high levels. They thus exclude terrorists and ideologically motivated offenders from their general theory and predict that ideologically motivated offenders do not commit 'routine' non-ideological crimes. Conversely, other criminologists (e.g., Blazak (2001) on strain theory, and Hamm (2007) on social learning theory), contend that the same factors are associated with both ideological and non-ideological crimes.

Relatedly, Smith and Damphousse note that terrorists often commit non-ideological crimes as necessary steps to complete their attack. For example, McVeigh committed robberies to gather the funds necessary to purchase fertilizer and materials that he used to build the bomb he detonated in Oklahoma City. Similarly, our discussion with a number of key informants in federal law enforcement charged with investigating terrorism found that in their experience animal/environmental rights extremists commonly committed non-ideological crimes to finance their lifestyles and/or operations. For example, they found that in many cases, these extremists engaged in frauds, larceny or "rip and return" offenses such as shoplifting parts/food for an operation or basic survival, and even counterfeiting of coupons or filing fraudulent customer complaints to acquire financial or logistical materials.

There are also a number of anecdotal cases that undermine Hirschi and Gottfredson's claims. Smith and Damphousse's (2009:

483; 485; 486; 492) case study of the environmental terrorist group "The Family" reveals that a number of this group's "terrorists" had been involved in "non-ideological" routine crimes, such as heroin addiction, and sexually abusive behavior, in addition to their ideological attacks. Relatedly, Dishman (2005) argues that recently both terrorist groups and criminal cartels have become more decentralized (and less hierarchal). Each thus has more "independence" which has led to the line between criminal and terrorist groups becoming blurred. Both groups are now more likely to engage in both ideological and non-ideological routine crimes. Dishman concludes that "many terrorist and guerilla movements are engaged in organized crime, and many profit minded criminals no longer have inhibitions about working with terrorists. Thus a criminal lead could very well trace back to a terrorist" (249).

Again, it is important to systematically investigate these competing claims using empirical data. A promising strategy to do so would be to examine the criminal histories of a sample of animal and environmental rights extremists. These data would be particularly valuable if they were able identify when each suspect became actively involved in the movement. This would allow us to examine whether environmental extremists, for example, have committed only ideological offenses, such as arson and vandalism.

5. Examining whether extremists "escalate" their criminal activities, and other significant policy issues

It is important to study whether the criminality of American animal/environmental rights extremists have "escalated" (for e.g., from non-violent civil disobedience, or vandalism cases) to violent arson or terrorist bombings on either the micro or macro-levels. Ackerman's (2003) threat assessment of ELF was partially prompted by environmental arson strikes that led some to query if the movement could escalate from property attacks to "intentional bodily harm" (144; see also Beck, 2007; Taylor, 1998). Only data collections efforts that include nonviolent ideologically motivated civil disobedience campaigns, property defacement and vandalism, as well as arson and bombings will be able to properly study this unexplored important issue.

Noted terrorism scholar David Rapoport (1984) has argued that violent terrorist conflicts have often been preceded by non-violent direct action illegal acts. Indeed, Monaghan's (2000: 258) study on the Animal Liberation Front (ALF) in England used a case study approach and stated that "impersonal attacks on property continued to account for ALF actions up until the early, 1980s, when a shift in tactics and targeting can be seen. Property damage was superseded by personal threats to, and actual attacks on, individuals" (258).

Rapoport's thesis is also consistent with both the hate-crimes literature which finds that bias-crime perpetrators "escalate" from less to more violent hate-crimes (Shively, 2005) and the general criminology literature which finds that offenders sometimes commit crimes sequentially and shoplifting generally precedes burglary, and burglary precedes robbery (Piquero et al., 2008). Finally, this thesis complements Smith and Damphousse's groundbreaking work on preparatory crimes. As noted, these scholars demonstrated how seemingly routine, non-ideological crimes (e.g., bank robbery) are often necessary steps (e.g., gather funds to build a bomb) that terrorists must take to complete their attack. Their work should be extended by examining whether non-violent ideological crimes similarly function as necessary stepping stones to more violent acts.

Other important policy-relevant questions include exploring how active animal/environmental extremists have been, whether the divergent crime types (e.g., sabotage, bombings, arson, etc) they commit co-vary on the micro or macro-levels, whether these patterns have changed over time, whether there are individual or regional variations in activity, and whether comparisons of criminal activity exist by ideology, or organizing characteristics (Taylor, 1998). It would also be worthwhile to study whether findings that other ideological extremist and terrorist groups/movements- like the domestic far-right- suffer from internal strife and violent acts perpetrated within the movement (for e.g., Freilich and Chermak, 2010 found that close to, 20% of the over 300 far-right homicides they identified were non-ideological but movement related which included internal slayings) apply to animal/environmental rights extremists. Again, while there are anecdotal suggestions that this is the case (see for e.g., Lee, 1995; Lee, 1997; Taylor, 1998; Smith and Damphousse, 2009), this issue has never been examined systematically. Finally, there is a need for scholars to systematically study repeated anecdotal "folk wisdom" claims about environmental and animal rights extremists who engage in illegal behavior, such as that they are more likely to have suffered from "troubled lives" or mental illness (Eagan, 1996: Taylor, 1998).

6. *Studying the relationship between suspects and groups/organizations*

Our literature review demonstrates that there is anecdotal, and some empirical, evidence that only small numbers of extremist organizations resort to organized terrorist or criminal activities. Importantly though, there is little empirical research about the organizational characteristics of extremist groups generally and environmental and animal rights groups in particular. This is because it is challenging to study animal/environmental rights extremist groups due to the movement's loose group structure, partial embracing of 'lone wolf and leaderless resistance' structures, and the creation of phantom groups (see Joosse, 2007; Leader & Probst, 2003). Thus, although there is great value in understanding the offending behaviors of individuals affiliated with extremist organizations, there is also a need for empirical understanding of the differences between environmental and animal rights extremist organizations that are criminal compared to those that are not.

Specifically, it would be valuable for future research to focus on identifying a sample of known extremist anarchist, environmental, and animal rights organizations, collecting data about those organizations, and coding key characteristics about their activities, structures, and networks. These characteristics could be systematically analyzed to begin shedding light on a host of unanswered important questions, such as: What factors are critical for explaining why some groups turn to terrorism and others do not? How does the criminal activity of individual extremist offenders relate to the nature and behavior of the organizations that they belong to? Are there certain kinds of organizational and relational factors that make it more likely that an organization will morph from being a criminal threat to being a homeland security threat? Why do ideologically similar organizations have very different criminal offending patterns? Do ideologically different organizations have different criminal offending patterns? How do organizations utilize criminal activity to accomplish terrorist objectives? Are there certain organizational and/or leadership structures that are more likely to lead to violent/terrorist offending? What external factors force organizations to adapt?

Conclusion

Animal and environmental rights extremists pose a serious problem to American public safety. Despite this threat and the severe financial damage they cause to society, there is little empirical research that systematically explores their criminal activities. This essay operationalized the terms "animal rights" and "environmental rights" extremists and discussed the criminal threat they represent to society. Next, based upon a systematic review of the social science literature important research gaps about these extremist movements were set forth. Specific research questions were also described that would lead to enhanced understanding of these issues. The next step is to develop a research strategy, that relies upon rigorous methods both quantitative and qualitative, to address these questions. The results promise to provide significant benefits for law enforcement agencies, crime analysts, policy makers, and scholars and other observers.

Notes:

[1] We operationalize these terms in the section titled "setting forth a research agenda"

[2] Lone wolf attacks are illegal incidents that are committed by a single political extremist. This type of attack encompasses both planned attacks committed by a single suspect) as well as presented opportunities, such as a routine call for service that brings a lone suspect in contact with a target s/he ideologically loathes.

References

Abbey, E., 1975. The monkey wrench gang. New York: Avon.

Ackerman, G.A., 2003a. Beyond arson? A threat assessment of the Earth Liberation Front. Terrorism and Political Violence 15(4): 143- 170.

Ackerman, G.A., 2003b. My reply to Perlstein and Taylor. Terrorism and Political Violence 15(4): 183- 189.

Anti-Defamation League (ADL)., 2006. Ecoterrorism: Extremism in the animal rights and environmentalist movements. [Online]: http://www.adl.org/Learn/Ext_/US/Ecoterrorism

Amster, R., 2006. Perspectives on ecoterrorism: Catalysts, conflations and casualties. Contemporary Justice Review 9(3): 287- 301.

Arnold, R., 1997. Ecoterror: The violent agenda to save nature. Bellevue: Free Press.

Beck, C.J., 2007. On the radical cusp. Ecoterrorism in the United States, 1998-, 2005. Mobilization: An international quarterly review 12(2): 161- 176.

Blazak, R., 2001. White boys to terrorist men: Target recruitment of Nazi skinheads. American Behavioral Scientist 44(6): 982- 1000.

Carlson, J.R., 1995. The future terrorists in America. American Journal of Police, 14(3/4): 71- 91.

Chermak, S.M., J.D. Freilich & D. Caspi.2009. Policymakers and law enforcement must consider the unintended consequences of their proposed responses to extremist and terrorist groups. In Frost, N.A., J.D. Freilich & T.R. Clear. Eds. Contemporary issues in criminal justice policy: Policy proposals from the American Society of Criminology Conference (pp. 139- 150). Belmont, CA: Wadsworth, Cengage Learning.

Chermak, S.M., J.D. Freilich, and J. Simone, Jr. 2010. Surveying American state police agencies about lone wolves, far-right criminality, and far-right and Islamic jihadist criminal collaboration. Paper under review.

Chermak, S.M., J.D. Freilich, and Z. Shemtob. 2009. Law enforcement training and the domestic far-right. Criminal Justice and Behavior 36(12): 1305-1322.

Cothren, J., B.L. Smith, P. Roberts, and K.R. Damphousse. 2008. Geospatial and temporal patterns of preparatory conduct among American terrorists. International Journal of Comparative and Applied Criminal Justice 32(1): 23- 41.

Dishman, C., 2005. The Leaderless nexus: When crime and terror converge. Terrorism and Political Violence 28: 237- 252.

Eagan, S.P., 1996. From spikes to bombs: The rise of eco-terrorism. Studies in Conflict & Terrorism, 19: 1-18.

Einwohner, R.L., 2002. Bringing the outsiders in: Opponents' claims and the construction of animal rights activists' identity. Mobilization 7(3): 253- 268.

Foreman, D., 1991. Confessions of an eco-warrior. New York: Harmony.

Freilich, J.D., and S.M. Chermak. 2009. Preventing deadly encounters between law enforcement and American far-rightists. Crime Prevention Studies 25: 141- 172.

Freilich, J.D., and S.M. Chermak. 2010. Introducing the United States Extremist Crime Database (ECDB), 1990-, 2009. Paper under review.

Freilich, J.D., S.M. Chermak & D. Caspi. 2009. Critical events in the life trajectories of domestic extremist white supremacist groups: A case study analysis of four violent organizations. Criminology and Public Policy 8(3): 497- 530.

Freilich, J.D., S.M. Chermak, and J. Simone. 2009. Surveying American state police agencies about terrorism threats, terrorism sources, and terrorism definitions. Terrorism and Political Violence 21(3): 450 475.

Freilich, J.D., N. A. P. Almanzar, & C.J. Rivera. 1999. How social movement organizations explicitly and implicitly promote deviant behavior: The case of the militia movement. Justice Quarterly 16 (3): 655-683.

Gruenewald, J., J.D. Freilich, and S.M. Chermak. 2009. An Overview of the Domestic Far-Right and its Criminal Activities." In Perry, B. & R. Blazak.(eds). Hate Crimes: Hate Crime Offenders (pp. 1-21). Westport: Praeger.

Hamm, M.S., 2007. Terrorism as crime: From Oklahoma City to Al Qaeda and beyond. New York City: New York University Press.

Handler, J., 1990. Socioeconomic profile of an American terrorist. Terrorism13:, 195- 213.

Hewitt, C., 2003. Understanding Terrorism in America: From the Klan to Al Qaeda. New York: Routledge.

Hirchi, T., and M.R. Gottfredson. 2001. Self control theory. Pp. 81- 96 in Raymond Patternoster and Ronet Bachman. (Ed). Explaining Criminals and Crime. Los Angeles: Roxbury.

Jarboe, J., 2002. The threat of eco-terrorism. Testimony before the House Resources Committee, Subcommittee on Forests and Forest Health. [Online]: www.fbi.gov.congress02/jarboe021202.htm

Joosse, P., 2007. Leaderless resistance and ideological inclusion: The case of the Earth Liberation Front. Terrorism and Political Violence, 19: 351- 368.

LaFree, G., and L. Dugan. 2007. Introducing the Global Terrorism Database. Terrorism and Political Violence, 19: 181-, 204.

LaFree, G., L. Dugan, and S. Fahey. (2007). Global terrorism and Failed States. In J.J. Hewitt, J. Wilkenfeld, and T.R. Gurr (eds). Peace and Conflict, pp. 39- 54. Boulder: Paradigm Publishers.

LaFree, G., L. Dugan, H. Fogg and J. Scott. 2006. Building a Global Terrorism Database. Final Report to the National Institute of Justice. May, 2006.

LaFree, G., L. Dugan, and R. Korte. 2009. The impact of British counter terrorist strategies on political violence in Northern Ireland: Comparing deterrence and backlash models. Criminology 47(1): 17-46.

Leader, S.H., and P. Probst. 2003. The Earth Liberation Front and environmental terrorism. Terrorism and Political Violence 15(4): 37-58.

Lee, M.F., 1995. Violence and the environment: The case of Earth First! Terrorism and Political Violence 7(3): 109-127.

Lee, M.F., 1997. Environmental apocalypse: The millennial ideology of "Earth First!"

Manes, C., 1990. Green rage: Radical environmentalism and the unmaking of civilization. Boston: Little Brown.

Liddick, D. R., 2006. Eco-terrorism: Radical environmental and animal liberation movements. Westport: Praeger.

Lum, C., L.W., Kennedy, and A.J. Sherley. 2006. The effectiveness of counter-terrorism strategies: A Campbell systematic review. http://www.campbellcollaboration.org.

Monaghan, R., 2000. Single issue terrorism: A neglected phenomenon? Studies in Conflict & Terrorism 23: 255-265.

Perlstein, G., 2003. Comment on Ackerman. Terrorism and Political Violence 15(4): 171- 172.

Rapoport, D.C., 1984. Fear and trembling: Terrorism in three religious traditions. American Political Science Review 18:

Rosebraugh, C., 2004. Burning rage of a dying planet: Speaking for the Earth Liberation Front. New York: Lantern.

Scarce, R., 1990. Eco-warriors: Understanding the radical environmental movement. Chicago: Noble.

Schwartz, D.M., 1998. Environmental terrorism: Analyzing the concept. Journal of Peace Research 35(4): 483- 496.

Shively, M., 2005. Study of literature and legislation on hate crime in America. Final Report to the National Institute of Justice, June, 2005.

Smith, B.L., 1994. Terrorism in America: Pipe bombs and pipe dreams. New York: State University of New York Press.

Smith, B.L., and K.R. Damphousse., 1996. Punishing Political Offenders: The Effect of Political Motive on Federal Sentencing Decisions. Criminology 34 (3): 289-321.

Smith, B.L., and K.R. Damphousse., 1998. Terrorism, Politics and Punishment: A Test of Structural-Contextual Theory and the 'Liberation Hypothesis.' Criminology 36(1): 67-92.

Smith, B.L., and K.R. Damphousse. 2009. Patterns of precursor behavior in the life span of a U.S. environmental terrorism group. Criminology and Public Policy 8(3): 475- 496.

Smith, B.L., K.R. Damphousse, F. Jackson, and A. Sellers. 2002. The Prosecution and Punishment of International Terrorists in Federal Courts: 1980-1998. Criminology and Public Policy 1(3): 311- 338.

Smith, B.L., and K.D. Morgan. 1994. Terrorists right and left: Empirical issues in profiling American terrorists. Studies in Conflict and Terrorism, 17: 39-57.

Stenz, T., 1990. Radical right vs radical left: Terrorist theory and threat. Police Chief, 70- 75.

Taylor, B., 1995. (Ed). Ecological resistance movements: The global emergence of radical and popular environmentalism. Albany: State University of New York Press.

Taylor, B., 1998. Religion, violence and radical environmentalism: From Earth First! To the Unabomber to the Earth Liberation Front. Terrorism and Political Violence 10(4): 1-42.

Taylor, B., 2003. Threat assessments and radical environmentalism. Terrorism and Political Violence 15(4): 173-182.

Trujillo, H R. , 2005. The radical Environmentalist Movement. pp. 141- 175. In Aptitude for destruction: Case studies of organizational learning in five terrorist groups, edited by B.A. Jackson, J.C. Baker, K. Cragin, J. Parachini, H.R. Trujillo, and P. Santa, Monica, California: Rand.

Varriale-Carson, J., 2009. The hazard of radical environmental and animal rights groups: The role of moral inhibitions in "monkey-wrenching." Unpublished PhD Dissertation Proposal. University of Maryland, at College Park.

Young, R.L., 2004. A time series analysis of eco terrorist violence in the United States:, 1993-2003. PhD dissertation, Sam Houston State University, Huntsville, Texas.

Zakin, S., 1993. Coyotes and Town Dogs. New York: Viking.

IX. The False Allure of Torture

Matthew D. Semel
John Jay College of Criminal Justice

Abstract

Methods employed by the United States to procure intelligence from human sources, known as HUMINT, have undergone increasing attention since the events of September 11th and the wars in Afghanistan and Iraq. After the attacks on the World Trade center and the Pentagon, the United States permitted passion to overrule reason and allowed interrogators to employ almost any techniques deemed necessary to gather intelligence from insurgents who do not play by the rules of war. This occurred in spite of the fact that the historical record does not support the use of harsh* interrogation techniques or torture. Recent history is replete with examples of torture producing false information. The historical evidence offers important insights for the national discussion about interrogation techniques and reveals that torture's allure is a false one. This short essay will provide an overview of some of the relevant historical material about interrogations in the military context, focusing primarily, but not exclusively, on the early to mid, 20th Century. (The interrogations refered to here are those conducted off the field of battle. Battlefield interrogations present their own unique logistical issues and concerns.) Lessons learned will be applied to the current conflict. And, while researchers cannot legally or ethically empirically test torture's effectiveness, more research is needed to study interrogation methods currently in use by the military. To date, there is almost no research about the efficacy of intelligence interrogations (Educing Information, 2006).

*The term harsh techniques, as used here, include torture and other practices that violate U.S. and international law.

Introduction

Experienced interrogators know the history of their art and this history includes many narrative accounts about the ineffectiveness of harsh techniques. The historical record describes the experiences of American POWs during four major wars: World War II, the Korean conflict, Vietnam and the first Gulf War. In addition, numerous books and articles, from open and declassified sources, depict how American interrogators treated enemy prisoners of war. Many of these accounts have been cited by journalists and others reporting about this issue, in print and on the internet. Most World War II interrogators interviewed have deplored the use of harsh techniques and openly dismiss their effectiveness.

Implicit in the Bush Administration's extreme approach to interrogations was the idea that the enemy faced by the United States was qualitatively different from past foes. This new threat not only ignored the rules of war but was fanatical in its approach to battle, advocating attacks on civilians and martyrdom as the ultimate act of piety. According to this argument, this enemy was resistant to traditional interrogation techniques and required "special" methods that would more readily "break" such fanatics. Similar arguments were made about the Japanese during World War II. However, during that war, the United States relied primarily on rapport-building techniques that tended to yield good results. Other methods were for the bad guys to use.

It bears emphasizing here that rapport-building, like the use of harsh techniques, has not been scientifically validated in the intelligence or military context even if the narrative and historical record overwhelmingly supports their effectiveness. I do not intend to endorse any one interrogation technique in this essay but seek to examine the evidence that exists about the efficacy of various interrogation practices used before, and subsequent to, September 11th, 2001.

With the continued release of new information about the Bush Administration's policy on interrogations and a pending investigation by Attorney General Eric Holder, several points have not been refuted by news reports. First, whether one agrees or disagrees with the prior Administration's policies, there appears to be no evidence, other than some anecdotal reports, that harsh interrogations produced good intelligence information.

For example, former Vice President Dick Cheney insists that harsh interrogations led to actionable intelligence. Cheney's contention is countered by experienced interrogators, some of the most prominent of whom have been two Air Force interrogators, Steve Kleinman and Matthew Alexander, (a pseudonym), and former FBI special agents Jack Cloonan and Ali Soufan. Recently Soufan wrote in the New York Times that supporters of harsh techniques have yet “to show that the techniques stopped even a single imminent threat of terrorism.” Soufan has been a frequent critic of the Bush policy both in print and as a witness before Congress.

Alexander has gone so far as to say that the Bush Administration's interrogation policies have led to the deaths of "hundreds if not thousands of Americans." Alexander, who served in Iraq, recounts that, day after day, captured foreign fighters told interrogators that they were inspired to come to Iraq after seeing what happened at Abu Ghraib and Guantanamo Bay. According to Alexander, many of the foreign fighters went on to become suicide bombers. (Alexander’s analysis may apply to foreign fighters in Afghanistan as well.)

The vice president has yet to clearly describe how harsh interrogations produced good intelligence or prevented an act of terror and has cloaked his reticence in national security concerns. Some supporters have pointed to the interrogation of Khalid Sheik Mohamed as an example of extreme techniques producing good intelligence. As has been reported widely, Mohamed was water-boarded dozens of times and reportedly gave up good information, although some have disputed the efficacy of water-boarding Mohamed, including Mohamed himself. He now claims he told his interrogators what they "wanted to hear," not the truth.

The bottom line? We don't know if torture or harsh techniques work and chances are we will never have a definitive answer. There may be cases where harsh techniques actually succeed in extracting actionable intelligence but this does not mean that rapport building techniques are deficient in comparison.

If rapport-building techniques and harsh methods work equally well it is axiomatic that the United States does not endorse methods proscribed by U.S. law or the Geneva Conventions. To do otherwise diminishes the moral standing of the U.S. and puts our troops in harm's way. This is not an endorsement of rapport-building; it is an acknowledgement that we do not have scientific evidence that validates one approach over another. In order for the U.S. to risk its moral stature and employ harsh techniques, at the very least, these techniques must be shown to work better and more quickly than rapport building strategies. This evidence does not currently exist, at least from open or declassified sources.

A second point seems undeniable. The Bush Administration did not ask seasoned interrogators what they believed were the most effective methods for gathering actionable intelligence. The irony in this fact is that the Administration sought the advice of so many individuals without appearing to consult front-line, experienced interrogators. In conjunction with a current study about military interrogation techniques I have spoken to two dozen interrogators from the Air Force, Army and Marines, both active duty and retired. Most of these experienced interrogators eschew the harsh tactics advanced by President Bush and his administration. They insist that rapport-building methods work best.

Third, a number of recent reports belie the theory that "fanatics" will not respond to rapport-building as an interrogation technique. Retired FBI special agents Jack Cloonan and Ali Soufan, both mentioned earlier, have openly spoken about their success using rapport building with senior Qaeda operatives. A number of other anecdotal reports describe the interrogations of Qaeda lieutenant Abu Zabaydah and suggest that more humane efforts, used by Soufan and colleague Steve Gaudin to extract information, yielded results while more aggressive questioning by CIA contractors did not. Shane (2008) recounts how a little-trained, novice interrogator from the CIA extracted important information from Khalid Sheik Mohammed by building rapport with the prisoner and this same CIA operative also had success with Zabaydah and Ramzi bin al-Shibh, the alleged intermediary between the September 11th hijackers and al Qaeda's leadership. Both provided important intelligence as a result of this rapport building approach.

The historical record also supports the contentions of these interrogators as well as Alexander, and Kleinman. Perhaps the most famous interrogator of any era was a Luftwaffe officer named

Hanns Scharff, the subject of a book written by Raymond Tolliver, called *The Interrogator*. Much has been written about Scharff, who used charm, wit and cunning to extract information from the mostly American airmen he interrogated during Worlds War II. Scharff is often cited as a counter to those who advocate harsh techniques. The coda to the Scharff story is that later in life he moved to the United States and spoke to many military audiences about his approach to interrogations. The Hanns Scharff Interrogator Translator Teams Association includes a small tribute to Scharff on its web site.

Scharff's methods were somewhat atypical; accounts of the treatment of U.S. POWs in World War II and the Korean War illustrate the defensive challenges of interrogation faced by prisoners. Both the Germans and the Japanese tortured Allied POWs captured over the course of the war and some estimate that, after being tortured, ten percent of American prisoners of war held by the Nazis cooperated in some way with their captors. Cooperation consisted primarily of confessions to fabricated war crimes.

During the Korean War, thirty-six American airmen confessed to a plot to bomb civilian targets after undergoing what was then called touch-less torture. These high value prisoners were isolated from all human contact but for their interrogators and at least one airman was held in solitary confinement for 10 months.

The North Koreans and the Chinese subjected these prisoners to stress positions, such as standing at attention for hours, repeated beatings and prolonged interrogation sessions during which questions were repeated over and over to disorient the subject. During the winter, prisoners were marched barefoot in the snow. Guards regularly threw food at prisoners and forced them to defecate in public. After becoming exhausted and demoralized, some airmen's resistance was overcome and they eventually "confessed" to war crimes. All the confessions elicited under these conditions were false and were procured primarily for propaganda purposes.

In one of the most sensational cases, Marine Corps Colonel Frank H. Schwable signed a written confession indicating that the United States was using germ warfare against China and North Korea (Meerloo, 1956). In his confession, Schwable provided the Chinese with names, dates, details of strategic meetings, and specifics of the alleged germ warfare program. His “admissions” occurred after weeks of continuous interrogations by teams of interrogators and degrading treatment and torture (Meerloo). After being repatriated, Schwable testified before a military Board of Inquiry. According to Merloo, Schwable stated: “*That is the hardest thing I have to explain; how a man can sit down and write something he knows is false, and, yet, to sense it, to feel it, to make it seem real” (21).*

The historical record is clear about one salient fact. The Koreans and the Chinese did not torture their American captives simply or primarily to elicit intelligence. They tortured U.S. soldiers in the hopes that they would convincingly confess to false charges or renounce the American political system. In some cases the soldiers did confess and endorse Communism, much to the shock of many Americans at home.

In his book, *Remembered Prisoners of a Forgotten War*, Lewis Carlson presents an oral history of American POWs in Korea. Carlson conducted interviews with Korean POWs in part to determine if the conditions of their confinement helped produce false confessions at higher rates than American prisoners in other wars. Carlson finds that the North Koreans used many of the same methods as the Soviet Union, and the U.S. subsequent to September 11, 2001, including beatings, starvation, sleep deprivation, exposure to extreme temperatures and "never-ending" interrogations. Marathon interrogation sessions can cause a subject to become so disoriented that the subject can no longer distinguish what he knows from what he does not know. These conditions, notes Carlson, caused prisoners to break down and "cooperate" with their interrogators to survive. For some, cooperation included falsely confessing to war crimes.

During the Vietnam War, the North Vietnamese elicited similar false confessions under similar conditions from American prisoners of war, including Senator John McCain of Arizona. Navy pilot Mike Cronin, who spent six years at the notorious Hanoi prison known as the Hanoi Hilton, was subjected to brutal interrogations during his time in captivity. Eventually Cronin did talk but, like other POWs including McCain, Cronin provided his captors with false or unimportant information. Cronin has publically insisted that "when you put people in this position, the information you get is not reliable."

Subsequent conflicts produced similar false confessions. At the height of the Vietnam War, North Korea seized an American Naval vessel, the U.S.S. Pueblo and held the 82-member crew captive for 11 months under severe conditions. The Koreans regularly assaulted the Americans, kept them blindfolded and questioned them over long periods of time. The commander of the ship, Captain Lloyd Bucher eventually "confessed" to war crimes after the Koreans threatened to shoot the members of his crew one-by-one while he watched. The statements elicited as a result of this threat were false. During the Gulf War in, 1991, Iraqi television displayed several downed U.S. airmen who publicly denounced the war against the "peaceful people of Iraq." Again the statements were elicited under torture and threats of death.

These events demonstrate again and again that even members of the best and most well-trained military in the world are not immune to torture and the often debilitating effects of captivity, particularly if injured when captured. They also demonstrate that the quality of information elicited under these conditions is suspect at best and at worst totally fabricated. Historically, harsh techniques seem to reliably produce unreliable information.

One American researcher, Albert D. Biderman, spent a considerable part of his career studying cases of false confession by U.S. military personnel. In, 1957, Biderman conducted a comprehensive examination of false confession cases on behalf of the United States Air Force and the CIA. He focused on one major question: what happened to U.S. personnel captured in Korea that caused them to "confess" to non-existent war crimes? (Biderman has gained renewed notoriety in the last few years as editor of *The Manipulation of Human Behavior*, what some have called the "Torture Handbook.") "

In accordance with the findings of other well known researchers for the CIA, human ecologists Harold G. Wolff and Lawrence E. Hinkle, as well as his own work, Biderman recognized that human behavior can be "manipulated" in a "controlled" environment, such as that in which a prisoner of war may find himself. The nation that holds prisoners of war has two major goals according to Biderman: to establish compliance and, in cases where prisoners may be used for propaganda purposes, to manipulate that compliance. The North Koreans and the Chinese, like their Soviet counterparts, gained compliance by undermining the prisoner's resistance, usually without the use of physical torture. Biderman organized the Chinese methods for gaining compliance into eight categories and those eight categories include the techniques, their "effects" and "variants."

Biderman contended that of all possible techniques, isolation works best to break down resistance in prisoners. Severe isolation can achieve the same results as other methods, such as starvation and sleep deprivation and can achieve those results in a shorter period of time. Within days, a prisoner experiencing isolation will begin to emotionally unravel and become a subject of intelligence that is worth little. When prisoners are subjected to complete or almost complete isolation, their psychological well-being rapidly begins to deteriorate. Long term solitary confinement can eventually induce psychosis and a complete mental breakdown. Isolation also has an added advantage; it leaves no marks on its victims. Biderman's findings suggest that, if isolation is used at all, its use must be measured and monitored. Too much isolation is not likely to produce accurate intelligence from a subject, a finding relevant to today's interrogations.

Biderman found that two other specific techniques also work well to establish compliance: threats of physical violence and the use of stress positions, techniques advocated and used after September 11. Stress positions, such as sitting at attention or standing for long periods of time, are particularly effective for compliance because the prisoner himself, not the interrogator or guard, is the source of the prisoner's pain. Stress positions cause the prisoner to "exaggerate" the power of the interrogator and convince a prisoner that his captor has the ability "to do something worse to him." Stress positions also allow the interrogator to assert that physical violence never entered the interrogation room; the interrogator need not lay a hand on the subject.

Regardless of the interrogation techniques used, Biderman believed that no subject could resist a determined interrogator and he supported this assertion with a review of intelligence gathering during World War II and the Korean War. The greater problem for an interrogator, according to Biderman, is evasion by a subject after he begins to talk. As a result of his findings, Biderman supported a change in the Military Code of Conduct which would allow American prisoners of war to engage with their interrogators instead of simply supplying name, rank and serial number. Biderman reasoned that most subjects will eventually talk and the military is wiser to train troops to evade their interlocutors, who were generally poor at detecting evasion or deception. Biderman's assertions are still true today and supported by law enforcement research on this subject. This research suggests, for example, that law enforcement officers are over-confident in their ability to detect deception. Are American military interrogators also over-confident in their ability to detect deception? If U.S. interrogators are better at detecting deception than their law enforcement counterparts, what practices does the military employ to enhance this skill?

Biderman's overall findings suggest that isolation, at least in its more extreme forms, and stress positions are not conducive to eliciting actionable intelligence during an interrogation. Training and research may be better focused on deception detection which is still subject to many myths. A search on Amazon will reveal a number of books that purport to teach the secrets of flushing out lies and liars, some written by former military interrogators. Most research literature to date on this subject, however, counters the view that deception is easily detected in another human being by physical cues.

It is understandable that the events of September 11, 2001 and increased threats of terrorism have prompted a desperate attempt to deal with a seemingly new type of foe. Those seeking to understand the perpetrators of the World Trade Center attack and their allies determined that the brutality on one side justified brutal measures in attempts to find and apprehend the perpetrators and prevent the next attack One of the Bush Administration's unstated reasons for endorsing harsh techniques was the belief that members of groups like the Taliban and Al Qaeda would not respond to traditional rapport-building techniques. The Bush

Administration reasoned that members of these groups, who exalted in death and raised it to a form of religious devotion, would never divulge information unless confronted by violence or extreme psychological pressures. Similar myths and prejudices were promulgated about the Japanese during World War and the Viet Cong during the Vietnam War. Experience and history have not shown these myths to be correct. Social science research, rather than myths and speculation, must be employed in our mission to prevent another September 11th and defeat those who portend to do us harm.

References

Biderman, A. D. (1956). Communist attempts to elicit false confessions from Air Force prisoners of war. *Bulletin of the New York Academy of Medicine, volume* number 33, 9, 616-625.

Biderman, A, D. (1963). *The march to calumny*. New York: Macmillan.

Carlson, Lewis. (2002). *Remembered prisoners of a forgotten war*. New York: St. Martin's Press.

Excerpts of interviews shown by TV in Iraq. (1991, January 21). *The Los Angeles Times*, p. A7.

Intelligence Science Board. (2006). Educing Information. Washington D.C.: National Defense College.

Meerloo, J.A.M. (1956). *The rape of the mind*. New York: Universal Library.

Shane, S. (2008, July 22). Inside the interrogation of a 9/11 mastermind. *The New York Times*, pp. A1, A12.

Sheehan, N. (1967, April 3). U.S. fears Hanoi is brainwashing American P.O.W.s. *The New York Times*, pp. A1, A4.

Toliver, R. (1997). *The interrogator*. Pennsylvania: Schiffer Publishing.

Wood, C. (2008, May 12). The story of the Pueblo. *The New American*, p.35.

X. What is Lone Wolf Terrorism?: A Research Note

Pete Simi

University of Nebraska, Omaha

Andrew J. Bringuel II

Federal Bureau of Investigation

Steven M. Chermak

Michigan State University

Joshua D. Freilich

John Jay School of Criminal Justice

Gary LaFree

University of Maryland

Lynn Maskel

University of California, San Diego

Abstract

Despite increased attention and concern, the discussion of "lone wolf terrorism" (LWT) is plagued by a striking absence of clear definitional parameters. The lack of conceptual clarity raises a number of important questions that we seek to examine in this essay. As such, the purpose of this essay is two-fold: 1) discuss the current status of the LWT concept and implications for continuing to use the concept in an uncritical and poorly defined manner; and 2) propose a research project aimed at clarifying the conceptual boundaries of LWT by examining the social-psychological characteristics of lone wolf terrorists as compared to other types of violent offenders.

Introduction

The summer of, 1999 was dubbed the "summer of hate." During the July 4th weekend of that year, Benjamin Smith, a lone gunman, set out on a three-day, two-state shooting spree killing two and injuring nine. A month later on August 10, Buford Furrow, another lone gunman, walked into a Jewish Community Center in Los Angeles, California shooting and injuring three and then killing an Asian-American postal worker nearby. Both Smith and Furrow were enmeshed in the white supremacist movement and were one-time members of the World Church of the Creator and the Aryan Nations respectively. Now a decade later, some would argue that we are witnessing another wave of far right violence. In a one-month period (between March and April, 2009), five law enforcement officers were killed in two separate incidents of right-wing extremist violence. A little more than a month later, George Tiller, a physician who performed abortions, was shot and killed in Wichita, Kansas. Scott Roeder, the gunman who allegedly shot and killed Tiller, is a longtime anti-abortion activist and has a history of participation in various far right causes. Less than two weeks after the Tiller murder, James Von Brunn, a veteran activist in the white supremacist movement, set out on a shooting spree at the Holocaust Memorial Museum in Washington DC killing an African-American security guard who made the mistake of opening a door for Von Brunn (Freilich & Chermak, 2009).

During this recent spate of extremist violence, Americans are struggling to determine how much of a threat this type of violence poses. Not surprisingly, extremist violence has also generated a new wave of media attention. The central storyline in much of this coverage has been the trend toward "lone wolf terrorism" (LWT). The focus on lone wolf terrorism, however, is more than media sensationalism. Law enforcement agencies, including the Federal Bureau of Investigation (FBI) and Department of Homeland Security (DHS), have indicated that lone wolf terrorism poses an increasing threat and that relatively little is known about this emerging brand of terrorism.

Despite increased attention and concern, the discussion of LWT is plagued by a striking absence of clear definitional parameters. At times, observers seem content using Justice Potter Stewart's famous dictum for judging pornography (i.e., "I know it when I see it"). There are a number of important issues that defining lone wolf terrorism raises. Should the term lone wolf be restricted to a single offender? Alternatively, does lone wolf terrorism include a small number of individuals linked together that operate outside of an extremist organizational command structure? Jeffrey Kaplan (1997), for example, combines lone wolf actors and small cellular structures as part of a larger strategy referred to as "leaderless resistance" (see Beam, 1992). Likewise, Turchie and Puckett's (2007) study of LWT includes Timothy McVeigh, despite substantial evidence that Terry Nichols and to a lesser extent played a significant role in the preparations of the attack (Michel and Herbeck, 2001; Jurgensmeyer, 2000). Including terrorists like McVeigh who are part of small cells with lone actor terrorists begs the question of whether there are important differences between a small group of terrorists operating outside of an organizational command structure and a single individual who commits violent acts without specific assistance (e.g., Buford Furrow and Benjamin Smith). This and other currently unanswered questions have significant implications for how we define and study lone wolf terrorism. At the most basic level, observers must decide whether LWT is an oxymoron. In other words, is the definition of terrorism incompatible with the idea of a "lone" actor committing "terroristic" violence?

One of the few previous studies of lone wolf terrorism suggests that a "narrow" definition of LWT is most appropriate (COT, 2007). A LWT is someone who, like a terrorist group, commits or plans acts of violence motivated by political ideology with the intention of intimidating a civilian population or government (COT, 2007). The LWT is differentiated from the terrorist group, however, along several dimensions: 1) the lone wolf does not belong to a network or organization; 2) the LWT is not influenced by a leader or hierarchy; and 3) the LWT conceives of and carries out their violence completely outside of any command structure. Although these criteria are reasonable, LWT's defining characteristics need to be analyzed as part of an empirical study that relies on a comparative methodology. Comparative methodologies allow researchers to assess the accuracy of definitional boundaries by utilizing between case assessments and are also critical to building and refining theoretical perspectives (Ragin, 1987; LaFree, 2007).

The purpose of this essay is two-fold: 1) discuss the current status of the LWT concept and implications for continuing to use the concept in an inconsistent and uncritical manner; and 2) propose a research project aimed at examining the social and psychological characteristics of lone wolf terrorists as compared to other types of violent offenders. The goal of the proposed project, in part, is to refine classificatory systems that analysts and other law enforcement personnel rely on as well as promote more nuanced analyses of terrorist behavior.

Origin of the term "Lone Wolf"

The concept of lone actors implementing violence in the name of or on behalf of larger movements is certainly not new. In the, 19th century, the Russian anarchist ideologue, Mikhail Bakunin, proposed a version of "propaganda by the deed" (1870) where single individuals or small groups were encouraged to assassinate members of the social order. Bakunin viewed the creation of hierarchical organizations as antithetical to their ideology and thus lone actor and small group violence was consistent with the spirit of anarchy.

Interestingly, the contemporary genesis of LWT is neither law enforcement nor academia but rather the U.S. white supremacist movement. The term lone wolf was popularized by white supremacists Alex Curtis and Tom Metzger (whose resist.com website features a snarling wolf on the front page) in the, 1990s. Louis Beam, a leading Klan and Aryan Nations representative, however, proposed a "point system" that awarded scores to would-be assassins based on the importance of their targets in the early-1980s (ADL, 2009). Other prominent white supremacist leaders such as William Pierce (now deceased), founder of the National Alliance and author of *Hunter* (a book which celebrated a fictional lone wolf but which the author dedicated to Joseph Paul Franklin, a real lone wolf) have also advocated lone wolf violence as a useful strategy at a time when white supremacists are greatly outnumbered and do not have the resources to wage a "full frontal attack."

White supremacists are not the only extremists who have advocated and used some version of the lone wolf model. Several scholars have noted that lone wolf tactics have been embraced by environmentalists and other far-left groups (Joose, 2007; Leader & Probst, 2004). Joose (2007) argues that the modern Environmental Liberation Front (ELF) movement is a prototype example of "leaderless resistance." The value of "leaderless resistance" is that it allows a network of individuals to commit acts in support of a common political objective even though there might be ideological differences between individuals working in independent cells. Although these scholars emphasize the threat of lone wolf tactics among far-leftists, other research indicates that state police officials are less concerned about lone wolf tactics occurring on the far left compared to such tactics being used by far rightists. For example, Freilich, Chermak, and Simone (2009) found that state police officials estimated close to 50% of criminal incidents involving anti-tax protestors, 21.4% involving Christian Identity adherents, and 28% involving freemen/sovereign citizens were committed as lone wolves. In contrast, only 4.5% of the respondents said that Animal Liberation Front (ALF), 9.5% for ELF, 6.7% for anti-immigration, and 8% for neo-Nazis usually committed their crimes as lone wolves.

Theodore Kaczynski (aka the Unabomber) who mailed 16 bombs over a seventeen-year period killing three and injuring 23 may be the prototype lone wolf terrorist. Although Kaczynski's motivation has been linked to his neo-Luddite politics, most observers agree that he had no known connections to any groups, authored his own personal manifesto, and lived in utter seclusion in a remote Montana cabin barely large enough for one person (Turchie & Puckett, 2007). In addition, Kaczynski definitely appears to have been a lone offender. What is less clear, however, is whether he was a terrorist. After his arrest Kaczynski was evaluated by psychologists and diagnosed with paranoid schizophrenia (Turchie & Pucket, 2007). Kaczynski's documented mental health problems raise the question of whether his violence was actually motivated by politics and thus appropriately viewed as terrorism or alternatively, whether his violence was primarily a manifestation of a mental health disorder. Other observers, however, claim Kaczynski was linked to the larger radical ELF movement illustrating that in some cases LWTs exhibit a co-presence of mental illness and political ideology. We also see this co-presence in a number of others cases such as former white supremacist Buford Furrow.

Interpreting the Lone Wolf

Although the lone wolf motif is a familiar one, how to interpret what lone wolf terrorism actually means is complicated. On April, 19, 1995 Timothy McVeigh detonated a homemade bomb that destroyed the Alfred P. Murrah Federal Building in Oklahoma City killing 168 people, including, 19 children, and injuring more than 500. The government's explanation for the incident rested on a lone wolf theory and, to this day, the official version of events states that McVeigh along with Terry Nichols and Michael Fortier acted alone. Years later, however, we know that McVeigh was deeply integrated into a potent culture of paranoia, conspiracy, and violence. His journey from learning extremist views to taking radical action was guided by a persistent network of white power activists (Wright, 2007; Hamm, 2001). McVeigh's involvement in this radical network warrants exclusion if a researcher adheres to the narrow definition of LWT discussed above.

The Oklahoma City bombing is a good example of the competing interpretations of lone wolf violence. Observers seem to offer two distinct interpretations. The first perspective views lone wolf terrorism as the work of isolated, deranged loners who typically suffer from psychological maladjustment. Characterological dysfunction, not politics, motivates these individuals to harm and kill innocent citizens. Lone wolves are "broken" individuals who perceive that they have been slighted and seek to use violence as revenge to address these wrongdoings. From this perspective, the term lone wolf terrorist is a misnomer, and, as such, these offenders are better classified as "spree," "rampage," or some other type of non-ideological violent offender. Using the term terrorist confuses the lone wolf's behavior with groups who seek to destabilize or overthrow an entire system, such as a government, or use violent tactics for achieving some other clearly expressed political goals (e.g., using plane hijackings in order to secure the release of "political prisoners"). Unlike the "true" terrorist, lone wolves are motivated by grievances that are primarily personal and do not extend into the broader, public realm of politics.

The second interpretation of lone wolf terrorism suggests that the problem with the term does not lie in the word terrorism but rather the word "lone." The focus on the lone wolf as pathological diminishes the importance of a broader network of extremist groups and the culture these groups create. Extremist group culture is where radical ideas are nourished and where radical action is generated. Although the groups that build and sustain extremist culture are typically informal, they are bound together by a basic agreement on key ideas (Jurgensmeyer, 2000; Post, 1998). The chatter about lone wolf violence over the past few months reveals several troubling tendencies. First, we continue to ignore where lone wolves come from; second, we continue to ignore how lone wolves maintain their radical beliefs; and third, we continue to ignore the possibility that lone wolves are not really alone. Extremists of any stripe typically form a community of like-minded believers who hope to change the world but who also recognize that just "getting by" is itself a major accomplishment for those whose beliefs are despised by the mainstream (Post, 2004; Simi & Futrell, 2009). The emphasis on the lone wolf betrays a general neglect of vibrant, albeit hidden, cultures that bring extremists together, helping them sustain their radical ideas, and, encourage the extremist violence enacted by groups and/or single individuals (Simi & Futrell, 2010).

In summary, our task in the proposed project will be to examine the extent to which lone wolf terrorism is, in fact, influenced by informal networks that link individuals together around extremist ideas or whether lone wolves are relatively isolated individuals who are more likely than members of terrorist groups to suffer from mental health problems and thus are better classified as non-ideological violent offenders.

Proposed Methodology

Despite widespread use of the term, the distinguishing features and characteristics of LWT remain unclear and the topic has received little systematic investigation. To examine lone wolf terrorism, it is critical to incorporate a comparative methodology (Ragin, 1994, 1987). The most significant previous studies of lone wolf terrorism (e.g., COT, 2007; Turchie & Puckett, 2007) neglected to utilize comparison groups and, thus, it is unclear how their findings regarding lone wolves compare to other types of offenders. These studies are also primarily descriptive and do not incorporate a fully systematic method for organizing and analyzing case study material and data.

Our primary question is essentially a practical one: is the term lone wolf terrorist helpful for criminal analysts and other law enforcement personnel or does referring to some offenders as lone wolves hinder our thinking and promote inaccurate ways of understanding violence? We have a number of sub-questions which we address later in the essay that specifically involve analyzing the nature of lone wolf violence.

To answer the research questions, we will compare lone wolves with three other categories of offenders: 1) members of American terrorist groups; 2) offenders who have committed violent acts that have been investigated as hate crimes as opposed to terrorism; and 3) non-ideological violent offenders such as serial murderers and serial rapists. The purpose of these comparisons will be to analyze whether lone wolves resemble other types of offenders or whether lone wolves possess unique characteristics thus necessitating a distinct classification.

The main points of comparison will involve two dimensions. First, each offender's life history will be analyzed using the psychological autopsy (PA) method (Shneidman & Farberow, 1961; Ebert, 1987; Lester, Yang, & Lindsay, 2004). Second, each offender's social network ties including the number of links and the types of relationships represented by these links (e.g., kinship, friends, coworkers etc.) will be analyzed.

Psychological autopsies have been employed to study suicide victims (Shneidman & Farberow, 1961), homicide investigations (Danto, 1979), and suicide bombers (Lester, Yang, & Lindsay, 2004) to name a few. The PA strategy involves reconstructing a subject's life from birth and using a number of data collection techniques such as interviewing key informants and reviewing secondary documents. Standard life history and demographic data including race/ethnicity, age, gender, and socioeconomic status is used to assess the subject's background and for the purposes of comparison to other research subjects in the sample. As part of the PAs, we will include some of the following categories: description of the subject's history (siblings, marriage, medical history etc.); history of subject's family; description of subject's lifestyle and personality; and nature of subject's interpersonal relationships. Our first task will be to create life history timelines for each offender that begins with his/her birth and moves forward until the date (s) of offending. Relatedly, our team will create event or incident timelines for each of the offenders. The incident timelines will, among other things, attempt to detail any information regarding pre-incident planning and pre-incident trigger (s).

Although a long tradition within the social sciences emphasizes the importance of engaging directly with research subjects through interviews and observation (Shaw, 1966; Weber, 1922; Whyte, 1943), studies of terrorism are characterized by a tendency to underemphasize or neglect their subjects' perspective. While exceptions certainly exist (e.g., see della Porta, 1988; Horgan, 2005; Hubbard, 1971; Gottschalk & Gottschalk, 2004; Post, Sprinzak, & Denny, 2003), many studies which do incorporate interviews employ clinical instruments (Victoroff, 2005) that while useful for assessing personality and other psycho-social characteristics are not well suited for gathering the actors' perspective about their own behavior and motives.

Despite a variety of methodological challenges posed by interviewing individual terrorists, we see significant benefits from incorporating primary interviews with members of this population. Gaining the perspective of any individual requires, to some extent, talking with him or her. In the cases where individuals are deceased, interviewing them is obviously not an option, however, many of the lone wolves and other offenders in our sample are still living. While some individuals may decline to participate, we expect that others will be willing to grant interviews. Given the difficulty of defining lone wolf terrorism, one source of information that has been neglected thus far is the offenders themselves. There is much to be learned by talking with these offenders including their perceptions regarding the factors that may have motivated their violent action.

Two of the most salient methodological problems associated with interviewing incarcerated terrorists include: 1) gaining access to the institutional environments where subjects reside; and 2) subject deception. Although the former issue is a serious logistical concern, our research team's partnership with the Behavioral Science Unit at the Federal Bureau of Investigation may help the researchers gain access to correctional facilities that might otherwise be unwilling, for security reasons, to grant access. The second problem involves data integrity and validity issues. Our research design's reliance on multiple data collection techniques and multiple data sources will provide "triangulation" (Denzin, 1978) and thus strengthen the research team's ability to assess data sources and verify findings. In addition, previous research suggests that criminal offenders are no more likely than anyone else to lie about their circumstances (Brezina, Tekin, & Topalli, 2009; Wright & Decker, 1994). The semi-structured organization of our interview instrument is consistent with past efforts to obtain the most valid and relevant information about the social and psychological circumstances that lead to their offending behavior (Huizinga & Elliott, 1996; West & Farrington, 1977).

Social Network Links and Lone Wolf Terrorism

What are the characteristics of lone wolves' social relational links? First, we are interested in determining whether lone wolves are connected to other extremists and, if so, what is the nature of those links? Second, what is the structure and content of lone wolves' primary and secondary groups (Cooley, 1902)? Are lone wolves connected to non-extremists such as kin, friends, and colleagues? When looking at the entirety of a lone wolf's social relations, what is the ratio of extremist-to-non-extremist links and how does this ratio compare to members of terrorist groups? At the same time, we also intend to investigate what portion of lone wolves are isolated "loners" as most descriptions of the Unabomber suggest?

The section of the study designed to determine whether lone wolves are embedded within a larger community of extremists will incorporate social network analysis (SNA), a methodological technique designed to examine the structural properties of a network such as which nodes have the greatest number of links, the centrality of various nodes, and whether the network is divided into relatively distinct clusters or cliques (Scott, 2001; Nooy, Mrvar, and Batagelj, 2005; Wasserman and Faust, 1994; Watts and Strogatz, 1998). SNA identifies interpersonal and interorganizational links.

One of the most widely researched issues using SNA is whether there are specific nodes that occupy central positions within the network (i.e., degree centrality) where centrality is understood as a sign of prominence, influence, or prestige (Wasserman & Faust, 1994). Our study will measure degree centrality of individual offenders by their "indegree," that is, their total number of incoming links. We will analyze betweenness centrality which measures where nodes are located in relation to other nodes. Nodes with high degree centrality scores serve as hubs while a high betweenness centrality score refers to a node that serves as a broker in the network located between two important constituencies. In addition, we will use SNA to examine whether the offenders in our sample are nodes in relatively distinct subgroups or cliques.

Data Sources

The sources of data we intend to use for this project include the following: interviews, information culled from existing datasets such as the American Terrorism Study (ATS) and the U.S. Extremist Crime Database (ECDB), and secondary data obtained through analysis of case files. The interview protocols will primarily focus on the offender's social network links prior to and during their involvement in terroristic behavior. The questions will be designed, in part, using secondary documents that detail the offender's life and his/her relationships. The interviews will be conducted with several goals in mind. First, we intend to use the responses to help map the offender's social network links and establish who the person was connected to and what types of relationships characterize the offender's connections. We also intend to examine whether the offenders were part of any clique formations and if so, were they central or peripheral members of these cliques. Second, we intend to use the interview format to gather information about their perspectives and motives. At this point, we have compiled a preliminary sample of lone wolves as well as the three comparison groups. Interviews with the entire sample will not be possible as some subjects are deceased (e.g., Timothy McVeigh). Other subjects may refuse to participate in the project. Because the psychological autopsy is designed for situations where the individual focal point is no longer living, this method is especially well suited for this type of project which involves populations that are hard to access.

Understanding the Characteristics of Lone Wolf Terrorism

The purpose of our analysis will be to provide specific answers to some of the following research questions. Are lone wolves motivated by a political ideology? In this respect, was Eric Rudolph's violence the work of a serial bomber as opposed to a far right activist? If Rudolph was, in fact, a serial bomber seeking revenge for personal slights, this means that his political views were at least secondary and potentially incidental to his violence. Likewise, are individuals like Benjamin Smith, Buford Furrow, and James Von Brunn, more like rampage shooters such as Seung-Hui Cho, the Virginia Tech University gunmen or adolescent school shooters like Columbine High School killers Dylan Klebold and Eric Harris? The ECDB will be used, in part, to answer this question. The ECDB provides data regarding extremists' strength of affiliation and the presence of a range of extremist indicators (e.g., group membership, tattoos etc.).

Another area we intend to explore with this research is whether specific "trigger" or catalyst events transpire prior to the lone wolf taking action. If so, are these events primarily personal slights or related to the extremist world which some of these lone wolves identify with? For example, the Illinois State Bar Association's refusal to accept Matt Hale' bar application reportedly provoked Benjamin Smith's shooting spree. In this case, Smith seems to have been acting on behalf of Hale and the white supremacist movement as opposed to a purely personal issue.

Following Turchie and Puckett's analysis of LWT (2007), we intend to investigate whether lone wolf violence may be a response to increased isolation from other extremists. The increased isolation may occur for a variety of reasons including personal turmoil and/or group rejection. As the lone wolf's isolation increases from other extremists, the lone wolf loses the support needed to "get by" in a world antagonistic to his/her extremism (Simi & Futrell, 2009). The loss of social support from other extremists may encourage the lone wolf to feel that enacting violent fantasies no longer poses a "high cost" in terms of jeopardizing his/her social network. Without the constraints of his/her ties to a larger social network, the lone wolf may feel emboldened to implement the violent fantasies that have been reinforced by his/her previous participation in extremist culture. At the same time, the lone wolf's increased isolation from other extremists means that he/she is no longer able to find cathartic releases for his/her anger relating to extremist beliefs. Coming together and participating in extremist culture with other like-minded adherents represents a type of "safety release valve" where extremists "blow off steam." When these opportunities are no longer available, the lone wolf may find that he/she is unable to continue coping in a world that he/she is fundamentally at odds with. As the lone actor's frustration mounts without any opportunities to vent his/her anger, the lone wolf finds the idea of "putting words into action" as the only way to resolve their inner turmoil (Simi & Futrell, 2010). At this point, the lone wolf may perceive taking violent action as a means to restore his/her ties to the extremist world.

Neurocognitive Factors

Alternatively, lone wolves may reflect a violent trajectory that occurs among a minority of extremists. It appears that many extremists are able to maintain their involvement over a long period of time without engaging in any intense episode of violence (Simi & Futrell, 2009). An even larger portion of extremists seem to "burn out" over time. Extremists, who burn out, are, for varying reasons unable to maintain their affiliations and/or beliefs and eventually exit the extremist lifestyle (Bjorgo, 1998; Blazak, 2001; Blee, 2002). The lone wolf may be a relatively rare type of extremist who experiences a diminished capacity over time to satisfy his/her extremist desires with nonviolent cultural practices such as, consuming propaganda, and, thus, finds it necessary to transcend fantasy by taking action. The transition toward the implementation of violent ideas may also have a strong neurological counterpart and, thus, understanding extremist pathways toward violence, such as, lone wolves, requires attention to neurological dimensions. Given the highly emotive content of extremist propaganda, extremist messages likely stimulate responses in a complex neural circuit involving the amygdala, the orbital frontal cortex, the anterior cingulated cortex, and other interconnected regions of the brain. Permanent dysfunction or temporary changes in the neural regions regulating emotion may increase a person's susceptibility to impulsive violent behavior (Davidson, Putnam, & Larson, 2000). Lone wolf violence, as is likely the case with all violence, results from a complex interplay socio-neurological processes which remain poorly understood.

The creation and consumption of extremist culture involves mental processing and components of the cognitive system. Violence of any sort requires violent scripts (Dodge, Price, Bachorowski, & Newman, 1990; Huesmann, 1998, 1988). Does planning and participating in terrorism, however, require more than the average violent script? As compared to interpersonal violence, terrorism, by definition, involves the potential to harm a large number of unknown people. This difference may require individuals to adapt existing violent scripts in ways that facilitate larger-scale acts of violence. Given the relatively low number of fatalities that result from lone wolf offenders (COT, 2007), does this suggest the lone wolf is an individual who is unable to effectively adopt a large-scale violent script?

Implications and Conclusion

Lone wolf terrorism remains an issue of significant concern. Even while writing this essay we witnessed another tragic incident of violence that some observers suspect was an act of lone wolf terrorism. On November 5, 2009, Major Nidal Hasan shot and killed 13 people and wounded another 30 individuals at Fort Hood, Texas. Evidence suggests the shooting spree was inspired, in part, by radical Islamic Jihadi ideology. The incident is still under investigation and the questions that remain unanswered regarding Hasan's motivations highlight our project's goals. Determining differences and similarities among violent offenders provides the basis for developing criminal classifications with greater accuracy and sensitivity. Determinations of this kind are also necessary for preventing overly broad characterizations that view all acts of violence as terrorism (lone wolf or otherwise). Currently we know far too little about individuals assumed to be lone wolves to be able to distinguish these offenders from members of terrorist groups as compared to more generic violent offenders.

The results from this study will be useful in terms of offender classification. The current lack of systematic empirical evidence regarding lone wolves encourages inconsistent assessments regarding offender characteristics and the nature of violent offenses. For example, despite evidence suggesting Timothy McVeigh participated in a wider network of white supremacists, McVeigh is often classified as a lone wolf (Turchie & Puckett, 2007). In terms of profiling and classifying criminal behavior, it seems reasonable to assume that fundamental differences may exist between an offense planned by three individuals and an offense planned by only one individual. If the lone wolf classification is going to be a meaningful concept, researchers need to establish clearer definitional parameters that will help determine when an incident of violence is the act of a lone wolf, a terrorist group, or a more generic violent offender.

References

Anti-Defamation League. 2009. "Extremism in America – Louis Beam." Downloaded October 20, 2009. Available at: http://www.adl.org/learn/ext_us/beam.asp?LEARN_Cat=Extremism&LEARN_SubCat=Extremism_in_America&xpicked=2&item=beam.

Beam, Louis. 1992. "Leaderless Resistance." (available at www.louisbeam.com).

Bjorgo, Tore. 1998. "Entry, Bridge Burning, and Exit Options: What Happens to Young People Who Join Racist Groups." pp. 231-258 in *Nation and Race: The Developing Euro-American Racist Subculture*, edited by Jeffery Kaplan and Tore Bjorgo. Boston, MA: Northeastern University Press.

Blazak, Randy. 2001. "White Boys to Terrorist Men: Target Recruitment of Nazi Skinheads." *The American Behavioral Scientist* 44(6): 982-1000.

Blee, Kathleen. 2002. *Inside Organized Racism: Women in the Hate Movement*. Berkeley: University of California Press.

Brezina, Timothy, Erdal Tekin, and Volkan Topalli. 2009. "Might not be a Tomorrow: A Multimethods Approach to Anticipated Early Death and Youth Crime." *Criminology*, 47: 1091-1129.

Cutler, Robert. 1992. *The Basic Bakunin: Writings 1869-1871*. New York: Prometheus Books.

Danto, B.L. 1979. "New Frontiers in the Relationship between Suicidology and Law Enforcement." *Suicide and Life Threatening Behavior* 9: 195-204.

Davidson, Richard, Katherine Putnam, and Christine Larson. 2000. "Dysfunction in the Neural Circuitry of Emotion Regulation – A Possible Prelude to Violence." *Science* 28: 591-94.

della Porta, Donatella. 1988. "Recruitment Processes in Clandestine Political Organizations: Italian Left-Wing Terrorism." *International Social Movement Research* 1: 155-169.

Dodge, Kenneth, Joseph Price, Jo-Anne Bachorowski, and Joseph Newman. 1990. "Hostile Attributional Biases in Severely Aggressive Adolescents." *Journal of Abnormal Psychology* 99: 385-392.

Ebert, Bruce. 1987. "Guide to Conducting a Psychological Autopsy." *Professional Psychology: Research and Practice*, v. 18:52-56.

Freilich, Joshua and Steven Chermak. 2009. "Preventing Deadly Encounters Between Law Enforcement and American Far-Rightists. *Crime Prevention Studies* 25: 141-172.

Freilich, Joshua, Steven Chermak, and Joseph Simone. 2009. "Surveying American State Police Agencies about Far-right and Islamic Jihadist Criminal Collaboration, Terrorism Threats,

Terrorism Sources, and Terrorism Definitions." *Terrorism and Political Violence,* 21 (3): 450-475.

Hamm, Mark. 2002. *In Bad Company: America's Terrorist Underground.* Boston: Northeastern University Press.

Huesmann, L. 1998. "The Role of Social Information Processing and Cognitive Schema in the Acquisition and Maintenance of Habitual Aggressive Behavior." In Human Aggression:

Theories, Research and Implications for Social Policy. eds. Russell Geen and Edward Donnerstein, p. 73-109. San Diego, CA: Academic Press.

Huesmann, L. 1988. "An Information Processing Model for the Development of Aggression." *Aggressive Behavior* 14: 13-24.

Huizinga, David and Delbert Elliott. 1986. "Reassessing the Reliability and Validity of Self-Report Delinquency Measures." *Journal of Quantitative Criminology*, 2: 293-327.

Jurgensmeyer, Mark. 2000. *Terror in the Mind of God: The Global Rise of Religious Violence*. University Press: Berkeley, CA.

Joose, Paul. 2007. "Leaderless resistance and ideological inclusion: The case of the Earth Liberation Front." *Terrorism and Political Violence*, 19: 351- 368.

Kaplan, Jeffrey. 1997. *Radical Religion in America: Millenarian Movements from the Far Right to the Children of Noah*. Syracuse, NY: Syracuse University Press.

LaFree, Gary. 2007. "Expanding the Domain of Criminology." *Criminology* 45, 1-31.

Leader, S.H. and P. Probst. 2004. *The Earth Liberation Front and Environmental Terrorism*. Retrieved from http://ww1.umn.edu.

Lester, David, Bijou Yang, and Mark Lindsay. 2004. "Suicide Bombers: Are Psychological Autopsies Possible?" *Studies in Conflict and Terrorism*, 27:283-295.

Michel, Dan and Lou Herbeck. 2001. *American Terrorist: Timothy McVeigh and the Oklahoma City Bombing*. Harper: New York.

Post, Jerrold. 2004. *Leaders and their Followers in a Dangerous World: the Psychology of* Political Behavior. Ithaca, NY: Cornell University Press.

Ragin, Charles. 1987. The Comparative Method: Moving Beyond Qualitative and Quantitative *Strategies*. Univ. of California Press.

Ragin, Charles. 1994. *Constructing Social Research: The Unity and Diversity of Method.* Pine Forge Press.

Shaw, Clifford. 1966. *The Jack Roller*. University of Chicago Press.

Shneidman, E.S. and N.L. Farberow. 1961. "Sample Investigations of Equivocal Deaths." In N.L. Farberow and E.S. Shneidman (eds.) in *The Cry for Help*, pp. 118-129. New York: McGraw-Hill.

Simi, Pete and Robert Futrell. 2010. *American Swastika: Inside the White Power Movement's Hidden Spaces of Hate*. Rowman & Littlefield: Lanham, MD.

Simi, Pete and Robert Futrell. 2009. "Negotiating White Power Activist Stigma." *Social Problems*, 56: 89-110.

Turchie, Terry and Kathleen Puckett. 2007. *Hunting the American Terrorist: The FBI's War on Homegrown Terror*. History Publishing Company: Palisades, NY.

Victoroff, Jeff. 2005. "The Mind of a Terrorist: A Review and Critique of Psychological Approaches." *Journal of Conflict Resolution* 49: 3-42.

West, Donald and David Farrington. 1977. *The Delinquent Way of Life*. London, UK: Heineman.

Whyte, William F. 1955/43. *Street Corner Society: the Social Structure of an Italian Slum*. Chicago: University of Chicago Press.

Wright, Stuart. 2007. *Patriots, Politics, and the Oklahoma City Bombing*. Cambridge, UK: Cambridge University Press.

Wright, Richard and Scott Decker. 1994. *Burglars on the Job. Boston*, MA: Northeastern University Press.

XI. Right-Wing Extremism and Military Service

Brent L. Smith

University of Arkansas

Andrew J. Bringuel, II

Federal Bureau of Investigation

Steven M. Chermak

Michigan State University

Kelly R. Damphousse

University of Oklahoma

Joshua D. Freilich

John Jay College of Criminal Justice

Abstract

Recent reports over the past year have suggested that right wing terrorists in the United States are more likely than other types of violent extremists to have served in our nation's military. Some of these reports and media accounts intimate that these extremists and potential terrorists have used their military training as a resource for training others in the movement. Other accounts suggest that military experience itself may be serving as part of the radicalization process. Unfortunately, none of these claims have been based on empirical data, relying instead on anecdotal evidence such as McVeigh-Nichols experience to bolster these arguments. The current article uses data from the Extremist Crime Database (ECDB) and the American Terrorism Study (ATS) to ascertain the extent to which right wing extremists, who have been indicted primarily in state courts, and right wing terrorists, who have been indicted in federal courts, have military service records. Accounts of noteworthy right-wing extremists and terrorists in the United States with military experience are also provided.

Introduction

During the past couple of years, concerns about efforts by right-wing extremist groups to recruit members from U.S. military personnel have received renewed attention. These concerns have existed for many years, rising periodically following significant incidents of right-wing domestic terrorism, only to subside when public concern about American terrorism wanes. The most recent presidential election, subsequent downturn in the U.S. economy, and a series of extremists' activities linked to civilians with prior military training has reignited calls for examination of this issue. Spurred by requests from groups monitoring right-wing activities in the United States, such as the Southern Poverty Law Center, both the Department of Justice through the Federal Bureau of Investigation (2008) and the Department of Homeland Security (2009) have issued "law enforcement sensitive" reports suggesting that right-wing recruitment of military personnel is indeed more real than imagined.

In particular, these reports drew two basic conclusions based upon a review of anecdotal information, recent extremist and terrorism related incidents involving members of the extreme right, and data drawn from FBI case files since the September 11 attacks. First, they contend that right-wing extremists actively recruit military veterans for membership. Implicit in this argument is that right-wing groups seek out those with military experience more than other types of extremist or terrorist groups. Second, both of these reports suggest that military experience provides an entrée into leadership positions within extremist or terrorist groups here in the United States. Both of these reports conclude that U.S. soldiers disillusioned with the wars in Iraq and Afghanistan are particularly vulnerable for recruitment by right-wing extremist groups.

The response to these reports was mixed – some contended that the military was not doing enough to address the issue, while others argued that suggesting that returning veterans might be disgruntled enough to consider joining an extremist group was an exaggeration and an attack on the integrity of our military servicemen and women. The current paper seeks to place these reports in context and assess the validity of these arguments using empirical data from two open source databases on American extremism and American terrorism – the Extremist Crimes Database (ECDB) and the American Terrorism Study (ATS).

Background

Concerns about military personnel becoming involved in American terrorism were an issue as early as the late 1960s. Generally, one would expect substantial variation regarding military background and political orientation. The extreme left, spearheading the anti-war movement of the 1960s and early 1970s, held a deep resentment of the military and veterans returning from Viet Nam. With the advent of an all-volunteer army in the mid-1970s, this resentment turned to suspicion regarding any military personnel who might have wanted to join leftist terror groups or participate in left extremism. In contrast, the extreme right saw the implementation of affirmative action in the military in the 1970s as an opportunity to attract white service members and veterans into the fold (Smith, 1994).

The activities of Frazier Glenn Miller in the early 1980s were among the first to attract national attention to this issue. Miller, who was discharged from the military for distributing Nazi literature to an undercover military intelligence officer (Turner, 1986), formed the Carolina Knights of the Ku Klux Klan in 1980. He is credited with converting the Carolina KKK from the traditional Klan robes to the more appealing military style uniforms of the survivalist movement. Miller subsequently changed the group's name to the White Patriot Party (WPP) and began focusing on providing paramilitary training to its growing constituency. As part of this strategy, Miller enlisted the aid of active duty military personnel from nearby Fort Bragg to provide much of the training.[1] The group's astounding growth and military connections attracted the attention of the Southern Poverty Law Center, which filed a lawsuit in 1985 demanding a Department of

---

[1] Indictment at 3, United States v, Stephen Samuel Miller et al. (87-2-01 thru 05 CR-3), U.S. District Court, Eastern District of North Carolina, Fayetteville Division.

Defense investigation into the WPP's ties to Fort Bragg. A federal judge eventually issued a court order prohibiting Miller from conducting any paramilitary training.[2] Miller and several other members of the WPP were eventually convicted of other charges related to their increasingly radical behavior.[3]

Despite Miller's conviction, his indirect influence on the growth of the militia movement in the 1990s is well documented (Martinez, 1988; Smith, 1994). The siege at Ruby Ridge, Louis Beam's call for "leaderless resistance," the conflagration at Waco, Texas, and fears of a "new world order" fueled the subsequent growth of the militia movement after 1992. When Timothy McVeigh and Terry Nichols bombed the Murrah Federal Building in Oklahoma City in 1995, all eyes once again focused on the extreme right's ties to the U.S. Army. While much can be debated about the radicalization of McVeigh and Nichols, one thing is certain – McVeigh's specialized military training was a key element in his ability to construct and detonate the Oklahoma City bomb.

Later that year, three white soldiers assigned to Fort Bragg were charged in the murder of two black men in Fayetteville, North Carolina. The Secretary of the Army, Togo West, responded by creating a task force on extremist activity. Although the task

---

[2] Bobby Person v. Glenn Miller, Jr. and the Carolina Knights of the Ku Klux Klan.

[3] Judgment in a criminal case, U.S. v. Robert Eugene Jackson, Douglas Lawrence Sheets, and Frazier Glenn Miller, Jr. (87-03247-01 thru 03-CR-S-4), U.S. District Court, Western District of Missouri, Southern Division.

force report issued in March 1996 "found minimal evidence of extremist activity in the Army,"[4] more detailed analysis of the task force's data and follow-up surveys independently conducted with military personnel revealed several notable findings. Presley (1996:1) for example, concluded that the recruitment of military personnel by the extreme right: (1) added a degree of legitimacy to their ranks; (2) provided militia group members requisite training in weapons and tactics; and (3) provided access to military equipment and munitions. The military subsequently clarified its policy on "active" and "passive" participation in extremist organizations.[5]

A decade later, the Southern Poverty Law Center once again brought the issue to the forefront in a 2006 report on neo-Nazi extremists joining the U.S. military for the express purpose of learning useful military skills and recruiting other service members (Holthouse, 2006). Within the next two years, both the Department of Justice and the Department of Homeland Security examined the issue, subsequently issuing the highly controversial reports summarized earlier (Federal Bureau of Investigation, 2008; Department of Homeland Security, 2009).

Other than the descriptive evidence from samples of cases drawn from FBI files (Federal Bureau of Investigation, 2008), little

---

[4] Office of the Assistant Secretary of Defense (Public Affairs). Army Task Force Report on Extremist Activity. DoD News Release No. 144-96. March 21, 1996.

[5] See Army Regulation 600-20 (Army Command Policy), Section 4-12 (Extremist Organizations and Activities). 18 March 2008.

empirical examination of the relationship between rightwing extremism and the military has been conducted. The goals of the current essay are to use data from the ECDB to determine the prevalence of military experience among far-right offenders who committed ideologically motivated homicide and compare this percentage to the percent of all inmates serving time for homicide who had served in the military. We will also use data from the ATS to determine whether empirical evidence exists to support two of the most common contentions from earlier reports, that (1) a greater proportion of rightwing extremist and/or terrorist groups have members with military training; and (2) that military training is associated with these members assuming leadership roles within their respective organizations.

Method

Very few domestic terrorism databases exist that have collected information on military involvement at the individual level. Among those that have are the *American Terrorism Study* (ATS), housed at the University of Arkansas, and the *Extremist Crime Database* (ECDB), housed jointly at Michigan State University and John Jay College, City University of New York. Both are affiliated with the DHS START Center of Excellence at the University of Maryland. The characteristics of these two databases are described below.

American Terrorism Study

The ATS began in 1988 when the FBI's Terrorism Research and Analytical Center provided a list of persons indicted under official "domestic security/terrorism enterprise" investigations as defined under the AG Guidelines for FBI Investigations. The FBI has provided subsequent lists of these defendants to ATS researchers through the U.S. House of Representatives Judiciary Subcommittee on Crime and, later, through Senate Judiciary Committee. Information on approximately 650 persons indicted in federal terrorism cases from 1980-2004 is available for analysis. Persons included in this database reflect the official definition of terrorism utilized by the FBI[6] and implemented through the regulatory application of the definition through the AG Guidelines for FBI Investigations. Although some modification to the definition and the AG Guidelines occurred during the period 1980-2004, the concept, as applied to this population of cases, has probably been one of the most consistently applied definitions of terrorism over time.

Data on nearly 400 variables relating to each person/group/incident from the FBI lists are extracted from the federal criminal court case files. Using FBI identifiers, the ATS

---

[6] The FBI, citing the Code of Federal Regulations defines terrorism as "the unlawful use of force and violence against persons or property to intimidate or coerce a government, the civilian population, or any segment thereof, in furtherance of political or social objectives" (28 C.F.R. Section 0.85), *Terrorism in the United States: 2002-2005*. Washington, DC: Federal Bureau of Investigation.

routinely categorized terrorists as “leftwing,” “rightwing,” “international,” “environmental,” and “single-issue.” Recoding of specific cases/groups into different categories is possible depending on the specific analysis needed. Regarding military involvement, the ATS database includes information on: (1) whether the indicted person was in the military at some point in time; (2) whether the person has any specialized military training (e.g., paratrooper); and (3) what their role was in the terrorist group. It should be noted that the number of persons identified having military service is probably underrepresented. However, we believe that any reporting/nonreporting error is random. Therefore, comparisons among group types and examinations of group roles should render reliable estimates.

Extremist Crime Database

Since 2006, Chermak (Michigan State University) and Freilich (John Jay College, CUNY) have received funding from the Department of Homeland Security directly as well as through START to build the ECDB – a relational database on the suspects, victims, events, and group characteristics of all known violent and financial crimes committed by far-rightists in the United States since 1990. In 2009 the ECDB expanded to include violent and financial crimes committed by jihadists and animal rights and environmental rights extremists in the United States. The ECDB is the first-of-its-kind database and unlike terrorism-focused databases, the ECDB includes violent and non-violent crimes, ideological and non-ideological attacks, crimes by groups and lone wolves, and cases tried both federally and under state-jurisdiction (see Freilich and Chermak, 2010).

The ECDB allows analytical comparisons of criminal activity by offenders based on group type, ideology, and organizing characteristics. By focusing on all crimes by extremists, the data allow for the comparison of criminal and extremist groups that do not employ terrorist methods with those that do, and differences in structural, network, and recruitment related variables can also be compared.

Data in the ECDB were collected using open-source methods. Incidents were identified from a wide-range of existing terrorism databases, official records, scholarly works, newspaper accounts and watch-group reports. Each identified incident was treated as a case study with the goal of compiling as much relevant open-source information as possible. Individual coders use this open-source information as the resource for identifying values for more than 500 variables, based on a coding scheme developed by Freilich and Chermak. Coded information for each case contains:

- incident variables including motivations of the event, criminal justice related variables, location variables, damage;

- suspect variables including demographics and military and prison experience, religion, position in group, and criminal history;
- victim variables including demographics, relationship to suspect, effects of crime, criminal history, provocation, alcohol/drug use; and
- group variables including structure, chain of command, network, community engagement, political engagement, location, membership, recruitment that prior research considers significant.

Results

First, we examined ECDB data to investigate the prevalence of military experience among far-right suspects who committed ideologically motivated homicide. The ECDB has identified 271 homicide incidents in the United States between 1990 and 2008 where at least one of the suspects adhered to a far-right belief system. These homicides included both ideologically (e.g., Oklahoma City bombing) and non-ideologically (e.g., a skinhead murdered his girlfriend in a domestic violence attack) motivated incidents. The 271 homicide incidents were committed by 589 individual suspects. Four hundred eighty three (82%) of these suspects were far-rightists, and 19 (5%) of these individuals had served in the military.

More interesting, and relevant, are the 116 (42%) of these homicide events that were ideologically motivated, and thus more comparable to "terrorist" behavior. These incidents include anti-government homicides, bias homicides, and other ideological homicide attacks committed by at least one far-rightist. These incidents were committed by 204 suspects, over 90% (188 individuals) of whom were far-rightists. Thirteen (6.9%) of these far-right suspects had military experience. The other 16 suspects collaborated with far-rightists to commit these ideological homicides. Only one of these individuals was known to have served in the military

Interestingly, the ECDB findings that close to 7% of far-right suspects committing ideologically motivated homicides had served in the military is lower than the latest Bureau of Justice Statistics (BJS) survey (Noonan & Mumola 2007) in 2004 which found that 12.3% of federal and state inmates serving time for homicide had served in the military.[7] We want to emphasize that the ECDB probably underreports offender involvement in the

---

[7] We derived this percentage by analyzing table 4 of this BJS report. In 2004 the total prison population was 1,4000,000 of whom 140,000 (10%) had served in the military and 1,260,000 had not served in the military. This table also inform us that 14.9% of the veterans in prison were incarcerated for homicide, and 14.9% of 140,000 inmates came to 20,860. In addition, table 4 inform us that 11.8% of non-veterans were incarcerated for homicide, and 11.8% of 1,260,000 inmates came to 148,680. Thus, the total number of inmates serving time for homicide were 169,540 of whom, 10,660 or 12.3% had military experience.

military. It is possible that the open sources we relied upon did not always report suspects' military service. In addition, the time periods of the ECDB and BJS are not the same. Nonetheless, this rough comparison of far-right suspects who committed ideologically motivated homicides to suspects serving time for homicides generally does not support the notion that far-rightists were more likely to have served in the military.

We next analyzed this issue with ATS data. We examined the proportion of "officially designated" terrorists who were identified as having military experience using ATS data. Table 1 supports the arguments made by previous reports and assessments that rightwing terrorists are more likely to have military experience than other types of terrorists. Overall, we were able to identify 10% (64 of 655) of the terrorists in the sample who had military training. (Once again, we want to emphasize that this overall percentage represents a minimum number.) Of these 64, they were disproportionately affiliated with rightwing groups. Nearly three-fifths (58%) of the terrorists with military background were linked to rightwing groups or causes (statistic not shown in table). Proportionally, rightwing terrorists were more than four times as likely to have military training as leftist terrorists (18% to 4%, respectively) and more than twice as likely to have military training as international terrorists indicted in federal courts (18% to 9%, respectively).

Table 1
Proportion of Terrorists Identified with Military Backgrounds

Military Service	Group Type					**Total**
	Left-wing	Right-wing*	Interna-tional	Environ-mental	Un-known	
Yes	4 (4%)	37 (18%)	18 (9%)	1 (3%)	4 (4%)	64 (10%)
No	111 (96%)	170 (82%)	192 (91%)	28 (97%)	90 (96%)	591 (90%)
Total	115	207	210	29	94	655

*Since all 3 single issue terrorists were "anti-abortion," they have been coded as "rightwing" and the single issue category has been deleted.

Of the 37 rightwing terrorists, no particular rightwing group dominated these statistics. No group having more than three members identified with military training. This finding is somewhat different from the 2008 FBI assessment that found that over 70% of military personnel with extremist affiliations were linked to three specific groups. The difference is probably attributable to two differences. First, the FBI assessment examined files involving "extremists," while the ATS uses only those cases where an officially designated federal "terrorism" incident has either occurred or was prevented. Second, the FBI assessment covers a more recent time period, 2001-2008, while the ATS cover the period 1980-2004. It will be interesting to see if, in the future, the extremists in the FBI assessment eventually turn to terrorism.

Next, we examined the demographic characteristics of the 64 terrorists identified as having military experience (tables not shown). As expected, almost all of the terrorists with military experience in the ATS were male. Only one female with military background was identified and she was affiliated with a rightwing group. Similarly, all 13 of the far-rightists with military experience in the ECDB were male and the BJS survey found that 99% of all inmates with military service were male.

Racially, all 37 of the rightwing terrorists in the ATS were White, as were all 13 far-rightists with military experience in the ECDB who had committed ideologically motivated homicide; while 3 of the 4 leftwing terrorists in the ATS with military experience were Black. Educationally, rightwing terrorists with military backgrounds were more disparate than other types. Nearly one-third (32%) of the rightwing terrorists with military backgrounds had a GED equivalent or less. All of the other terrorists (leftwing, international, and environmental) with military backgrounds had at least a high school diploma.

Finally, using ATS data, we examined two issues relating to the effect of military experience on one's role in a terrorist group. First, we wanted to assess whether military experience in general was associated with leadership roles in terrorist groups.

FBI and DHS assessments in 2008 and 2009, respectively, had suggested that military experience was particularly valued by members of the extreme right and that such experience was more likely to propel these members to leadership roles. Overall, we found that military experience is strongly associated with the assumption of leadership roles among terrorist groups that have targeted the United States (see Table 2). In the total sample of 655 terrorists examined, nearly one-fourth (22.6%) were classified as "leaders" or "subordinate leaders," while for the other three-fourths (77.4%), no evidence could be found that these remaining members had ever assumed a "leadership" or even "subordinate leadership" role in the group. When comparing leaders with cadre members, approximately seven percent (37 of 507) of the cadre members were found to have military experience, while nearly twenty percent of the leaders (27 of 148) had military experience. In essence, those with military experience were more than twice as likely to assume leadership roles in American terrorist groups. These differences are highly significant.

Table 2
Proportion of Terrorist Leaders and Cadre with Known Military Backgrounds

Military Service	Group Role		Total
	Leader	Cadre	
Yes	27 (18.2%)	37 (7.3%)	64 (9.8%)
No	121 (81.8%)	470 (92.7%)	591 (90.2%)
Total	148 (100.0%)	507 (100.0%)	655 (100.00%)

$\chi^2 = 15.57$, df =1, $p < .001$

Table 3
Proportion of Rightwing and Other Terrorists with Known Military Backgrounds* by Group Role

Group Type	Group Role		Total
	Leader	Cadre	
Rightwing	17 (45.9%)	20 (54.1%)	37 (100%)
All Other	10 (37.0%)	17 (63.0%)	27 (100%)
Total	27 (42.2%)	37 (57.8%)	64 (100.00%)

*Excludes 3 persons with military experience whose group affiliation was not known.

$\chi^2 = 0.51$, df =1, p = NS

Finally, we wanted to ascertain whether this pattern applied to all terrorists or was specific to rightwing terrorists. Earlier reports had suggested that the extreme right particularly valued those with military experience for their leadership skills. To determine this, we only analyzed those with military backgrounds and compared rightwing terrorists against other group types (see Table 3). We found only slight differences between the proportion of rightwing terrorists with military backgrounds (45.9%) and other terrorists with military backgrounds (37.0%) who assumed leadership roles. Although in the predicted direction, these differences were not statistically significant. While not conclusive, these findings suggest two things. First, over the past 25 years, rightwing terrorist groups have been more likely than other American terrorist groups to attract members with military backgrounds. Second, and in contrast, once enlisted into the ranks of a terrorist group, military experience has similar effects on one's role regardless of group ideology. Those with military experience were all more likely to rise to leadership roles, regardless of whether the domestic group was rightwing, leftwing, or environmental. This pattern characterized international terrorists in the sample as well.

Conclusions

This essay attempted to assess the validity of recent DHS, DOJ and Southern Poverty Law Center reports that the extreme right had focused upon recruiting persons with military backgrounds. To accomplish this, we used two noted open-source databases, the American Terrorism Study and the Extremist Crime Database. Although the small number of persons with military backgrounds in the samples precludes an assessment of changes over time, we are able to confirm a couple of findings noted in the earlier reports. First, rightwing terrorists are significantly more likely to have military experience than any other category of terrorists indicted in U.S. federal courts. Among terrorists included in the American Terrorism Study, thirty-eight of the 207 right-wing defendants (18%) indicted in federal courts from 1980-2004 had military backgrounds. This percentage was twice as high as for international terrorists in the sample and it was more than four times higher than the percentage of other domestic terrorists with military experience.

Second, our data suggest that the extreme right has recruited those with military experience with the expectation that these individuals would become leaders within their organization. Over 40% of rightwing terrorists with military experience assumed some position of leadership within their respective terrorist group. Those with military experience were more than twice as likely to assume a leadership role. However, it should be noted that although the extreme right recruited a significantly greater percentage of members with military backgrounds, military experience has similar effects on leadership roles regardless of the ideological motives of the terrorist group. Those with military experience were much more likely to achieve leadership status regardless of the type of group with which they were affiliated – whether leftist, rightist, environmental, or international.

Finally, different findings from the ATS data and the ECDB data are noteworthy. While interpreting differences using two different data sources can be risky and must be applied with caution, the variation between the patterns of military involvement among rightwing extremists (ECDB data) and rightwing terrorists (ATS data) are suggestive of the interaction and impact of ideological commitment. The ECDB revealed that only 5% of the homicides committed by rightwing extremists involved persons with a military background. This proportion increases to seven percent when considering only homicides that were ideologically motivated. Shifting to ATS data, which by definition includes only cases that are labeled as terrorism by the FBI, the percentage of rightwing persons with military experience increases to eighteen percent. Roughly speaking, these three statistics reflect increasing levels of ideological motivation – from simply crimes committed by far rightists, to ideologically motivated homicides committed by rightists, to terrorism committed by rightists. With each increase in ideologically motivated behavior, we also note an increase in participation by those with military experience. While this pattern may be regarded as merely conjecture at this point, it does support the notion that military experience provides some extremists with a skill set that allows them to progress to more dangerous levels of indiscriminate violence. Further examination of these findings is warranted.

References

Department of the Army. 2008. Army Regulation 600-20, Personnel – General: Army Command Policy. Washington, DC: Department of the Army.

Department of Homeland Security. 2009. Rightwing Extremism: Current Economic and Political Climate Fueling Resurgence in Radicalization and Recruitment (Unclassified). Washington, DC: Department of Homeland Security, Office of Intelligence and Analysis.

Federal Bureau of Investigation. 2008. White Supremacist Recruitment of Military Personnel since 9/11 (Unclassified). Washington, DC: FBI Counterterrorism Division.

Freilich, Joshua D., and Steven M. Chermak. 2010. Introducing the Extremist Crime Database (ECDB), 1990- 2009. Paper under review.

Holthouse, David. 2006. A Few Bad Men. Montgomery, AL: Southern Poverty Law Center.

Martinez, Thomas. 1988. Brotherhood of Murder. New York: McGraw-Hill.

Noonan, Margaret E., and Christopher J. Mumola. 2007. Veterans in state and federal prison, 2004. Bureau of Justice Statistics, Special Report. U.S. Department of Justice, office of Justice Programs. May 2007, NCJ 217199.

Presley, Stephen M. 1996. Rise of Domestic Terrorism and its Relation to United States Armed Forces. U.S. Marine Corps Command and Staff College. Found at http://www.fas.org/irp/eprint/presley.htm.

Smith, Brent L. 1994. Terrorism in America: Pipe Bombs and Pipe Dreams. New York: State University of New York Press.

Turner, John. 1986. The Ku Klux Klan: A History of Racism and Violence. Montgomery, AL: Southern Poverty Law Center.

XII. Making Bullets Dance: Drugs and "Small Players" in Small Wars

Erich Wagner

Federal Bureau of Investigation, Special Agent

United States Marine Corps, Lieutenant Colonel

Abstract

The Long Range Threat Assessment of potential U.S. intervention into areas where widespread drug usage and trafficking flourish in religio-social environments where notions of invulnerability exist is likely. Similarly, the overwhelming number of conflicts today are civil wars, occurring at a much higher rate among drug producing countries than non-drug producing countries. While "kinetics" – active killing – is estimated as only twenty percent of the solution to the endeavor of countering irregular challenges, it is paramount for the warfighter, the policeman, the humanitarian and the diplomat to understand a persistent characteristic of many such conflicts and cultures, which, in some corners of the world, are increasing: drug-induced warriors, who may or may not believe they "can make bullets dance."

If today's counterinsurgent fighter does not understand the mental state and perceptions of his opponent, he will falsely assume that the enemy will act in a "logical and rational" manner to protect his life and limb. Understanding the means in which his martial doctrines harmonize with his prevailing system of cultural beliefs is important. Knowing that an opponent may not view himself as capable of dying – or does not care if he does – can help professional militaries and constabulary forces assess the extent to which the enemy may take risks or act unpredictably in combat, which in turn will aid in the formulation of strategies and tactics to defeat him.

The strategists' "**So What?**" question centers on the varying effects of different methods to alter a combatant's mindset (whether insurgent or counter-insurgent): religion, hypnosis, drugs (alcohol, cocaine, amphetamines, tranquilizers, etc.) all obviously have different individual effects. When preparing for the new paradigm of "wars amongst the people," an analysis that includes a deduction of the enemy's "freedom of action, physical strength, or will to fight." If countering irregular threats requires that military intelligence is capable of extrapolating the particular character of the conflict, its context, and its participants, then intelligence specialists must not negate the impact of drug use on their opponents. If intelligence analysts are better familiarized with the psychological underpinnings of the enemy's nature, they are better prepared to understand, counter, and exploit his actions and intents.

Problem statement:

Links between drug-financing and insurgencies are well documented and researched. Similarly, many historians and anthropological scholars have written on societies and military conflicts where "small" players invoke invulnerability paradigms into their fighting cultures. There are many reports and historical anecdotes of "small" players in small wars fighting under notions of invulnerability, but *never has there been an academic study of the hybrid linkage of psychoactive substances and such notions in the current operational environment (COE) of today's battlefields.* Monographs addressing combatants' mannerisms resulting from drugs in the COE simply do not exist.

Approach:

This monograph presents a cursory overview of some historical instances of "small" warriors using drugs and then follows with case studies and interviews of combatants in such operational environments.

Results:

Psychotropic drugs play a fundamental role into bringing individuals into a state of mind to kill or to self-destruct, while invulnerability perceptions fuel ethnic violence because of the strategic advantages they portend. They also contribute to breaking down will and abet subjugation to a cause or an act contrary to nature. Consumption of psychoactive drugs, whether licit or illicit, is only likely to increase. Drugs and their patterns of use in asymmetric irregular need to be well-studied in conflict zones.

- Action reports from units engaged with drug/invulnerable combatants need to be emphasized post-conflict, and these reports need to be utilized to build a knowledge database for interagency awareness.

- Analyses of contemporary usages of amulets and talismans indicate considerable invulnerability resonance in many areas of the world where political violence and long range threats appear most likely.
- Drugs are utilized as a "drug substitute" for empowering a “combat narcosis” before battle.
- The vast majority of suicide bombers and terrorists today utilize drugs to facilitate or enable themselves.
- Combatants exposed to drug use and inured to violence will have the most difficulty adjusting to a life free of violence.
- Drug abuse can hinder reintegration, increase criminality, and threaten the peace-building process.
- Disarmament, demobilization, and reintegration (DDR) programs need to be prepared to deal with significant drug-related problems amongst internally displaced peoples and ex-combatants.
- Tactics, Techniques, and Procedures must be adapted to address this phenomenon.

Conclusions:

A cross-agency counterinsurgency plan that does not address the insurgent drug use will only prolong the duration and cost of conflict settlements and subvert efforts to build a stable nation in the future. The rising phenomenon of drug stimulated “small” players must not be viewed solely as a criminal problem, but a shared criminal-social-military conundrum.

Do you know why our forefathers were so brave in those battles? We smoke this substance, and it fills your heart with courage, making you as strong as a lion.

Unidentified Zulu[1]

Soon after 11:00 am on the morning of March 29, 1879, eleven Zulu regiments (*impis*) – about 21,000 warriors in prime physical condition – would surge from the misty valleys of northern Zululand and throw themselves with courageous abandonment at the small British laager of Kambula. The *impis*, veterans of the greatest defeat in the history of British arms, chanted "We are the Boys from Isandhlwana!" as they advanced, salivating about the anticipated orgy of bloodletting akin to the one two months previous in which they would soon partake. Zulu courage was already legendary amongst their red-coated foes by this stage of the short war: "They came on with the ferocity of tigers, never halting, never wavering . . . no soldiers in the world could be more daring," declared one British officer. Doubtless, every wide-eyed British soldier watched the humming, swishing, black mass appear and deploy in five columns to their front, acutely understood their formidability.

The *impis*, however, failed to coordinate their charges. By 6:30 pm, 2,200 Zulus lay dead. The *impis* charged with distinct over eagerness into the fray, and characteristic tactical

[1] Ian Knight, "Secrets of the Dead: The Mysteries of Zulu Dawn: A consideration of some questions raised by the recent TV programme," Anglo Zulu War Historical Society, http://www.anglozuluwar.com/el/members/journal-11/secrets-of-the-dead-the-mysteries-of-zulu-dawn/, accessed September 15, 2009.

coordination was absent. It is quite probable those warriors who had committed themselves to acts of extraordinary courage had ingested some South African cannabis containing unusually high levels of the chemical stimulant, tetrahydrocannabinol (THC), a powerful hallucinogen, which many warriors carried in their snuff horns around their necks. In addition, warriors sometimes ingested a hallucinogenic mushroom containing a toxin called muscimol, which researchers speculate might have made them utterly fearless, believing themselves impervious to British bullets.[2] The pre-battle rituals, combined with chemical stimulants, heightened and enhanced their aggressive tension and eagerness to bloody their spears, perhaps causing the attack to be discoordinated.[3] It has been suggested that the use of stimulant drugs by the Zulus, while it may have emboldened them for battle, may have been responsible ultimately not for their victory, but for their defeat at Kambula.[4]

Fast forward a century and 29 years, and geographically shift from the misty plains of *KwaZulu* Natal to the urban behemoth of Mumbai, India. From November 26-29, 2008, ten

---

[2] Botanist Ben-Erik van Wyk of Rand Afrikaans University in Johannesburg, South Africa, as quoted in *Secrets of the Dead: Day of the Zulu*, PBS, 2002.

[3] Ian Knight notes that "At the battle of Kambula, the attacking Zulu army as a whole was clearly seen by the British to go through the final ritual preparations about three hours before the battle. This was the optimum time suggested by the scientists for any such drug application to take effect.

[4] Ian Knight, "Secrets of the Dead: The Mysteries of Zulu Dawn: A consideration of some questions raised by the recent TV programme," Anglo Zulu War Historical Society, www.anglozuluwar.com/el/members/journal-11/secrets-of-the-dead-the-mysteries-of-zulu-dawn/, accessed September 15, 2009.

members of *Lashkar-e-Taiba*, a Pakistan-based militant organization closely linked to Al Qaeda, battled Indian commandos for 60 hours and killed 173 people while wounding another 308. The heavily built men had utilized steroids to build a tougher physique, as well as cocaine and lysergic acid diethylatnide (LSD), to stay awake and keep on fighting despite life-threatening injuries without food or sleep.[5]

Today, in the increasingly unstable environments characterized by religious/ethnic/sectarian strife around the world, it is statistically likely that potential foes will be emboldened with feelings of invulnerability from courage-inducing drugs.

At the dawn of this relatively young 21st Century, policymakers, military and police planners, intelligence specialists and humanitarian organizations are constantly attempting to stay ahead of the rapidly changing security environment in order better to quell insurgencies and kill, capture or convert their actors. The necessity for soldier-diplomats to function as conflict-resolvers and negotiators in the Fourth Generation Warfare ("4GW"), asymmetric environment is greater now than ever before in our nation's history. In the context of warring groups in this setting, the requisite for sophisticated approaches in defusing volatile tensions under duress is critical. Military and police decision makers must be sagacious, understanding as fully as possible the

[5] Bruce Crumley, "Were the Mumbai Terrorists Fueled by Coke?," *Time*, 3 December 2008.

nature of the enemy. Combatants are more and more of an ambiguous, "non-state" character: insurgents, guerrillas, rebels, militias, terrorists, criminals, warlords, drug cartels, gangs and similar irregular groups and organizations that operate sub-nationally to transnationally, in failing or failed states or ungoverned areas. Collectively, this disparate group of irregular and comparatively untrained enemy can be rightfully termed "small" players.[6] In the use of this term, I contrast them to "strong" players, those of the side with the greatest material resources at their disposal – *i.e.*, the side with numerical superiority in population, territory, industrial resources, financial power, and conventional military forces, especially in firepower.

Literature is voluminous comparing and contrasting the multiplicity of differences between conventional and irregular warfare throughout history, and the plethora of published thought on how to be victorious in such environments is legion. However, one persistent and little-noticed element in the history and geography of warfare during the past half-millennium has been virtually overlooked in contemporary discussion on the nature of these "small" players: the recurring, often bizarre, and rapidly increasing presence of psychoactive substance[7] use amongst

---

[6] The Marine Corps *Small Wars Manual* further defines small wars as "those operations in which a trained regular force is opposed by an irregular and comparatively untrained enemy."

[7] "A psychoactive substance is any chemical that can alter a person's perceptions, feelings, behaviors, or thoughts. A psychoactive substance can be a medicine, plant

irregular fighters and the persistent presence in many warrior cultures of invulnerability notions – sometimes a result of, or enhanced by, pseudo-religious rituals yoked with opiates.[8]

"So What? Does it Really Matter?"

> *Who are these drug users, and what kind of drugs are they using, and what is their role in the insurgency up there?*
>
> **Dan Senor, Senior Advisor, CPA addressing question to Brigadier General Mark Kimmitt, Deputy Director for Coalition Operations, 22 April 2004, regarding Fallujah**[9]

The Long Range Threat Assessment of potential U.S. intervention into areas where widespread drug usage and trafficking flourish in religio-social environments where notions of invulnerability exist is likely.[10] Similarly, the overwhelming number of conflicts today are civil wars, occurring at a much higher rate among drug producing countries than non-drug

---

derivative or industrial product. Psychoactive substances used will vary from setting to setting." See "Rapid Assessment of Alcohol and Other Substance Use in Conflict-affected and Displaced Populations: A Field Guide," UNHCR, World Health Organization, 2008.

[8] Colin Robert Flint, *The Geography of War and Peace*, (New York: Oxford UP), 242.

[9] Coalition Provisional Authority Briefing, April 22, 2004; www.defenselink.mil/transcripts/transcript.aspx?transcriptid=2522, accessed 5 August 5, 2009.

[10] Marine Corps Long Range Threat Assessment, 2008-2028, Defense Intelligence Report, December 2008.

producing countries.[11] In the next five to ten years, U.S. forces will be engaged in areas of the world where instability threatens national interests: Africa, Southeast Asia, South Asia, and the Middle East. As of this year, 177 states were identified as "failing," of which 38 were classified as "alert" and 93 as "warning". Today, such fragile states, if neglected, could pose mounting risks for the United States. Such geography often devolves into vast ungoverned areas, breeding grounds for the irregular threats that we fear the most: criminal networks, international terrorists, ethnic strife, and genocide. While "kinetics" – active killing – is estimated as only twenty percent of the solution to the endeavor of countering irregular challenges, it is paramount for the warfighter, the policeman, the humanitarian and the diplomat to understand a persistent characteristic of many such conflicts and cultures, which, in some corners of the world, are increasing: drug-induced warriors, who may or may not believe they "can make bullets dance."

Every student of the art of war can recite Sun Tzu's admonition to combatants throughout the ages: "Know the enemy and know yourself, and you can fight a hundred battles without defeat."[12] One Marine commanding officer recently lamented how little we actually understand of the character and motivation of the

[11] Paul Kan, *Drugs and Contemporary Warfare*, (Potomac Books: Virginia, 2009), 1.
[12] Sun Tzu, *The Art of War*, (Radford: Wilder Publications, 2008), 52.

enemy, admonishing "we must get to know him."[13] If today's counterinsurgent fighter does not understand the mental state and perceptions of his opponent, he will falsely assume that the enemy will act in a "logical and rational" manner to protect his life and limb. Knowing that an opponent may not view himself as capable of dying – or does not care if he does – can help professional militaries and constabulary forces assess the extent to which the enemy may take risks or act unpredictably in combat, which in turn will aid in the formulation of strategies and tactics to defeat him.

The strategists' "*So What?*" question centers on the varying effects of different methods to alter a combatant's mindset (whether insurgent or counter-insurgent): religion, hypnosis, drugs (alcohol, cocaine, amphetamines, tranquilizers, etc.) all obviously have different individual effects. When preparing for the new paradigm of "wars amongst the people," campaign planners utilize intelligence preparations of the battlefield (IPBs), an analysis that includes a deduction of the enemy's "freedom of action, physical strength, or will to fight."[14] In evaluating the enemy, however, counterinsurgents sometimes fail to look at the nucleus of the enemy's nature. If countering irregular threats requires that military intelligence is capable of extrapolating the particular

---

[13] Glen Butler, "Know the Enemy? Still Struggling to Identify Our Foe and His Battle Doctrine in this Long War," *Marine Corps Gazette*, August 2009, 40-46.
[14] U.S. Joint Chiefs of Staff, Joint Publication (JP) 5-0, Doctrine for Planning Joint Operations (Washington, DC: U.S. Government Printing Office [GPO], December 2002, draft 2), IV-12.

character of the conflict, its context, *and its participants*, then intelligence specialists must not negate the impact of comparative social thought, accomplished through an understanding of the cultural rituals, taboos, perceptions, and drug use of their opponents. In particular, how do these local belief systems translate to the fighter and his notions of invulnerability, and is that notion heightened by an accepted, ignored, or promoted usage of psychoactive substances? Finally, what tactical, technical and procedural implications do substance-generated bravery of "small" players predict for the capabilities needed to meet these challenges, and how do we adapt to counter them?

Several recent Department of Defense publications call for such an examination. A 2008 Pentagon report evaluating the potential for adversaries to exploit advances in Human Performance Modification (HPM), and thus create a threat to national security, recommends "that the U.S. maintain awareness of popular supplements, and develop intelligence about popular and military applications of [pharmaceuticals] in potential adversaries' cultures."[15] The influence of drugs on local communities is addressed in the July 2009 Marine Corps *Cultural Generic Information Requirements Handbook* (C-GIRH), which

---

[15] E. Williams et al., "Human Performance Modification," The MITRE Corporation, JSR-07-625, March 2008, 38, www.fas.org/irp/agency/dod/jason/human.pdf, accessed July 18, 2009.

provides Marines a foundation for beginning to understand foreign cultures.

While the aforementioned publications discuss illegal drugs and their impact, it is interesting that Field Manual (FM) 3-24, the new U.S. Army/U.S. Marine Corps manual for counterinsurgency operations fails to mention drug-induced or invulnerability inspired opponents.

"*Has this been Studied Before*?" - Methodology and Contributions to the Field of Counterinsurgency Studies

Links between drug-financing and insurgencies are well documented and researched. Monographs addressing combatants' mannerisms resulting from invulnerability notions, drugs, or a combination of both, do not exist.

To date, Dr. Paul R. Kan, Professor of National Security Studies at the U.S. Army War College at Carlisle Barracks, is the only scholar who has taken a serious look into the strategic and tactical effects of drugged non-state actors on the modern battlefield.[16] Kan feels the "lack of a serious examination of the role of drug usage and their impact on small wars is surprising." His topical premise that "the complexity of many ongoing and persistent conflicts in the post-Cold War is partially attributed to the widespread presence of drug intoxicated irregular fighters"

---

[16] Paul Kan, "Webs of Smoke: Drugs and Small Wars," *Small Wars and Insurgencies*, Vol. 17, No. 2, June 2006, 148.

underscores the tactical planning requisite for cognizance of this phenomenon. "No Western military," he notes, "has developed a doctrine to outline the ways to cope with intoxicated combatants."[17]

If the essence of maneuver warfare is defeating the enemy's will rather than his ability to fight, then defeating an opponent's mind is a paramount requirement. Understanding what drives "small" players, physically as well as mentally, is, as Colin S. Gray suggests, "of greater significance" in irregular warfare because of its unpredictability. Because the "small" player is inherently disadvantaged, he seeks to increase his strength by any "asymmetric" means available. Exploiting notions of invulnerability through drug use is just one of these resources.

An in-depth discussion and analysis is merited. Combining operational lessons learned with historical, geographic, religio-cultural examples, gives the counterinsurgent forces a mental map for navigating foreign cultures in an expeditionary environment. In order to influence current operating concepts and further advance our counterinsurgency mindset, we must not let the tactics, techniques and procedures (TTPs) and previous historical lessons learned fade as they have with the American military after previous small wars.

---

[17] Paul Kan, *Drugs and Contemporary Warfare*, 15.

This monograph will present case studies of insurgents enhancing invulnerability notions through the use of opiates.

Drugs

> *Defeating the enemy's will. That is the essence of maneuver warfare, that you defeat the enemy's will to fight rather than his ability to fight. But how do you defeat a man's mind?*
>
> **David A Grossman**

> *We used to take drugs like marijuana or amphetamines before going to the battlefront. They made us very brave to attack and kill our enemies. Our commander used to buy these drugs from across the border...eventually my system got used to them.*
>
> **Ophelia, Liberian female soldier**[18]

Warfare's long saga provides many examples of drugged warriors in combat. Human performance modification (HPM) is the alteration of human physiology to enhance, sustain, restore, or degrade physical, cognitive, or emotional performance through the pharmaceutical drugs and supplements (vitamins, traditional medicines and herbs).[19] These substances bring about either physiological or psychological changes in consciousness and mood

---

[18] "Liberia: Drug Abuse on the Rise." *IRIN*, UN Office for the Coordination of Humanitarian Affairs, December 10, 2008.
[19] E. Williams, 38.

that the user may find pleasant (*e.g.* euphoria) or advantageous (*e.g.* increased alertness, stamina, and courage). The psychopharmacological model suggests that some individuals, as a result of short or long term ingestion of specific substances, may become excitable, irrational, and may exhibit violent behavior. The most relevant substances in this regard are stimulants, barbiturates and phenylcyclo-hexylpiperidine (PCP).[20] A lengthy bibliography exists examining the relationship between these substances and violence.

What drives a warrior to want to use drugs during times of conflict? Man has a desire to overcome his natural weakness and susceptibilities, and psychoactive substances have been used since the dawn of time to alter mood, perception, behavior and stamina. Kan ascribes that anything which mitigates the fear of death in such atmospheres "outweighs the possibility of impairment, illness, or injury in the minds of many combatants who consume drugs."[21] Any advantage to be obtained for this end is sought.

The history of warfare is replete with examples of soldiers seeking and utilizing drugs as battle aids. Norse Berserkers with sworn allegiance to the god Oden fortified themselves with hallucinogenic mushrooms mixed with mead that caused them to disregard wounds in battle, act like wild animals and conduct feats

---

[20] Paul Goldstein, "The Drugs/Violence Nexus: A Tripartite Conceptual Framework," *Journal of Drug Issues*, 15 (1985): 493-506.

[21] Paul R. Kan, "Drug Intoxicated Irregular Fighters," *Strategic Studies Institute*, March 2008, 4.

of incredible strength.[22] The ancient Assyrians, Egyptians, and Greeks reportedly utilized opiates before and during battles to sustain or enhance bravery and courage.[23] In 470 B.C, the Greeks defeated the Persians on the plains of Marathon. They fought on a field of fennel and this led to the belief that fennel inspired courage and strength. As a result, Greek and Roman soldiers chewed fennel seeds before entering battle. Alcohol and rum fortified many a warrior in the past, depressing the self-protective reflexes and inducing the appearance and feeling of courage, and were deemed of such value that their stores were actively defended even in the heat of battle.[24] When Holland became the world leader in gin production, the widespread use of this beverage by soldiers led the expression "Dutch Courage" to express the resulting effect. Napoleon's military exploits were also responsible for introducing thousands of French soldiers to hashish. The Emperor was so concerned that he prohibited its usage because troops became "victims of violent delirium. . ." Drugs helped many an army overcome the perpetual soldiers' plague: boredom in a combat environment. The American experience in Vietnam was the first war in which drugs were plentiful. John Keegan writes that "the American Army's widespread addiction to [marijuana] in Vietnam,

---

[22] Howard D. Fabing, "On Going Berserk: A Neuro-chemical Inquiry," *Scientific Monthly*, November 1956, 234.

[23] M. Goldsmith, *The Trail of Opium (The Eleventh Plague)*, (London: Robert Hale, 1939).

[24] During the famous Battle of Rorke's Drift in 1879, the British defenders, although outnumbered 33:1, assigned a guard to protect the garrison's rum ration.

deeply troubling though it was to the conscience of the nation, may therefore be seen, if not as a natural, certainly as a time-honored response to the uncertainties with which battle racks the soldiers." Boredom, peer pressure, availability, fear, and commander's approval – or lack of disapproval – all contributed and fostered such use. The history of wartime pharmacological use among conventional forces has been well documented, and grew dramatically during the 20th Century. Suffice it to say amphetamines and its derivatives are prescribed to this day in certain professional combat units.

The canvas across the spectrum of conflict presents a picture more and more inclined towards unconventional fights, where massed professional armies are less and less likely to meet on the battlefield. While the threat of traditional warfare remains, insurgencies and irregular fighting styles have become the *flavor de jour*. Whether independent self-medication or mystical, traditional concoctions, "small" warriors in particular have a colorful history of fighting under intoxication. The level of combatant abuse is constrained by social, religious, cultural and legal factors, as well as availability.[25] Drug consumption among combatants in such environments has effects that military leaders and policymakers must take into account. These regions are prone

---

[25]MacDonald, 148.

for widespread usage and availability of drugs, utilized to embolden and strengthen the individual actors.

Drug supply in today's wars falls into one of four categories: traditional/local drugs, transshipped, looted, and manufactured.[26] These categories which Kan establishes are not necessarily exclusive to a single conflict, and combatants often obtain their illicit drugs from an amalgamation of different sources.[27] The convergence of large segments of today's insurgencies with elements of organized crime offer increased opportunities for consumption and availability to small players.[28] In many areas of the world, from Columbia to Central Eurasia to Afghanistan to Chechnya, these players are bankrolling the majority of their operations through the narcotics trade and develop a Darwinian foothold in the local economy. In some areas, the host nation state is complicit in facilitating such activities.[29] Similar drug trafficking activity is flourishing in the tribal belt that includes northwestern Pakistan, and it is providing huge amounts of cash to the Pakistani Taliban and Al Qaeda. With the Taliban now controlling large swaths of Afghanistan,

---

[26] Kan, "Drug Intoxicated Irregular Fighters: Complications, Dangers, and Responses," 9.
[27] Ibid, 9.
[28] Christine Jojarth, *Crime, War, and Global Trafficking: Designing International Cooperation*, (Cambridge: Cambridge UP, 2009), 92.
[29] Bruce Riedel, who chaired the Obama administration's interagency review of policy toward Afghanistan and Pakistan, notes "Our whole effort at developing security in Afghanistan was undermined by having a Ministry of Interior that was interested in facilitating the drug trade rather than combating it." Josh Meyer, "U.S. Increasing Counter-narcotics Efforts in Afghanistan," *Los Angeles Times*, July 20, 2009.

traffickers and their networks pay the militants as much as half a billion U.S. dollars per year to grow and protect the poppy fields, smuggle the drugs and run sophisticated processing labs and drug bazaars locally and in neighboring countries.[30] Afghan drug traffickers with ties to the Taliban have been placed on the "joint integrated target list" by U.S. forces, giving them the same target status as insurgent leaders for capture or kill priority.[31]

Pervasive use of illicit drugs on the battlefield is characteristic of the protracted conflicts, largely fought by nonprofessional combatants amidst an international system characterized by globalization. "Small" players have easy access to all five classes of drugs of natural or synthetic origin for a variety of combat uses: depressants, narcotics,[32] hallucinogens, stimulants and steroids. Drugs are, in a sense, a form of exchange used by militants to trade for vehicles and arms. In many areas, indiscriminate self-medication with powerful psychoactive pharmaceutical drugs is increasingly common.[33] Polydrug use is also on the rise, where fighters mix different intoxicants in quick succession.[34]

---

[30] Gretchen Peters, *Seeds of Terror: How Heroin is Bankrolling the Taliban and al Qaeda*, (New York: Thomas Dunne Books, May 2009), 4.

[31] James Risen, "Drug Chieftains Tied to Taliban are U.S. Targets," *The New York Times*, August 10, 2009.

[32] The term narcotic currently refers to naturally occurring substances derived from the opium poppy and their synthetic substitutes.

[33] MacDonald, 149.

[34] MacDonald, 148.

All the Chechen terrorists who committed the 2004 Beslan School Siege were drug addicts who injected heroin and morphine and other analgesics to keep them alert and courageous. The long list of medicines and narcotics included diazepam, phenobarbital, codeine, morphine, and ephedrine with promedol. Autopsies revealed blood concentrations far exceeding lethal doses, which criminologists believe account in part for the brutality of the mass murders that occurred, and the terrorists' ability to withstand numerous gunshots before succumbing to Russian security forces' fire.[35]

The recent intensification of piracy along the Somali coast and the Gulf of Aden provides another example of drug induced "4GW" actors. Muslim high-seas bandits in this region promote the use of courage-inducing drugs.[36] High on stimulants and lacking discipline, their kidnapped crew members are sometimes not best-served, one lucky captive remembering the raiders became "like demons."[37]

---

[35] "Beslan Terrorists Were 'High on Drugs'," *Mercury*, October 18, 2004; "Beslan School Attackers Were Drug Addicts," *Healthcare Customwire*, October 17, 2004; and Viktor Baranets, "The Bandits at Beslan 'Psyched Themselves Up' With Drugs," *Moscow Komsomolskaya Pravda*, September 28, 2004, 6.

[36] Maxim Tkachenko, "Russian Warship Apprehends Somali Pirates," CNN, April 20, 2009.

[37] Robyn Hunter, "Somali Pirates Living the High Life," *BBC News*, October 28, 2008. See also Shashank Shekhar, "'Pirates Took Drugs All night, Slept Whole Day,' IndianExpress.com, November 25, 2008, www.indianexpress.com/news/pirates-took-drugs-all-night-slept-whole-d/390087, accessed September 10, 2009 and "Somali Pirates Terrorized Nigerian Crew," Reuters, June 10, 2009, www.reuters.com/article/latestCrisis/idUSL8699904, accessed September 10, 2009.

Today, militant drug usage, rampant amongst all sides fighting in Western, Central, and Eastern Africa, has reached unparalleled magnitudes. Analgesics and stimulants include marijuana, cocaine, ephedrine and *khat*.[38] Sexual violence by armed groups in The Democratic Republic of Congo over the last decade has been the setting for some of the most repulsive atrocities in the history of warfare. Drugs are commonly used among Congolese militiamen. Here, systematic rape as a *tactic* of war is often perpetrated by drug-crazed child- warriors, high on marijuana. One guerrilla explained "getting high makes it easier to raid and pillage villages."[39]

The 2009 Failed States Index ranks Somalia highest for the second year in a row. The chewing of an amphetamine-laced leaf known as *khat* is so intrinsic in Somali culture that it is a daily ritual which impacts the country's decades-long civil war. Many militants chew this leaf for courage, while others gain a sense of stimulation (compared to the drive of speed in some varieties) to escape the effects of combat.[40] A 1997 study of UN operations in Somalia notes the profound second-order effects of insurgents' *khat*-induced courage in wartime environments:

---

[38] Marijuana has been shown to be a CNS stimulant that affects euphoria.
[39] Matthew Clark, "Congo: Confronting Rape as a Weapon of War," *The Christian Science Monitor*, August 2, 2009.
[40] H. Halbach, "Medical Aspects of the Chewing of Khat Leaves," *Bull World Health Organ,* 1972; 47(1):21–29.

> The armies of the clans were fortified … *khat* ... [which had] the benefits of suppressing hunger and imparting the user with alternate senses of invulnerability, irritability and anxiety. It was *khat* that gave the clan's gunmen their surly demeanor. The clan militias placed a *higher* premium on obtaining *khat* than on obtaining food [emphasis added].[41]

Chief Warrant Officer 3 Michael Durant, USA (ret.), pilot of Black Hawk Helicopter Super Six Four, was shot down during the October 3, 1993 military operation in Mogadishu and held prisoner for eleven days. He recalls khat gave the Somalis "a feeling of euphoria and made them utterly fearless in combat." In captivity, Firimbi, his full time warder, did the 'fist pump gesture to explain [to Durant] what [khat] did for him."[42]

Having interviewed over 8,000 militia personnel in Somalia, Michael Odenwald concludes that drug-related problems, mainly relating to the use of *khat*, have reached proportions formerly unknown to the country.[43] Odenwald found that *khat* is used by a significant majority of young combatants, and is by far the most abused drug in East Africa compared with hashish, tablets

---

[41] Michael F. McCarthy, "Not Quite War: The Link Between Operational Protection and the Principles of MOOTW: An Examination of Somalia Operations," (Newport, R.I.: Naval War College, November 14, 1997).

[42] Interview conducted with Michael Durant, March 21, 2010.

[43] Michael Odenwald, et al., "The Consumption of Khat and Other Drugs in Somali Combatants: A Cross-Sectional Study," (2007) *PLoS Medicine*, 4 (12), 1959-1972

of any sort, alcohol, inhalants, and *bangi* (hemp) seeds. This suggests that conflict has been associated with increased substance misuse, and there is growing evidence that *khat*-related business is one source of income for civil war factions in southern Somalia.[44] However, perhaps the most dangerous effect of *khat* misuse is that it significantly exacerbates poverty levels and has a negative impact on the living standard of the Somali people, who already live in one of the poorest countries of the world. While drugs are not officially acknowledged as a problem in Somalia, it is interesting to note that *Al-Shabab*, the fundamentalist, Al-Qaeda linked militant group of Somalia, for religious reasons and command and control abilities, has banned the use of *khat* to the great dismay of many potential recruits.[45] *Khat* is also grown in many areas in Iraq, and was prevalent in Iraq amongst the Shi'a Madhi Militia as well as widespread use amongst the Sunni population.

The distinction between crime and war becomes more blurred in drug-producing and trafficking countries where non-political violent acts occur on a large scale.[46] The Mexican government is currently engaged in a brutally violent form of internal small war against narco-cartels which threaten, by some

---

[44] S. Grosse-Kettler, *External Actors in Stateless Somalia.* Bonn (Germany): Bonn International Center for Conversion; 2004.
[45] David H. Shinn, "Somalia's New Government and the Challenge of *Al-Shabab*," Combating Terrorism Center at West Point, March 2009, Vol. 2, Issue 3, www.ctc.usma.edu/sentinel/CTCSentinel-Vol2Iss3.pdf, accessed 12 September 2009.
[46] Jojarth, 94.

intelligence analyses, the very existence of the nation-state itself. Many cartel killers also use the highly addictive crystal methamphetamine, the same drug that has torn through American suburbs in recent years, contributing to the gruesomeness of the drug-related violence, which includes beheadings, skinnings and other mutilations. "Meth exaggerates the worst of people's characters. It makes them more violent and more ruthless," one detoxified, former cartel thug remembers. "When you give it to hired killers, you can get some really evil people." Many of the cartel lords end up paying their lieutenants with narcotics in lieu of cash, as is common with drug dependent militias.[47] The Mexican government has tactically attacked this problem by decriminalizing the possession of drugs to challenge the cartels as they seek to preserve their hold on members, who previously feared leaving for apprehension of being purged from within if it became known they were attempting to quit the habit.[48]

Middle East – Iraq and Afghanistan

Now the terrorists are bringing the drugs with them.

Waleed Sharka, a member of the Iraqi National Assembly[49]

---

[47] Ioan Grillo, "Drug Use Spreads Through Mexico's Streets", GlobalPost, June 19, 2009.
[48] Louis E.V. Nevaer, "New Threat to Mexico's Drug Cartels: Rehab Centers," *New America Media*, September 12, 2009.
[49] Jonathan Finer, "Iraq Used For Transit Of Drugs, Officials Say," *The Washington Post*, June 12, 2005.

The abuse of pharmaceutical drugs, widely available in the Middle East, is skyrocketing, due to availability on the black market and through private pharmacies, nourished by globalism, the stresses of the war, porous borders, and the lack of strict government regulation.[50] Methamphetamines are readily available in these regions. More illegal amphetamines are being seized in the Gulf, a 2008 United Nations report noted, than in the United States, China and Britain combined.[51] Heroin addiction is rampant, especially in Afghanistan, and hashish is considered a rite of passage.

Post-war Iraq has many of conditions which facilitate the expansion of drug use. The inflow of drugs is partially associated with the significant increase in Iranian pilgrims visiting Shi'a shrines in Najaf and Karbala.[52] Iraqi Shi'a communities have been hit especially hard in Iraq, where they tend to be poor and many of the youth frustrated and depressed.[53]

There was widespread abuse of prescription drugs by Iraqi insurgents, and one U.S. Marine felt that "whoever was organizing

---

[50] Mudhafer al-Husaini and Erica Goode, "Prescription Drug Abuse Rises Among Iraqi Troops," *The New York Times*, December 21, 2008.
[51] Habib Shaikh, "Saudi Tops in Abuse of Stimulants in Gulf," *Khaleej Times*, July 3, 2008.
[52] Robert Looney, "The Business of Insurgency: The Expansion of Iraq's Shadow Economy," 5, http://web.nps.navy, (accessed July 15, 2009); see also Jonathan Finer, "Iraq Used For Transit Of Drugs, Officials Say," *The Washington Post*, June 12, 2005.
[53] Aqeel Hussein and Colin Freeman, "Heroin Trade Thrives on Back of Chaos and Terror in Iraq," *London Sunday Telegraph*, September 4, 2005.

the insurgency was pushing the drug use on these fighters."[54] Saddam's *Fedayeen* used illegal drugs prior to attacks to incite religious fervor and instill courage. Numerous reports from Iraq mention the use of methamphetamines and other Amphetamine-Type Stimulants (ATS) or designer drugs by insurgents, and their hideouts and fighting positions routinely were littered with drug paraphernalia. "Unbelievable amounts of drugs" were found.[55] "We found in a lot of the insurgent houses," Marine First Sergeant Darrell Carver recalls of The Battle of Fallujah (2004), "bottles of adrenaline and syringes covering the floor. I would be comfortable to say more [insurgents] used drugs than didn't from the amount of syringes and adrenaline we found."[56] Both Carver and First Lieutenant Michael Liguorni felt that at least half of the fighters were drugged, while fellow Lieutenant Cosmo Calvin, felt "safe to say that nearly 100 percent were doped up."[57] Al Qaeda in Iraq (AQI) hideouts were frequently found littered with drug paraphernalia like crack pipes and needles, and some dead bodies had hypodermic needles on them.[58] After one firefight in the

---

[54] Interview with First Sergeant Darrell Carver, USMC, June 30, 2009.
[55] Bill Gertz and Rowan Scarborough, *Washington Times: Inside the Ring*, December 17, 2004.
[56] Carver.
[57] James Hider of the *Times* report, Fallujah and Tony Perry, "Fallouja Insurgents Fought Under Influence of Drugs, Marines Say," *Los Angeles Times*, February 13, 2005.
[58] Paul Kan, "Drugging Babylon: The Illegal Narcotics Trade and Nation-Building in Iraq," *Small Wars & Insurgencies*, Vo. 18, Issue 2, June 2007, 222. See also, Tony Perry, "Fallujah Insurgents Were Addicted to More than Mayhem," *Los Angeles Times*, January 13, 2005. Lieutenant Colonel John Sullivan, USMC, was responsible for

Diyala Province, U.S. soldiers found half-filled atropine (synthetic adrenaline) syrettes on one-fourth of the dead AQI terrorists and cocaine in their fighting positions: they had used the cocaine for preconditioning and the atropine for sustainment.

Pharmaceutical drugs in the Middle East are often referred to by the color or appearance of their tablets or capsules, their name and long-term effects largely unknown.[59] One of the illegal drugs used and abused among Iraqi insurgents is *Sifr Wahid* ("Zero One") because of the "0.1 stamped onto one side of the pill." Accessible through numerous drug smuggling networks in the region, it is diluted in one form or another into at least six different qualities. *Saleeb* ("Cross" because of the two lines forming a cross on one side of the pill), is a legal drug, commonly given to members of AQI for heightened stimulation.[60]

Shi'a members of *Jayish al-Mahdi* (*JAM*), Muqtada Al-Sadir's Mahdi Army, were so routinely fortified with drugs that they are commonly referred to locals as *Jaysh al-wardi* ("The Pink Army") after the color of the pharmaceutical *Trihexyphenidyl* (Artane) they consume.[61] Before conducting offensive operations,

---

removing dead insurgents from "cleared areas" in Fallujah, and told the author of finding needles on some corpses.

[59] MacDonald, 148.

[60] Interview conducted with member of Marine Corps Command and Staff College, May 4, 2009. Interviewee wishes to remain anonymous.

[61] Lieutenant General Mieczyslav Bieniek, Polish Army, as quoted in "Coalition Troops Seize $30 Million in Heroin," *The Washington Times*, October 11, 2004.; On the street, Artane, Valium and other drugs are known by nicknames, including "the capsule," "the eyebrow" and "the cross." When Iraqi police officers talked among themselves about the

many *JAM* members would take between three to six Artane pills, labeled to treat poor muscle control of Parkinson's Disease. Artane alters unusual nerve impulses, relaxes stiff muscles, and causes behavioral and physiological effects while it lessens fear and instills a sense of invulnerability in the user. Widespread use of this drug is almost unheard of elsewhere around the globe.[62] Usage began in Iraq before their war with Iran "when some athletes started using the drug in training."[63] The artificial courage that the tablet produces prepared *JAM* fighters for fatal missions and increased their willingness to fight coalition forces.[64] According to a State Department analyst, perhaps as high as 85 percent of *JAM* members use Artane, while sometimes fighting each other for the pills. The desire for Artane was so high amongst these black-clad fighters that intramural gunfights erupted over

---

drugs, they referred to them as "appetizers" or "takeout." Artane was by far the most popular drug abused by the addicts, with Valium a close second. Other drugs included Ativan and Mogadon, also tranquilizers, Somadril, a muscle relaxant drug in the same class as Artane, and codeine cough syrup. Unlike some tranquilizers and drugs like cocaine or heroin, Artane does not produce physical addiction, but can produce psychological dependence. Also see "Iraq's Muqtada al-Sadr: Spoiler or Stabiliser?", Middle East Report No. 55, July 11, 2006, www.ciaonet.org/pbei/icg/icg007/icg007.pdf, accessed September 9, 2009.

[62] Keith Humphreys, a professor of psychiatry at Stanford University School of Medicine, as quoted by Mudhafer al-Husaini and Erica Goode, "Prescription Drug Abuse Rises Among Iraqi Troops," *The New York Times*, December 21, 2008.

[63] Nazar Amin, a psychiatrist at Sulaimaniya University, as quoted by Mudhafer al-Husaini and Erica Goode, "Prescription Drug Abuse Rises Among Iraqi Troops," *The New York Times*, December 21, 2008.

[64] Colonel Karim Sultan, police chief in Karbala, quoted in James Hider, "Iraqis Drugged, Brainwashed and Sent to Die for Bin Laden", *Times Online*, March 22, 2004. See also Chris Hughes, "Exclusive: Iraq Fanatics' Kill Pill," *Mirror UK*, December 1, 2005 and Sharon Behn, "Al-Sadr Militia Pumping Up with Drugs," *The Washington Times*, October 5, 2004.

their supply. "There was a firefight in a mosque where two factions of Sadr's guys shot each other to pieces over amphetamines," the analyst said, citing eyewitness reports...."[65]

One State Department analyst reported from Najaf that Al Sadr's militia "give their suicide bombers barbiturates, and the amphetamines are for street fighters who are facing off with the U.S." to induce feelings of power.[66] Both the British and the Americans faced Mahdi militia in Najaf and Basra on such "kill pills." These methamphetamine filled courage-drugs were given to insurgents to instill fearlessness when taking on heavily-armed Coalition forces. Users feel a huge surge of stimulation – "superhuman" confidence 10 to 15 minutes after they had taken a dose. Members of *JAM* "have been known to stand in front of U.S. armored vehicles and open fire almost oblivious to the tank's guns," armed only with AK-47s.[67]

Dr. Amatzia Baram, Director of Center for Iraq Studies at University of Haifa, reports that Muqtada al-Sadr even sanctioned hashish use by *JAM*. In 2006,

---

[65] Behn, "Al-Sadr Militia Pumping Up With Drugs," *The Washington Times*, October 5, 2004.

[66] Sharon Behn, "Al-Sadr Militia Pumping Up with Drugs," *The Washington Times*, October 5, 2004.

[67] Chris Hughes, "Exclusive: Iraq Fanatics' Kill Pill," *Mirror UK.*, 1 December 2005. In an email to the author on October 21, 2009, Dr. Amatzia Baram, related that one of his students at Ft. Leavenworth, Kansas, an Iraqi interpreter who helped investigate JAM prisoners, noted that in the battle with the Marines in the cemetery and around the Najaf shrine in November 2004 he was told by prisoners that they were given "pink pills" that made them oblivious to danger. The Marines, he remembered, were surprised to see that many JAM fighters were quite reckless and threw themselves into battle without any effort to take cover.

Muqtada was asked by some of his commanders whether it was true that in one of his recent meetings with the Imam Mahdi, the latter allowed the use of *hashishat al-Imam* (The Imam's Hashish). Muqtada replied that indeed, in a recent meeting between him and the Hidden Imam the latter approved of such use. The communiqué never appeared on Muqtada's own website. Rather, it was reported and reproduced on sites hostile to Muqtada and theoretically could easily be a forgery. However, while Muqtada's office took great care to deny many embarrassing claims that Muqtada had issued non-Islamic communiqués, this particular communiqué relating to his meeting with the Imam Mahdi and to the use of drugs has never been denied. Furthermore, as I was told by a diplomat from a state in the Far East, his embassy in Baghdad reported that Muqtada was supplying his men with drugs that strongly influence their behavior.[68]

[68] Amatzia Baram, "Muqtada al-Sadr, the Mahdi and Shi'i Messianic Expectations," (essay, no date), www. turcopolier.typepad.com/sic_semper_tyrannis/files/muqtadah_and_the_mahdi.doc, accessed 22 October 2009. "This is a letter from Muqtada to his commanders in reply to a question they addressed to him. The letter is from a website and it looks and feels genuine, using his signature, letterhead and language. However it is appearing in a site hostile to Muqtada. Theoretically, it could be a forgery. If so, it was done extremely well. So we are left with some doubt." It must be noted, however, that many scholars do not believe this story, doubting that Muqtada al-Sadr would publicly admit having met the Mahdi, and that the form of the "fatwa" seems exaggerated. See Reidar Visser, "The Sadrists of Basra and the Far South of Iraq: The Most Unpredictable Political Force in the Gulf's Oil-Belt Region?," (*Norwegian Institute of International Affairs*, 2008), 10.

The militiamen wanted to know whether this was just a rumor or a true report because the use of hashish by the Mahdi Army's men reportedly had a negative influence on discipline. Clearly, the inquiry implied displeasure with the consumption of the drug, so Muqtada's reply must have come to the militiamen as a shock: he confirmed that in a recent meeting he had with the Imam Mahdi, the Imam authorized the taking of hashish. Sadr further requested that it be provided free or at a discounted price to members of *JAM*.

In Afghanistan, evidence suggests that the use of hashish has been ubiquitous among combatants, as it has been for other groups in the population.[69] The Taliban has maintained a hypocritical, confusing range of attitudes towards drugs and drug usage: sometimes draconian, sometimes ambivalent, sometimes accepting. While their operations are funded by the production and transportation of narcotics, they banned the use during their in-power years. Nevertheless, they continue to sanction it and utilize it when they see fit. Dr. Nader Alemi, Director of Mental Health at Mazar-iSharif's General Hospital and former Taliban doctor, estimates that he treated "at least 1,000 soldiers and commanders of the regime" for depression with antipsychotic medication after 1998.[70] One Northern Alliance soldier, captured by the Taliban,

[69] Email correspondence with David Macdonald, 8 September 2009.
[70] Jeffrey Gettleman, "Taliban Had the Blues, Says an Afghan Doctor," *Los Angeles Times*, 11 March 2002.

related how the Taliban recruited him with heroin-laced cigarettes, which caused him to feel fearless and led to his addiction.[71]

Al Qaeda is principally funded by the drug trade to the tune of $800 million per year. While Al Qaeda leaders use drugs, they are not typically heavy drug users, understanding the need to remain under control. Utilization and addiction of drugs usually occurs in the lower ranks of such organizations, and Al Qaeda is no exception. In Afghanistan, Al Qaeda members frequently "freebase" cocaine, a process of purifying cocaine by dissolving it in a heated solvent and separating and drying the precipitate, and then either taken intranasally (snorted) or burned and inhaled, causing feelings of euphoria.[72] Al Qaeda safe houses in Kabul, after the Taliban fell in November 2001, contained amphetamines.[73] Ramzi Hashem Abed, a captured member of the Al Qaeda affiliate *Ansar Al-Islam*, told investigators that prior to operations in Iraq leadership would "give us pills, something like hashish and opium, and tell us we would not feel the operations we were carrying out," referring to the rape rooms and assassination attempts in which he participated.[74] Similarly, Hussein Al-Ahmad, a Kuwaiti pop-singer who dramatically joined Al Qaeda, escaped

---

[71] McDonald, 51.
[72] Personal interview with Trace Kirk, Quantico, Virginia, March 15, 2004.
[73] Scott Peterson, "Marine, Insurgent Tactics Evolve," *The Christian Science Monitor*, November 17, 2004.
[74] Excerpts from the investigation of Ramzi Hashem Abed, a captured Iraqi terrorist, which aired on Al-Fayhaa TV on August 12, 2005, and Al-Iraqiya TV on August 7, 2005, www.centcom.mil/archives_extremistssay.htm, accessed May 3, 2008.

and returned after working for sometime with the terrorists. Al-Ahmad said "that those who call themselves 'Mujahideen' in Afghanistan are just drug addicts," noting that he "was surprised" as soon "as he started [his] military training, [he] was hit by drug consumption."[75]

The use of mind-altering substances and other performance enhancing pharmacology is not limited to jihadists. In Iraq and Afghanistan, large numbers of indigenous security forces – one of the planks in a successful counterinsurgency campaign – are also partaking of such substances. "The long duties, the suicide attacks and the killing are all factors that drive the security force members toward Artane and other drugs," one Iraqi doctor told *The New York Times* in December 2008.[76] "They take it so that there is no anxiety, no fear," he said, "so they can break down doors and enter houses with no shame."[77] On *jeundi* (Iraqi soldier) estimated that one out of three soldiers in his army unit take Artane or other drugs while on duty. Jalal Ammar, an Iraqi police officer, said "probably 30 percent" of his fellow officers used Artane and other medications. Nevertheless, the Iraq Interior Ministry concerned with police affairs, emphatically denied that abuse of prescription drugs was rampant, adding that any member of the security forces

---

[75] "Pop-Singer Turned Militant Tells His Story," CBS News Investigative Roundup, July 16, 2008. See also, Abd-al-Razzaq al-Najjar and Ibtisam Sa'id, "Former Kuwaiti Singer Flees Afghanistan, Says 'Mujahidin Take Drugs'," *Kuwait Al-Watan*, July 15, 2008.

[76] Mudhafer al-Husaini and Erica Goode, "Prescription Drug Abuse Rises Among Iraqi Troops," *The New York Times*, December 21, 2008.

[77] Ibid.

found using such substances "will be dismissed from our ministry forever."[78]

Currently the use of drugs among soldiers of the Afghan National Army (ANA) and police of the Afghan National Police (ANP) is of major concern for the future development of these forces. According to doctors and Afghan government officials, fighters in Afghanistan have long relied on drugs for courage or to kill pain. Many of them started using hashish when fighting with the *mujahideen* against the Soviets. Some were paid or rewarded for their fighting with hashish, which they consumed before going into battle. When there was no hashish, one Afghani remembered, some of them would smoke dried snakes heads and scorpion tails.[79] Military advisors to the ANA are sometimes very frustrated by the drug use amongst those they mentor. Usage occurs even amongst Afghan Special Forces troops.[80] One Marine ETT (Embedded Training Team) member building the force surmised that "if they introduced drug testing to the Afghan army, we would lose probably three quarters to 80, maybe 85 percent" of the recruits."[81]

> You get over here, and you walk into
> a whole squad of ANA smoking

---

[78] Ibid.

[79] David MacDonald, *Drugs in Afghanistan: Opium, Outlaws and Scorpion Tales* (New York: Pluto, 2007) xix.

[80] Personal interview with U.S. Army Special Forces Intelligence officer.

[81] John D McHugh and others, *The Hashish Army* (London: Guardian Films, 2009), www.journeyman.tv/?lid=59545, (6 min.).

> hashish. . . . They don't understand that the use of drugs affects the way that they accomplish their mission. Ultimately it affects their ability to protect their nation and get Afghanistan on its feet.[82]

A British Army advisor told BBC, "The first thing the ANA do in a break in the fighting is . . . go get 'stoned'....Hash or opium. One or the other. Soon as they get two minutes, they start smoking it and passing it around, laughing and joking, and then a minute later their running towards bullets."[83] "It's having them understand that as a policeman you can't be high," Marine Corps First Lieutenant Dan Nagourney lamented, ". . .but they don't understand that concept."[84] Covert hashish use among the ANA is so prevalent that the Marines adopted a "don't ask, don't tell" policy unless they were directly confronted with the problem.[85]

In February 2009, the British Foreign Ministry announced its concern about the levels of drug abuse among Afghani police.[86] To escape from the psychological pressure of facing Taliban militants, the police who are responsible for stopping the drug

---

[82] John D McHugh and others, *The Hashish Army* (London: Guardian Films, 2009), www.journeyman.tv/?lid=59545, (6 min.).
[83] Unidentified British advisor, *Jack, A Soldier's Story* (London: www.vbs.tv, 2008).
[84] Claire Truscott, "Training, Drug Use Major Issues for Afghan Police," *AFP*, October 5, 2009.
[85] Dion Nissenbaum, "Afghan Soldiers Way Below Standard, Esasperated Mareins Say," *McClatchy Newspapers*, March 24, 2010.
[86] Martin Patience, "Drug Abuse Hampers Afghani Police," *BBC*, February 18, 2009.

trade actually become its clients.[87] Two high-level police officers reported independently of each other that "up to half of all police in local police posts take hashish . . . or opium to while away the time when on night duty."[88] The Government Accountability Office (GAO), the investigative arm of Congress, reported in March 2010 that almost half of the new police recruits tested positive for drug use.[89] Recently in Kandahar province, one third of the police recruits failed their drug tests, while it is estimated that 60 percent of the Afghan police in the country's southern province of Helmand use drugs.[90] The majority of those who tested positive had used cannabis or opium.

Because of the heavy negative stigma in Muslim countries regarding drug usage, soldiers and policemen are hesitant to seek treatment and are often reluctant to reveal their military status. In such socio-religious environments is almost impossible to know the size of the problem because of the security situation and because of spiritual disgrace.

Using Drugs to Turn Children into Soldiers

> *On a playground, children are harsh to each other, and they fulfill their own needs all the*

[87] "Cops, Troops in Ranks of Addicts," Chicago *Tribune*, October 1, 2008, 11.
[88] McDonald, 152.
[89] David Wood, "GAO: In Afghanistan's Counter-Drug Campaign, The Police Are A Problem," March 9, 2010, www.PoliticsDaily.com, accessed March 9, 2010.
[90] "Cops, Troops in Ranks of Addicts," 11. See also, Martin Patience, "Drug Abuse Hampers Afghani Police," *BBC*, February 18, 2009.

time. You give them an AK-47 and it's a whole different story. You combine the fact that they are on drugs, they behave as if they are on a playground and it's terrifying.

Major Jim Gray, Royal Marines[91]

They gave me pills that made me crazy.

Thirteen year old Liberian soldier[92]

Children, as a result of their malleability, are a militia recruiter's dream, and more and more are becoming combatants by being pumped with drugs.[93] They are valued less than adult soldiers because they are immature and inexperienced. 60 percent of the non-state armed forces (77 of 129) employ child soldiers, with numbers reaching 300,000 boys and girls under the age of eighteen worldwide as of 2002.[94] The ultimate goal of organizations that employ child troops is to foster dependency so the child feels bound to the group. The percentage of these induced through dependency is unknown, but it is indisputable that warlords, through the use of drugs – the most common being barbiturates, cocaine, and amphetamines – are able to control

---

[91] "Child Soldiers: Implications for U.S. Forces," Seminar Report, Center for Emerging Threats and Opportunities Marine Corps Warfighting Laboratory, (Quantico, VA: 2002).

[92] "EASY PREY: Child Soldiers in Liberia," Human Rights Watch/Africa, September 1994.

[93] "Children at Both Ends of the Gun," UNICEF website, accessed September 21, 2009.

[94] "Child Soldiers: Implications for U.S. Forces ," Seminar Report, Center for Emerging Threats and Opportunities Marine Corps Warfighing Laboratory, (Quantico, VA: 2002).

children's behavior and harness their natural, childlike tendency towards fearlessness.[95] The most common drug is gunpowder, which supposedly removes fear. Called "brown-brown" by the Liberians and Sierra Leoneans – concoctions include mixing heroin or cocaine with gunpowder – create youthful rebels "incapable of realizing their own mortality, . . fearless and more compliant, with addiction the end result."[96] Former Liberian child soldiers recall being drugged on a mixture of cane juice and gunpowder or with "bubbles," an amphetamine which is supposed to make them "strong and brave," which produced in some children "a burning desire" to go out and get drugs."[97]

> Kids are often supplied with drugs; marijuana is the most common drug, but kids are given cocaine too, and cane juice and gunpowder, which can cause brain damage. Also the kids talk about being given "bubbles," a tablet that is apparently an amphetamine, an "upper." The theory apparently is that if a kid is intoxicated he'll be braver to jump over his friend's body and keep shooting.

---

[95] P.W. Singer, *Children at War* (New York: Pantheon Books, 2005), 6.
[96] Ibid, 81-82.
[97] "EASY PREY: Child Soldiers in Liberia," Human Rights Watch/Africa, September 1994.

One spoke of having some drug put into his eyeball "so that you wouldn't see the people you killed, and you wouldn't think about it."[98]

Ishmael Beah, a former child soldier of Sierra Leone, related his story to an audience at Marine Corps University in June 2002. He was kept "high" on drugs and alcohol, weakening his inhibitions and facilitating the indoctrination effort. Beah explained, "You were always drugged and you pretty much fought constantly. And when you were not fighting, you were using drugs."[99] Kati Marton, former Chief Advocate for Children in Armed Conflict, United Nations, noted that child soldiers are often given amulets, "which they are told would make them impervious to bullets," making them "among the world's most fearless and brutal fighters."[100]

It was estimated that over eighty percent of the 7,000 children who fought in the Sierra Leone Conflict had used cocaine or heroin.[101] In Sri Lanka and Burma, children were given amphetamines and tranquilizers to lessen fear and create a feeling of invulnerability and then used for "human wave" attacks that

98 "EASY PREY: Child Soldiers in Liberia," Human Rights Watch/Africa, September 1994.
99 "Child Soldiers: Implications for U.S. Forces ," 23.
100 "Child Soldiers: Implications for U.S. Forces ," 23.
101 Singer, 81.

resulted in massive casualties.[102] A 2003 United Nations' report estimated that SBUs (Small Boy Units) accounted for an 80 percent of rebel – and government – forces in Liberia, both of which were users of freely available marijuana and crack.[103]

Along America's southern border, Mexican authorities acknowledge a new weapon utilized by the bloodthirsty cartels in their intrastate conflict: *sicaritos*, or child assassins. Many of those doing the killing and being killed are 13-14 year old children on the fringes of society, who are almost certain to be high on crack cocaine.[104] The cartels find thousands of candidates amongst the poor and disenfranchised in towns, easily exploited because of their natural immaturity and fearlessness and the easy access to marijuana, cocaine and heroin.[105]

Suicide Bombers and Psychoactive Substances

American Marines and French Legionnaires painfully realized the abilities of drugged suicide bombers on the morning of October 23, 1983. Aziz al-Abub, psychiatrist and member of Hezbollah, gave "cookies laced with drugs" to suicide bombers

---

[102] Mike Wessells, "Child Soldiers," *Bulletin of the Atomic Scientists*, Chicago, November/December 1997, http://pangaea.org/street_children/africa/armies.htm, accessed September 21, 2009.

[103] Jan Hennop, "Liberia: Peace at Last?," African Security Analysis Program Situation Report, Institute for Security Studies, September 8, 2003, 3.

[104] Tom Leonard, "Mexico Drugs War: Cartels Recruit Child Assassins," (*Telegraph UK*, March 25, 2009).

[105] Renee Montagne, "Mexican Drug Cartels Recruiting Young Men, Boys," (*National Public Radio*: March 24, 2009).

who destroyed U.S. Marine barracks and French headquarters in Beirut.[106] The reality of intoxicated suicide bombers has continued to increase dramatically since that fateful morning.

While pre-existing religious violations, faith obligations, revenge motives, and familial bonds are exploited, drugs are also routinely utilized to facilitate the recruitment of suicide bombers.[107] Kuwaiti officials acknowledged in June 2009 that they had discovered "youths going to fight in Afghanistan who . . . were . . . trained to become suicide bombers when under the influence of drugs."[108] Unsuccessful female suicide bombers in Israel, Iraq, and Chechnya have stated they were given drugs prior to their suicide missions.[109] Anti-Russian militants in the North Caucasus are using drugs to create "zombified" suicide bombers, a Moscow newspaper recently charged.[110] Suicide bomber schools in various parts of the Caucasus are attracting "drug specialists [from the Middle Eastern countries] for the preparation of *shahid* suicide bombers," in order to indoctrinate their students quicker

---

[106] Yossef Bodansky, *Target America & the West: Terrorism Today*, (New York: S.P.I. Books, 1993), 31.

[107] Paul Gill, "Suicide Bomber Pathways in Comparative Perspective," *Paper presented at the annual meeting of the Midwest Political Science Association 67th Annual National Conference, The Palmer House Hilton, Chicago, IL*, April 02, 2009 www.allacademic.com/meta/p360734_index.html, accessed January 4, 2010.

[108] "Drugs, suicide bombers, ruthless militants...rendezvous with 'Jihad', The Arab Times, June 8, 2009, www.zawya.com/Story.cfm/sidZAWYA20090608065233/Drugs,%20suicide%20bombers,%20ruthless%20militants...rendezvous%20with%20'Jihad'%20/.

[109] Yoram Schweitzer, "Palestinian Female Suicide Bombers: Reality vs. Myth," Jaffee Center for Strategic Studies, Tel Aviv University, August 2006.

[110] Paul Goble, "North Caucasus Militant Using Drugs, Not Religion, to Produce Suicide Bombers, Moscow Paper Says," *Georgian Daily*, September 16, 2009.

through “stupefaction of the consciousness of their pupils . . . with the help of narcotics.” “Chechens are turning . . . young girls into zombies using psychotropic drugs,” Vladimir V. Putin's senior adviser on Chechnya stated in July 2003.[111] Similarly, militants in Kashmir are being given heavy doses of mind-altering substances to infuse them with courage and "take away the pain" before launching a terror attack on security forces in Jammu and Kashmir.[112]

During the 1980s and early 1990s, thousands of young, angry and zealous foreign Muslim volunteers flocked to the training camps in Afghanistan and Pakistan to learn the art of combat. Fatah recruited Rima Tannous, of the female hijackers recruited from the Popular Front for the Liberation of Palestine, by making her drug dependent.[113] The Turkish government has maintained that the Kurdistan Workers' Party (PKK) brainwashes recruits who are “sent into armed clashes under the influence of drugs. [PKK] leaders keep them under the influence of drugs so as to prevent them from seeing the reality.”[114]

---

[111] Steven Lee Myers, “Female Suicide Bombers Unnerve Russians,” *New York Times*, August 7, 2003.

[112] “Fidayeen Take Drugs Before Terror Attacks,” *Daily Excelsior*, October 21, 2003.

[113] Rex A. Hudson, “Sociology and Psychology of Terrorism: Who Becomes a Terrorist and Why,” (Washington, D.C.: Federal Research Division, Library of Congress, September 1999).

[114] Rex A. Hudson, “Sociology and Psychology of Terrorism: Who Becomes a Terrorist and Why,” (Washington, D.C.: Federal Research Division, Library of Congress, September 1999).

Captured insurgent/terrorist leaders in areas such as Yemen, Horn of Africa, Afghanistan commonly admit the most characteristic method of drugging suicide bombers is by spiking drinks, usually tea.[115] Al Qaeda routinely gives psychotropic drugs – sedatives followed by euphorics – to recruit non-consenting women to be prospective suicide bombers and to increase their courage to engage in suicide attacks against coalition and indigenous forces in Iraq. AQI uses Artane on its operatives to give suicide bombers a sense of invulnerability. *The Times* (of London) revealed in March 2004 that AQI used drugs to brainwash men and women in Iraq to create suicide bombers.[116] The process involves the use of drugs in combination with hypnosis:[117] the routine is introduction to drugs (if not already an addict), convincing them martyrdom is the way to salvation, training (sometimes of short duration while still under influence), and then execution of the mission.[118] An Iraqi police officer told *The Times* that Al-Qaeda is increasingly recruiting young Iraqis via intoxication, "drugging them before sending them out to commit

---

[115] Personal interview with Trace Kirk, Quantico, Virginia, March 15, 2004.

[116] A captured Al Qaeda in Iraq (AQI) document entitled "Analysis of the State of ISI," date unknown, discusses in depth the psychological side of the "martyrs" coming to Iraq, and the depth of their "despair and hopelessness" which would logically lead to ideal candidates for drug introduction. This document can be located on the West Point Harmony Database, ID: NMEC-2007-612449.

[117] James Hider, "Iraqis Drugged, Brainwashed and Sent to Die for bin Laden," *The Times* (London), March 21, 2004.

[118] *Arab Times*, 08 June 2009, www.zawya.com/providertracker.cfm?http://www.arabtimesonline.com/arabtimes/index.asp&provider=arabtimes

terrorist acts against their own people, . . . seduce[ing] them with money," then "using drugs on them until they are half conscious."[119] A 2008 report from Diala, Iraq, stated local officials estimated "nearly 97 percent of [female] suicide bombers carried out their attacks under the influence of drugs."[120]

Numerous reports attest to Al Qaeda and the Taliban seeking mentally ill and physically disabled individuals, coercing them through drugs. They also actively recruit pre-existing drug users and those exhibiting signs of dejection and despair for operations.[121] One Moroccan woman from the hometown of two suicide bombers accused Al Qaeda of "exploiting desperate people who take psychotropic drugs."[122] According to one open-source report, an Afghan coroner estimated ninety percent of persons who had carried out suicide bombings in Kabul were disabled or mentally ill.[123] Suicide bombers in Afghanistan and Pakistan have been given soporifics to calm them before an attack, or to increase

---

[119] Radio Free Europe, "Iraqi Police Say Al-Qaeda Recruiting Iraqis to be Suicide Bombers," Iraq Report, 26 March 2004, Volume 7, Number 11, www.rferl.org/content/article/1343063.html, accessed 8 August 8, 2009.
[120] "Revenge, Illiteracy Push Up Female Suicide Bombers' Number in Diala," Al Bawaba (Middle East) Ltd., June 8, 2008, www.iraqupdates.com/p_articles.php/article/33524, accessed September 21, 2009.
[121] Mentally Disabled Female Homicide Bombers Blow Up Pet Markets in Baghdad, Killing Dozens," Associated Press, February 1, 2008; also, "Al Qaeda: Creative Recruiting for Suicide Bombers," STRATFOR, May 5, 2008.
[122] "Al Qaeda targets US diplomatic offices in Morocco as jihad intensifies," Militant Islam Monitor.org, April 14, 2007, www.militantislammonitor.org/article/id/2819, accessed September 21, 2009.
[123] Sonya Fatah, "Taliban recruiting vulnerable groups to carry out suicide attacks," *Toronto Globe and Mail*, May 7, 2007.

their courage and numb them of their actions.[124] Dr. Brian Glyn Williams describes 2007 bombers in Afghanistan:

> Several of the bombers apprehended . . . were carrying mind-altering hallucinogens or sedatives, which they had been told to take to calm their fears during their last moments of life. Others, including a Taliban bomber who was arrested while pushing his explosives-laden car toward its target after it ran out of fuel, appear to be inept beyond belief. Coalition troops who have spoken of seeing bombers blow themselves up far from their convoys have characterized it as the act of drugged or mentally unstable bombers.[125]

Dr. Colin Ross, an internationally renowned researcher, author and lecturer in the field of psychological trauma, suspects the number of suicide bombers programmed with drugs may be "close to 100 percent."[126]

In 2004 in southern Thailand, for example, an al-Qaeda-linked terrorist force, armed mainly with machetes, launched mass suicide assaults upon three police stations. According to the nation's public health minister, Sudarat Keyuraphan,

---

[124] President Hamid Karzai told reporters noted "terrorist leaders are recruiting drug addicts to carry out attacks and that some may not even realize they are being sent on suicide missions." See Griff Witte, "Suicide Bombers Kill Dozens in Afghanistan," *The Washington Post*, January 17, 2006; also Suicide Attacks in Afghanistan (2001-2007), United Nations Assistance Mission in Afghanistan Report, September 9, 2007.
[125] Brian G. Williams, "The Taliban Fedayeen: The World's Worst Suicide Bombers," *Terrorism Monitor* Volume: 5 Issue: 14, July 19, 2007.
[126] Gordon Thomas and Thomas G. Whittle, "The Terror Doctors," *Freedom* Magazine, August 2004.

"methamphetamines and other illegal drugs [were found] in their bloodstream."[127] In Kashmir, suicide bombers, called *fedayeen*, are administered drugs before their missions. According to an Indian Army major general, "The *fidayeen* come in pairs, sometimes three, and at times four in numbers. They inject themselves with drugs before the assault."[128] In Afghanistan, captured suicide bomber handbooks instruct their human weapons to be under the influence prior to attacks.[129] The Central Java Police reported that it became evident after the Second Bali Bombing (2005) that suicide bombers were dependent addicts, users of psychotropic drugs and other addictive substances and not simply people from underprivileged family backgrounds.[130]

Suicide attacks are going to be more common, and suicide bombers are going to be less inhibited and more apt to complete their mission, or, in some other instances, disoriented and "loopy." Oftentimes insurgents and terrorists are poor at gauging dosages when drugging up for suicide attacks. Rania, a 15-year old female suicide bomber captured in August 2008 in Baqouba, Iraq, was initially unable to talk to police because she had been given so

---

[127] "New Clues Emerge on Identity of Militants Behind Violent Attacks in South Thailand," *Politinfo.com*, May 1, 2004.

[128] Ashok K. Mehta, "Jammu & Kashmir: Shadow of the Fidayeen," *The Pioneer*, July 30, 2003.

[129] Personal interview with former Special Forces ETT member, June 20, 2009. Interviewee wishes to remain anonymous.

[130] "Central Java Police Chief: Terrorists Recruiting Drug Addicts as Suicide Bombers," *Jakarta Kompas*, October 15, 2005.

many drugs.[131] In May 2009, an AQI Syrian suicide bomber was arrested before detonating himself in the middle of a crowd of worshippers at a mosque in the city of Kirkuk, Iraq. The bomber was so drugged out of his senses he could not depress the trigger and was tackled by Kurdish security forces. This 19-year old man proved to be very smart and cooperative with Coalition forces after detoxification.

Islam: Notions of Invulnerability and Drug Intoxication

Religious beliefs have strengthened warriors throughout history. These, when coupled with notions of invulnerability, and strengthened by intoxication are as applicable in today's "4GW" as ever before. Of specific world religions, Islam's position on intoxicants is of most interest to policy planners and military operators as we envision tomorrow's conflicts.

It would seem unlikely that the more fundamentalist Islamic non-state actors would use any type of intoxicating drug, as this is forbidden in the Koran, and upheld in the *Hadith*, the recorded sayings and actions of the Prophet Mohammad. Although open to slightly different interpretations in different Islamic states,

---

[131] "Pictured: The Dramatic Moment a 15-Year-Old Iraqi Suicide Bomber Gave Herself Up, *Times*, (*Daily Mail Online*, www.dailymail.co.uk/news/article-1049021/Pictured-The-dramatic-moment-15-year-old-Iraqi-suicide-bomber-gave-up.html <http://www.dailymail.co.uk/news/article-1049021/Pictured-The-dramatic-moment-15-year-old-Iraqi-suicide-bomber-gave-up.html> , August 26, 2008), accessed October 23, 2009.

the official position remains that intoxicants are *haram* (forbidden). Most schools of Islam believe that the prohibition of alcohol in the Koran is applicable to other mind-altering substances, including narcotics, as they clouded the mind and distracted it from the path of God. There are exceptions, however. Mystical Sufi Muslims believed spiritual enlightenment was obtainable through a state of altered consciousness, and permitted the use of hashish to this end.[132] It is interesting to note that under the reign of the Ayatollah Khomeini in Iran, "Wine and all other intoxicating beverages are impure, but opium and hashish are not.[133] Opium "balls" are still common wedding gifts for newlyweds in Afghanistan.

While "there is a very strong anti-drug culture among Salafists," as French terrorism expert Roland Jacquard notes,[134] cases involving jihadists around the globe illustrate that consuming drugs supports short-term goals sometimes outweighs the purer edicts of Islam.[135] Kan asserts that "powerful sectarian leaders have turned a blind eye to their followers' participating in the drug trade."[136] Veteran FBI Special Agent Trace Kirk has interviewed or interrogated 125 detainees at Guantanamo Bay and over 500

---

[132] Martin Booth, *Cannabis: A History*, (New York: Macmillan, 2005), 49.
[133] Robert Dreyfuss and Thierry LeMarc, *Hostage To Khomeini*, (New York: New Benjamin Franklin House, 1980) 92-95.
[134] Bruce Crumley, "Were the Mumbai Terrorists Fueled by Coke?," *Time*, December 3, 2008.
[135] Kan, *Drugs and Contemporary Warfare*, 96.
[136] Paul Kan, "Drugging Babylon: The Illegal Narcotics Trade and Nation-Building in Iraq," *Small Wars & Insurgencies*, Vo. 18, Issue 2, June 2007, 227.

insurgents/terrorists worldwide, spanning three continents over the last 33 years as a Federal investigator: the preponderance of these were Muslims. Of the non-Muslim born fighters Kirk interviewed who had converted to Islam, many, if not all, were drug users or had a history of drug use in their past. One captured Afghani insurgent leader told Kirk that because of jihad, the "ends justify the means."[137]

As in all religions, contradictory pressures shape obedience (or not) to the Islamist's dictate. Regardless, in harsh subversion of Islamic ethics, terrorists and insurgents have cashed in on producing and trafficking drugs while also using them to stimulate their operatives. From alcohol to hashish to opium to heroin and a relatively new torrent of pharmaceutical intoxicants, drug use is part of Islamic culture and society. Interestingly, the Taliban's most recently captured code of conduct manifesto, *Rules and Regulations for Mujahidin,* fails to even mention opium or narcotic use. The glaring omission of drug use in the code may reflect the Taliban do see this as a problem among their insurgents. It may also reflect that drugs have become so common among insurgent groups as to be an insolvable problem better left unaddressed.[138] Illustrative of this conundrum, mainstream Taliban commanders in Peshawar in 2006 warned hashish shop owners to shut down their

---

[137] Personal interview with Trace Kirk, Quantico, Virginia, March 15, 2004.
[138] "Understanding Afghan Culture: Analyzing the Taliban Code of Conduct: Reinventing the *Layeha"*, (Newport: Department of National Security Affairs Naval Postgraduate School, August 6, 2009), 12.

business or face Islamic punishment. The problem, however, was so endemic and accepted among the local Taliban fighters, and the adverse reaction to this proclamation so quick and intense, that the hashish shops remained open, although barbers were still forbidden to shave beards or play music.[139]

Yossef Bodansky, former director of the Congressional Task Force on Terrorism and Unconventional Warfare and author of *The Secret History of the Iraq War*, believes that "For the Iranians, it has been very important to make sure that each and every operation is a success, and they are therefore willing to bolster zeal with chemicals." "[Islamic] terrorists use drugs to reach their goals, but they don't believe in drugs," a former K.G.B. officer told *Vanity Fair* in 2002. "Terrorists see themselves as super people, above the law, and drugs allow them to manipulate all other people."[140] The Northern Alliance has said that American turncoat John Walker, for example, was a heavy hashish user.[141]

Overcoming the Muslim existence denial mindset poses a challenge for nation builders and counterinsurgency forces when attempting to solve the problem of drug abuse in Phase IV, post-conflict operations. Dr. Abbas Fadhil Mahdi is not alone in his confidence that "There is no drug problem in Iraq. We have immunity against addiction ... [as] Islam protects people from

---

[139] Ismail Khan, "Drug Ban Divides Militants," *Karachi Dawn*, March 21, 2006.
[140] Maureen Orth, "Afghanistan's Deadly Habit," *Vanity Fair*, March 1, 2002.
[141] Evan Thomas, "A Long, Strange Trip To The Taliban," *Newsweek*, December 17, 2001.

indulging in such illicit, harmful intake of substances. And unlike in the West and in America, we have cohesive and supportive extended families. So there is no problem with drugs."[142] The established Islamic dishonor surrounding narcotics use discourages addicts from seeking help.

> The drug problem in Iraq is like the early part of an epidemic, a rising storm, and if it increases we cannot withstand the severity because we have no infrastructure to control it, no experience in treating it. But it is almost impossible for us to know the size of the problem because of the security situation and because it is kept in the dark. Until recently, these things were not spoken about.[143]

Operational Implications for Countering Drug-Induced Insurgents with Feelings of Invulnerability

> *Only superman could go faster than a bullet, and you're only invulnerable until you're not.*
>
> **Murphy's Law**

Psychologists generally agree that humans have four natural, primitive, automatic, inborn response reactions when faced with interpersonal danger. These options are (1) Stay and fight;

---

[142] Jonathan Finer, "Iraq Used For Transit Of Drugs, Officials Say," *The Washington Post*, June 12, 2005.
[143] Jonathan Finer, "Iraq Used For Transit Of Drugs, Officials Say," *The Washington Post*, June 12, 2005.

(2) Flee; (3) Posture to intimidate the perceived aggressor; or (4) Submit. When preparing operational battle plans, most modern military staffs analyze the Enemy's Most Probable Courses of Action (EMPCOA), which are partly derived from intelligence predictions of the opponent's proclivity towards one of these options: in other words, how the enemy will react to attack. How, then, can counterinsurgent planners use social science to exploit cultural characteristics to defeat insurgents?

"Small" players harboring invulnerability notions or hyped-up on opiates display altered, non-natural, non-rational predisposition towards aggression, and often show an enhanced presence of absence of empathy for others. When the "fight or flight" response of the Limbic brain (the automatic nervous system) is activated in psychoactively altered insurgents or fighters believing themselves bullet-proof, the resulting response is abnormally weighted towards the fight option, away from their natural survival instinct. This increased sense of invincibility encourages them to attack to the death. That paramount requirement of defeating the opponent's mind – *his will to fight* – is correspondingly much more difficult, if not impossible. The factors contributing to his "killing enabling process" – a term measuring the average soldier's psychological enablement to kill, coined by Lieutenant Colonel David Grossman, U.S. Army (ret.), author of *On Killing* – are abnormal and unpredictable.

Attempting to outwit the irrationally arrogant fighter and foster him into submission or flight responses with traditional, rational, tested means is therefore limited, and TTPs must be modified and new thought processes explored if the goal is to disable his capacity to resist by other than kinetic means.

Drugs chemically alter the combatant's risk to reward thought pattern. Donald Horowitz, Professor of Law and Political Science at Duke University, pens "a major theme of the violent enterprise is risk reduction. Angry or aroused people are not necessarily heedless of risk. An impressively wide range of variables affects the rioters' calculation of risk. Among these are supernatural beliefs in invulnerability. . . [which lower] inhibitions on violent behavior . . [through] war spells, as well as charms, religious passages, and amulets that are supposed to impart invisibility or invulnerability to those who use them. . . Frenzy, disinhibiting mania, and amok-like behavior are also recognizable in riots. Their furious quality may have the effect of maximizing the advantages enjoyed by the aggressors, but it may also convince them, to their fatal detriment, that risks do not exist."[144] If the insurgents develop a belief of invulnerability, the group will no longer believe it needs to negotiate with the government.[145]

---

144 Horowitz, 526-527.

145 Navin A. Bapat, "Insurgency and the Opening of Peace Processes," *(Journal of Peace Research*, Vol. 42, No. 6: 2005), 699-717.

Utter disregard of risk creates a more violent and dangerous battlefield environment for combatants and non-combatants alike, and makes peaceful outcomes more distant. Fighters with clouded minds are less predictable and looking for fights. Insurgents whose senses of pain have been dulled by prescription medications and whose inhibitions have been reduced are an enemy that is going to be more reluctant to surrender or submit to capture. Behavior of fighters in Fallujah, recalled by veterans as "fanatic," "supernatural," and "bizarre," included suicide charges and insurgents strolling down the middle of the street screaming at the top of their lungs while firing a weapon. Methamphetamines are consumed in almost every region of the world, and the corresponding violence associated with its use is unparalleled. Acts of enemy bravery under such substances during operations are going to be more commonplace than in engagements with sober combatants.

Robert B. Charles, Assistant Secretary of State for International Narcotics and Law Enforcement Affairs in the Bush Administration, wrote that "the value of proving that insurgents are drugged when they explode, raises some poignant questions for everyone. The questions are worth asking; answers are worth pursuing. If the link is real, it tells us a lot."[146] He queries,

---

[146] Robert Charles, "Iraq and Drugs – Opening a New Front in the war on Terror," December 16, 2005,

> What does the possible link mean operationally? Not much in terms of stopping a VBIED or mobile suicide attacker, since there is little difference between an insurgent exercising murderous irrationality and an insurgent exercising drugged-up murderous irrationality. On the other hand, implications for intelligence gathering, cross-fertilization of drug-related and insurgent-related information, increased counter-drug training for . . . police, greater reliance on DEA and other counter-drug experts in country, and a potential for leveraging this connection to find more bad guys could be real.[147]

Drug induced fighters or "small" players with notions of invulnerability increase the likelihood of unpredictability on the battlefield and place coalition forces at greater risk of physical harm. "Invulnerable" fighters under emotional human performance modification can exhibit any of the following characteristics: heightened proclivity to take risks and disregard self preservation; abnormal perceptions of pain; increased religious conviction; decreased empathy; extremely aggressive tendencies; erratic behavior; exaggerated strength; and increased mental alertness. Ethnic aggression heightened by drugs can produce

---

http://counterterrorismblog.org/2005/12/iraq_and_drugs_opening_a_new_f.php, accessed August 1, 2009.

[147] Ibid.

"angry violence," which deviates from the standard military professional's call of duty motivation. As a result, as we have seen, the levels of such violence can escalate abnormally and desensitize the perpetrators, making them blind to everything but their destructive goal. Congolese child fighters, experiencing drug-induced fearlessness, "no longer saw people as people but as animals, and they could do anything they had to do, the implication being that drug taking made it possible to commit atrocities such as killing family members and cutting off peoples' limbs."[148] Drug-induced combatants are often inured to violence, operating on almost an unfathomable plane of reality. One boy soldier said that he would do "just about anything that was ordered" when on drugs, that "I became stronger . . . I was no longer human . . . I could do anything."[149] On the other hand, depressants may be used to calm suicide bombers who might "flake" at the decisive moment.

In Operation IRAQI FREEDOM (OIF), Coalition Forces observed a variety of mannerisms resulting from drug induced invulnerability notions amongst irregular fighters. "Doped" fighters often demonstrated little or no tactical acumen: they maneuvered, but not in a smart manner; frontal assaults were common. They exhibited little patience or control of fires, and were more prone to unaimed shots. Amphetamines enable the

---

[148] Sue Loughlin, "A Preliminary Assessment of Past and Current Drug Use Among Former Child Ex-combatants in Sierra Leone," Report for UNICEF, August 2000, 4.
[149] Singer, 82.

body to continue functioning despite mortal wounds, prolonging life. The "discipline" of the enemy was something that left a lasting impression on the Marines, according to Patrick O'Donnell in his book on Fallujah, but that discipline was not altogether a result of raw courage and religious steadfastness: nearly all the grunts he was embedded with faced AQI fighters with zombie-like relentlessness who "were high on a cocktail of drugs."[150] First Sergeant Carver, USMC, recalled that it was easy to differentiate those combatants who were on drugs compared to their sober counterparts. They were more resilient in their reaction to gunshot and shrapnel wounds, and "didn't fall as quickly."[151] As a result, on the second day of the fight, to counter such fighters, "word came down to focus on head shots, as body shots were not good enough," as opposed to the centers-of-mass gold-standard Marines had always been taught on rifle ranges.[152] First Sergeant Carver proudly noted that his "Marines didn't miss." He describes a scenario during Fallujah: "One insurgent, after sustaining a fragmentation grenade and two gunshots to the chest still was in a "fighting mood after we entered the room. He was definitely hopped up on something, and we found bottles of adrenaline and

---

[150] Paul Monk, *We Were One: Shoulder to Shoulder with the Marines Who Took Fallujah* (Cambridge: De Capo Press, 2006), 95.
[151] Phone conversation, First Sergeant Darrell Carver, June 30, 2009.
[152] Special Operations units have increasingly transitioned to making central nervous system shots standard operating procedures as a result of drugged insurgents.

syringes all around."[153] In "Queens," – a lair for terrorists and jihadists on the south side of Fallujah – Carver encountered many fighters who "didn't act like they were mentally there."[154] Captain Russell Thomas, USMC, a tank platoon commander attached 2nd Reconnaissance Battalion also in "Queens," engaged multiple insurgents fighting with syringes and tourniquets in their arms. In one such scenario he recalls:

> We shot a tank round [two simultaneously from different angles at a brick house (medium size, one level)] and then moved to our next target. As we began to move we received fire from the house, so I traversed over to the impact hole where my tank round penetrated the house and saw muzzle flashes, we engaged with 7.62 and .50 Cal and shot another tank round into the house and again began our move. We received additional gun fire and I traversed over to see where it was coming from and 3-5 insurgents were coming out of thc house with AK-47's. They all had syringes and tourniquets in their arms and were bloody (ear drums had to have been blown out). We cut them down as they charged our tank.[155]

---

[153] Phone conversation, First Sergeant Darrell Carver, June 30, 2009.
[154] Phone conversation, First Sergeant Darrell Carver, June 30, 2009.
[155] Personal interview with Russell Thomas, Quantico, Virginia, March 22, 2010.

Captain Timothy Strabbing, USMC, relates another story from Fallujah:

> I had "one of my Lance Corporals engage an insurgent about 40m away with his M249. He had probably 5-7 center of mass hits against this insurgent, who stood and took the shots and proceeded to run back around the corner of the building. If he was not "amped" up on drugs, there is really no way he would have stood there, taken the shots, and then run back behind cover.[156]

Within 48 hours of this incident, Strabbing's Marines came across a substantial medical and drug "cache" which included a duffel bag of drugs, which his corpsman[157] verified were "not your standard morphine/medical supplies." These were classified as amphetamine-type narcotics, and the Marines were confident from insurgent actions witnessed that they were using these to aid in their boldness and aggression throughout the fight. "One guy described it as like watching the *Night of the Living Dead*," corpsman Peter Melady said. "People who should have been dead were still alive." Another corpsman, Quinton Brown, said "It

---

[156] Email correspondence, Captain Timothy Strabbing, May 11, 2009.

[157] "Corpsmen" are U.S. Navy medical personnel serving in Marine Corps units.

reminded me of the stories you hear about people on PCP who just keep going."[158] Most of the reports I heard or read while in theater attributed this behavior to heroine, liquid adrenaline, or amphetamines.[159]

U.S. Army Sergeant David Bellavia's reflection about anticipating the upcoming fight in Sadr City, a Shi'a suburb of Baghdad, is indicative of what counterinsurgents encounter and will encounter against stimulant-induced foes:

> We'll be facing fighters hopped up on dope again. If this is true, these guys are going to be hard to kill. In Muqdadiyah, my squad watched a drug-crazed Mahdi militiaman charge . . . [a] Bradley [fighting vehicle]. The gunner blasted him with coax machine-gun fire, shredding his legs. He tumbled off the Bradley and flopped face up onto the street. As we approached him, he started to laugh. The laughter grew into a hysteria-tinged cackle, then ended with a bone-chilling keen. That froze us cold. Watching us with wild eyes, he then pulled a bottle of pills out of a blood-soaked pocket and drained its contents into his mouth. Then he went for something under

---

[158] Tony Perry, "NARCOTIC FERVOR: Fallujah Insurgents Were Addicted to More Than Mayhem," *New Hampshire Union Leader*, January 13, 2005.
[159] Personal interview with Lieutenant Colonel John Sullivan, USMC, 29 October 2009.

his jacket. Thinking he was about to detonate a bomb vest, three of us opened fire and riddled him with bullets. We shot and shot until he finally stopped moving.
A few minutes later, as two men carried the shattered husk of that Mahdi militiaman to the helicopter. "To our astonishment, he was still alive. Blood bubbles burbled up through his mangled nose and mouth. Blind, in agony, he still managed to scream through broken teeth and punctured lungs." We later discovered the Mahdi militia had gained access to American epinephrine -- pure adrenaline that will keep a heart pumping even after its owner has been exposed to nerve gas or chemical weapons. A dude with that in his system is almost superhuman. Short of being blown to pieces with our biggest guns, he'll keep fighting until his limbs are severed or he bleeds out.[160]

Strategic Considerations of Invulnerable and/or Drugged "Small" Players in the COE

To be successful on the frontier, a man has to deal with the hearts and minds of the people, and not only with their fears.

[160] David Bellavia, *House to House*

Thomas Henry Thorton[161]

Finally, what does the convergence of psychoactive narcotics and local invulnerability beliefs in small wars mean strategically? What directions for the future missions can we elicit? As Robert Charles noted regarding implications on the operational side, there are corresponding implications on the strategic side as well.

While simply stopping the flow and access of drugs to local fighters is an obvious goal, such a "war on drugs" obviously is not a realistic panacea for a globalized world, especially since many of the intoxicants are home-grown, traditional drugs linking the fighter to the traditions of his ancestors and the mystical elements of animistic religions. Today, the bulk of the global cultivation of opium and coca is taking place in conflict zones.[162]

> In situations where nation building and stability operations are mandated, the main goal of governments in responding to these conflict environments should be to reduce the level of violence through a reduction of the use of drugs. By lowering the

---

[161] Christian Tripodi. ""Good for One But Not the Other": The "Sandeman System" of Pacification as Applied to Baluchistan and the North-West Frontier, 1877-1947." The Journal of Military History 73, no. 3 (2009): 767-802. Retrieved September 8, 2009, from Military Module. (Document ID: 1796459451).

[162] Svante Cornell, "Narcotics and Armed Conflict: Interaction and Implications," *Studies in Conflict & Terrorism*, 2007, 30: 207–227.

> demand for drug use, command and control can be strengthened among irregular forces, thus increasing the likelihood of adherence to the parameters of any possible peace accord.[163]

Recruiting militia members for violence is facilitated through the proclivity of drugs in today's most dangerous regions. Whether "paid" with narcotics as in the Congo or Central and South America, or lured with drugs in Iraq, such chemistry dramatically increases the pool of "qualified applicants" to a cause.

All combat commanders are taught from day one to "orient the map to the enemy's point of view." Facing a drug-induced foe can alter tactical mission planning. Many rebel forces that rely on stimulant drugs do not focus on the traditional military targets or strategic choke points such as airports or harbors, but rather installations and terrain that are related to drug trafficking, such as roads where drugs are transported.[164] Such a break from typical notions of warfare, Kan notes, "requires a greater understanding of the levels of drug-trafficking influence and varying degrees of combatant drug use."[165] Initial objectives for counterinsurgent forces should include securing infrastructure such as pharmacies, clinics, hospitals, and other lootable structures which are tactically

[163] Kan, "Drug Intoxicated Irregular Fighters," 29.
[164] Odenwald, 1968.
[165] Kan, *Drugs in Contemporary Warfare*, 9.

strategic for warlords who command drug-incentivized militias. Likewise, security forces should patrol along known drug trafficking routes, which are crucial lines of support for drug-fueled combatants. Turf wars between factions for drug fertile land can lead to increased levels of violence, and need to be identified by planners. Massacres in Columbia between "small" players vying for valuable resources were often the product of such land acquisition goals.

The presence of large numbers of drugged children on today's battlefields will have an impact on the existing "warrior code" of western armies with regards to ability and proclivity to engage in kinetic action. Killing children creates a conflict between morality and necessity. Potential hesitation to kill could have the same harmful outcomes for today's counterinsurgent as it did for the French in 1890. French Foreign Legionnaires faced female warriors of the Kingdom of Dahomey, and as a result of their hesitation to kill women, many of the French soldiers delayed before shooting or bayoneting them, resulting in many of the Legionnaire casualties.[166] Similarly, U.S. soldiers in the Battle of Mogadishu (1993) were reluctant to shoot at women who were either being used as human shields or attacking them. There is no doubt that Western militaries will continue to encounter child soldiers in many different environments, and face the "lose-lose"

---

[166] Dave Grossman, *On Killing: The Psychological Costs of Learning to Kill in War and Society* (New York: Little, Brown and Company, 1995), 175.

conundrum of engagement (and the images that will emerge on the world media) or jeopardize force protection. Psychological preparation for troops, and those responsible for counseling them after these encounters, must be implemented. Military operations will require more briefings and role-play scenarios for units going into combat on the possibility – nay, likelihood – of using lethal force on youthful, drugged-up adversaries.

In order to attain costless advantages over adversaries and to influence their attitudes and behavior, counterinsurgent forces must take full advantage of the potential of information operations necessary to counter and delegitimize drug usage in the Muslim world. Counterinsurgent commanders need to ask themselves, "What collective behavior are we attempting to get the populace to engender?" The answer to that question should help shape campaign design, particularly with respect to the civil information portion of the campaign. A core message of Information Operations (IO) should be flooding the populace with information that their fighters are not impervious to the kinetic laws of physics in combat. In order to break the myths, the standing beliefs of local insurgents' invulnerability should be aggressively challenged by an IO campaign – led by the local indigenous forces[167] – which engages local nationals and community leaders.

---

[167] Using indigenous forces to this end only is the most effective method of disseminating information, while simultaneously bolstering their credibility in the eyes of the locals.

Counterinsurgents need to proliferate information of insurgent drug use and partner with local religious authorities to isolate the insurgents morally in terms of their legitimacy, in the attempt to shape civilian perceptions that may mold their willingness to assist friendly forces or, conversely, not assist insurgents. Fallujans' civic and religious leaders repeatedly expressed their concern to Marine commanders about the serious drug problem, asserting that the drug use by those engaged in the violence was something that needed to be addressed.[168] As one expert noted from the French Algerian experience, "…one of the main weapons of anti-insurgent warfare is to find and magnify internal differences."[169] Letting the populace know that these fighters are not invulnerable, and that narcotic usage equates to *haram* in Islam for example, should be standard IO operating procedures. Such an information campaign could help break the myths and the standing beliefs of insurgents that they are invulnerable, divert local support away, while alerting fighters to the adverse medical repercussions of drugs physically and mentally. For example, if Coalition Force loudspeakers in southern Iraq had blared the message that consuming "pinky" drugs are un-Islamic and cause impotence, as several captured

---

[168] Coalition Provisional Authority Briefing, 22 April 2004; www.defenselink.mil/transcripts/transcript.aspx?transcriptid=2522, accessed 5 August 2009.

[169] Edgar O'Balance, *The Algerian Insurrection; 1954-1962,* (London, UK: Faber, 1967), 205.

members claimed, by highlighting the known concern that *JAM* fighters already have, could militant actions have been changed? Gretchen Peters, author of *Seeds of Terror: How Heroin Is Bankrolling the Taliban and al Qaeda* advises

> There has to be a lot more publicity about the fact that these self-described 'Holy Warriors' are committing *haram* in the name of Islam. I think most Afghans and Pakistanis would be appalled by this. We, the West, have been hesitant to wade into Islamic waters and discuss these issues. To the extent that we allow the enemy to define himself as religiously motivated, the Coalition has lost half the battle. It's going to be very difficult for locals to partner with someone whose actions define him as an infidel. Their activities are not something that most Afghans and Pakistanis support. We need to hold a mirror to their actions.[170]

It is interesting to note that as a result of local indignation to acts of pedophilia committed by the Taliban, Taliban leaders told their field commanders to constrain their more egregious

[170] Phone conversation with Gretchen Peters, September 16, 2009.

instances of pedophilia, because their tendency to take and sodomize young boys was losing them popular support. Such indignation against drug use should be exploited in cases of "religious insurgencies."[171]

From a purely Machiavellian point of view, can the furious, berserk-like qualities created by drugs/talismans be exploited by counterinsurgent forces? One of the age-old quandaries of small war generals was the fear that the enemy would not "come out and fight." Of course guns and bullets are no respecter of persons, so if kinetics are deemed the primary solution for breaking an insurgent standoff, can such notions be used to an advantage for destroying such fighters in a similar manner that challenges to insurgent masculinity were when blared from Coalition vehicles during Iraq? Similarly, intoxicated cadres of militants who require ever-increasing doses of courage-pills, pose command and control problems for insurgent commanders. The trained snake can sometimes bite the master. As one Afghan soldier working with the Soviets stated, "if the commanders refused to come up with the hashish, they would face the wrath of armed soldiers."[172] Awareness of the side effects of enemy drugs on individual insurgents is valuable to the strategic planner. One of the common consequences of *khat* consumption amongst Somali fighters, for

---

[171]No author, "Religion and Insurgency," www.smallwarsjournal.com/blog/2007/05/religion-and-insurgency/, accessed October 17, 2009.

[172] Kan, *Drugs in Contemporary Warfare*, 56.

example, is reported sleepless nights.[173] Special Operations units in Somalia routinely planned raids to fall around known *khat*-chewing hours.[174] Marine Corps Second Lieutenant, Adam Mathes remembered that the drug induced foreign insurgents at Fallujah exhibited "hyper-energy in the morning and early afternoon, possibly after a fix, and then less energy as the day wore on."[175]

Anecdotal reports offer little comfort for those who must make the critical decisions in wartime environments. Counterinsurgent forces need to partner with forensic specialists in combat environments – not just headline producing spectacular hostage scenarios – to routinely drug test captured insurgents and autopsy cadavers in order to provide information to intelligence specialists. Multi-agency verification needs to improve, and currently is not at hand. Merajudin Pathan, governor of Afghanistan's Khowst province, related to Gretchen Peters that he was confident almost all the suicide bombers were high on drugs. To no avail, he made repeated requests to get drug-testing kits from the American Embassy in 2007, so that he could determine what types of narcotics were being utilized.[176] Kan shares Pathan's pain in this regard. "What is needed is greater cooperation among agencies of the Department of Defense, Department of Justice,

---

[173] Odenwald, 1969.
[174] Personal interview with Gunnery Sergeant Will Falcon, USMCR, May 26, 2010.
[175] Tony Perry, "Fallujah Insurgents Were Addicted to More than Mayhem," (*Los Angeles Times*: January 13, 2005).
[176] Phone interview with Gretchen Peters, September 16, 2009.

Department of Treasury, and Department of Homeland Security to monitor and assess the ways drugs are being used by irregular forces so that new strategies can be added to the plans of conventional forces who [*sic*] may intervene in such operational environments."[177] Tracking and recording combatant drug usage and their sources will prepare tacticians and strategies for encounters with "hyped" combatants by developing early warning signals in order to adjust their tactics in appropriate environments. Supply and demand of drugs in conflict environments is directly related to the types of users and the availability in the geographic location. Intelligence networks of supporting agencies like the CIA, FBI and international organizations like INTERPOL must be coordinated to include integrity of the drug supply as a key concern.[178] Combat intelligence centers need to map the type of drugs being used amongst combatants in ways similar to large city police departments. The FBI Laboratory which provides forensic analysis support services to the FBI has never tested bomber remains for possible drug use. Toxicology reports should be completed – regardless of the prosecutive demand – to create such a mapping database.

Investigators can often increase their success in the interrogation room by utilizing the drug usage theme. Kirk has

---

[177] Kan, "Drug Intoxicated Irregular Fighters," 6.

[178] Bryan A. Liang, "Pigs, Drugs, and Terrorists," Institute of Health Law Studies, November/December 2008, http://safemeds.typepad.com/files/pigs-drugs-and-terrorists.pdf, accessed September 29, 2009.

found this to be "a very effective tool" for investigators to exploit when dealing with Muslim fundamentalists, especially opportunistic true believers, or those who have joined to enhance wealth, power, control, property or other narcissistic supplies. The drug them provides an acceptable reason to confess and many Islamists seize upon it to project blame and explain away unorthodox actions contrary to social mores. Many fighters admitted to Kirk they would not have acted in such manners normally, but were induced by the influence of drugs. Kirk maintains knowing about the proliferation of drug use amongst true believers will help investigators and interrogators look into the psyche of such people and differentiate between their internal and external "selves."[179]

Part of the strategy of attacking police and military forces with guerrilla tactics is to induce a heavy-handed response in the hopes of polarizing the community and gaining popular support. The best a disciplined counterinsurgent force can hope to do to mitigate the success of this strategy is to be precise through fire discipline, utilizing the least amount of force possible for a given situation. In the case of the irregular war in Iraq, the use of stimulants by insurgents was met with an increase in the degree of lethal force used by coalition forces. Notionally, if the counterinsurgent shoots someone with an M4 rifle (small, 5.56

---

[179] Personal interview with Trace Kirk, Quantico, Virginia, March 15, 2004.

caliber round), and he keeps advancing, the counterinsurgent will incrementally increase to a larger caliber round with more kinetic energy to end the engagement. Higher caliber rounds are inherently less accurate, therefore increasing the potential for collateral damage in such environments. The trauma induced when a soldier faces an enemy that is hopped up on drugs, both for the fear of his/her personal safety, and for using extreme levels of violence to kill that enemy, also rises.

Drugged, religious "small" warriors of the past have led to requirements for changes in weaponry. Do we need heavier bullets to stop drugged insurgents in today's conflicts? The experience campaigning against the Moros in the Philippines from 1902-1913 led the U.S. Army to adopt the Colt .45 as its new sidearm to replace the .38 caliber revolver. The Moros used native drugs that inhibited the sensation of pain and put them in an altered state of consciousness prior to battles, and the .38 rounds would not adequately stop them.[180] Many after action reports from Iraq noted that there were instances where insurgents, especially those under the influence of drugs, were not stopped by single shots.[181] Captain Michael A. Little, USMC, noted that many Marine units

> had cases where they shot guys
> with 240Gs [a 7.62mm caliber

---

[180] L.A. Rutledge, "Trial by Fire:38 vs. Moros," *1985 Handgun Annual* (Los Angeles, Ca: Petersen Publishing Company, 1985), Volume 2, 136.
[181] "Lessons for Leaders" (Revision 3): A compilation of reports for new commanders," Marine Corps Center for Lessons Learned, March 14, 2007.

> weapon], six and seven times and they were still coming. Heard one story from, I believe it was 2nd Battalion 2nd Marines, they shot a guy twice with a Barrett .50 Cal and he was still coming. A lot of people said there were a lot of drugs used, to get [the enemy insurgents] hyped up.[182]

Other veterans recall watching insurgents in Fallujah who had been shot at close range return fire and hurl grenades at Marines who stormed their strongholds. Corpsman Quinton Brown recalled "We actually shot four or five guys multiple times and they got up and moved across the room."[183] U.S. Special Operations Command have transitioned almost exclusively to higher caliber, "match grade" ammunition with greater kinetic energy yielding increased stopping power through consistent, rapid fragmentation which shortens the time required to cause incapacitation of enemy combatants.[184]

---

[182] Interview with Captain Michael A. Little, Marine Corps Center for Lessons Learned, February 10, 2005, "Effectiveness of the M-16 Family of Weapons: A Summary of Collected Lessons, Observations, Interviews, After Action Reports and Relevant Documents from OEF, OIF-I, and OIF-II," Marine Corps Center for Lessons Learned V 7, May 9, 2005.

[183] Tony Perry, "Fallouja Insurgents Fought Under Influence of Drugs, Marines Say," *Los Angeles Times*, February 13, 2005.

[184] "Corps to Use More Lethal Ammo in Afghanistan," *Military Daily News*, February 15, 2010, www.militarydailynews.com/2010/02/corps-to-use-more-lethal-ammo-in-afghanistan, accessed March 3, 2010.

Challenges of drugs use must be realized when raising "native," host-nation security forces. Proper drug screening procedures must be in place during the recruitment phase, and routine screening must be implemented as a standard from the beginning, and the importance of this standard instilled by advisors to indigenous officers. As we have seen, drug use is currently an enormous problem for recruiting Afghani police. Also, from a human rights perspective, western advisors to these local forces must be constantly alert to drug-related incidents of their troops. Reports exist of Iraqi policemen taking Artane among other drugs for experiencing similar effects as those of JAM insurgents, while another report shows an Iraqi Forces intelligence interrogator consuming drugs before sessions to inhibit scruples against torture. Mark Moyar, professor of national security affairs at the U.S. Marine Corps University, recently suggested staffing indigenous Afghani forces with Coalition or U.S. leadership, vice just embedding them with advisors, to overcome the dearth of an effective officer corps.[185] Such an action would serve a dual purpose, as it would go far towards ameliorating the drug problem which is exacerbated within ANA ranks by unconcerned "native" leadership.

[185] Dr. Mark Moyar, speech at the U.S. Marine Corps Forum on Counterinsurgency Leadership in Afghanistan, Iraq, and Beyond, National Press Club, Washington D.C., September 23, 2009. Advisors rate over 65 percent of ANA leadership as poor.

Because of the high levels of corruption in the COE, and the proclivity of many indigenous security forces to partake of performance enhancing drugs, counterinsurgent policy planners must understand that enforcement through "native forces" is more complex. Host nation security forces sometimes profit from the drug market, or they themselves are emboldened by consumption, making anti-drug enforcement exponentially more difficult because of inherent disinclination to stop it. Many police forces in troubled spots know the pharmacies which distribute narcotics, but choose to look the other way, or have an agreement with the dealers to sell the drugs to service members.[186]

Detainee protection extends beyond simple abuse by indigenous security forces. During most military operations, doctors and nurses are not on the frontlines. Therefore, it is paramount that military medics/corpsmen be trained to identify and aid detainees captured and held on the forward edge of the battle area. Such medical personnel and small unit leaders must pay particular medical attention to persons being interrogated or awaiting interrogation for adverse signs of drug usage, acute intoxication or life-threatening overdose. Hyped-up detainees must avoid becoming overheated. Artane, for example, may cause decreased sweating which could lead to heat stroke in hot weather or with vigorous exercise. Use of psychoactive drugs has many

[186] Mudhafer al-Husaini and Erica Goode, "Prescription Drug Abuse Rises Among Iraqi Troops," *The New York Times*, December 21, 2008.

negative repercussions, to include death, insanity, sterility, and seizures. Cases of withdrawal can be severe, inducing vomiting, insomnia, diarrhea, depression, fatigue, and psychosis. Recently, Army medics in Afghanistan have been routinely administering Naloxone, a drug used to counter the effects of opioid overdose, to any detainee who they suspect under the influence of opiates.

Narcotic consumption has led to unpredictable fighting, the commission of atrocities, and to the prolonging of intrastate violence. As a result, policy makers and military planners must account for the presence of non-rational combatants as a characteristic of armed conflict in operational assessments. In this vein, Sabine Collmer, a social scientist focusing on military sociology issues, believes the drug induced complexities of child soldiers in irregular wars could easily lead to a situation where peacekeeping soldiers unwillingly prolong a conflict because of their reluctance to kill youth.[187] Conflict resolution is inherently more difficult, and frequently humanitarian operations are directly hampered by the deleterious influence of narcotics, both on the fighters and the refugees. Ethnic atrocity killings are exacerbated by drug-induced militants such as exemplified in Yugoslavia or Rwanda, where warlords needed to secure drugs in order to pay

---

[187] Collmer, 10-11.

their fighters.[188] Drug usage not only aids in combatant stimulation, but in combatant economic subsistence. Giving up sources of drugs and their inherent economic viability can be counterproductive to peace accords. Drug addicts and traffickers will seek to prosper in new capitalist economies that often exist in war torn environments. In some cases, resurgence of violence has resulted post-conflict as a result.[189] Kan suggests that drug use is "an influential factor on a variety of issues that complicate efforts to reach ceasefires and political settlements," and illustrates that in modern times there are no settled conflicts where there has been widespread drug usage amongst belligerents.[190] If the demand for drug use amongst militia members can be reduced, the potential for increasing the likelihood of adherence to the parameters of any potential peace accord corresponding increases.[191] Youth who are likely to be recruited for warfare and are active in conflict zones who have been exposed to drug use and inured to violence, will then have the most difficulty adjusting to a life free of violence. The "West Side Boys," the notorious gang of child soldiers in Sierra Leone, enjoyed playing a sort of lottery game in a drugged-

---

[188] John Mueller, *Remnants of War* (New York: Cornell UP, 2004), 89-92; Mats Berdal and David Malone (eds.), *Greed and Grievance: Economic Agendas in Civil Wars* (Boulder: Lynne Rienner Publishers, 2000), 13.
[189] Gail Wannenburg, "Organized Crime in West Africa," *African Security Review* 14, No., 4, (2005), 7.
[190] Kan, *Drugs and Contemporary Warfare*, 73.
[191] Kan.

induced state in which they determined which part of their victims' bodies they would cut off next.[192]

Counternarcotics operations must be approached with caution, and an understanding of the fragile political, economic and social stability of the regions must be evaluated. The international coalition in Afghanistan is partnering with think-tanks and scholars around the world today as the realization that simple eradication of poppies is not a viable solution in and of itself. Sometimes, David MacDonald admonishes, "although the availability of a wide range of drugs in certain areas has contributed to the problem, restricting the availability of one drug can easily lead to the search for a substitute, perhaps more harmful than the one replaced."[193]

Widespread drug abuse affects the peace-building process as a whole.[194] Infectious diseases increase. The disruption of livelihoods and social/familial networks may make displaced peoples vulnerable to substance use or involvement in the drug trade.[195] Militants who have been drugged by warlords to make them "brave" will need to be rehabilitated post-conflict. They will need to go to clinics and flush the drugs from their system, and

---

[192] Sabine Collmer, "Child Soldiers—An Integral Element in New, Irregular Wars?," *The Quarterly Journal*, (Vol 3., no. 3, 2004), 8.
[193] MacDonald, 148.
[194] Kingma K. Post-war societies. In: Pauwels N, editor. *War Force to Work Force: Global Perspectives on Demobilization and Reintegration.* Baden-Baden (Germany): Nomos; 2000.
[195] Catherine Todd, Naqibullah Safi, and Stephanie Strathdee, "Drug use and harm reduction in Afghanistan," (*Harm Reduction Journal*: 2005) 7(2): 13.

participate in mental health programs to integrate them back into society, while works programs need to be available to keep them from recidivism. In such settings, future disarmament, demobilization, and reintegration (DDR) programs need to be prepared to deal with significant drug-related problems amongst internally displaced peoples and ex-combatants. This is going to entail a "whole of government approach." In Afghanistan, the government's program to disarm, demobilize and reintegrate ex-combatants was alerted to the problem of drug dependency among ex-fighters. In exchange for their guns, it was deemed likely that the rehabilitated combatants would simply spend the money earned on drugs.[196] Anthropologists can aid in this process through identifying cultural and religious misunderstandings or hesitancy to rehabilitation. For example, many Afghani addicts believe that the only way to be "cured of heroin addiction" is to have a complete blood transfusion, while for others, the stigma of acknowledging such problems personally or within the local communities prevents them from ever seeking aid.[197] Former child soldiers exposed to drugs during combat could be especially affected by PTSD and other psychiatric disorders.[198]

---

[196] MacDonald, 182.
[197] MacDonald, 148.
[198] Odenwald, 1970.

Drug abuse can hinder reintegration, increase criminality, and threaten the peace-building process.[199] Conflict and post-conflict environments will see an increase in crime as a result of drug-induced locals.[200] "This kind of medicine pushes them to commit more crimes," including carjackings, murders, assaults, and familial abuse, said one Iraqi police officer.[201] Many ex-combatants turn to drug trafficking or banditry, as some examples show.[202] The bulk of the drug arrests by Liberia's Drug Enforcement Agency are ex-combatants.[203] If criminals have been released by the opposing side during the course of the conflict, then a narcotics problem is proportionally higher. Abu Musab al Zarqawi recruited drug users to his cause during his time in a Jordanian prison.[204] Saddam Hussein, like Slobodan Milosevic, emptied his prisons, scattering drug abusers, who were pre-conflict confined to prisons and hospitals, into the general population. Omar Zahed, the leader of the Iraq police's anti-drugs squad, stated that "Most of our criminals take these tablets before they act. It

---

[199] Ibid.

[200] Paul Collier, "Demobilization and Insecurity: A Study in the Economics of the Transition From War to Peace," *Journal of International Development,* Volume 6 Issue 3, November 15, 2006; 343 – 351.

[201] "Iraq: Iraqi Officials Fear Abuse of Medicines Is Fueling Crime," *Boston Globe*, January 30, 2004.

[202] UNODC. *The Drug Nexus in Africa.* Vienna: United Nations Office for Drug Control and Crime Prevention; 1999. Available: www.unodc.org/pdf/report_1999-03-01_1.pdf., accessed September 19, 2009.

[203] "Liberia: Drug Abuse on the Rise." *IRIN*, UN Office for the Coordination of Humanitarian Affairs, December 10, 2008.

[204] Jean-Charles Brissard, *Zarqawi: The New Face of Al Qaeda* (New York: Other Press, 2005), 49.

stops them feeling any scruples or fear."[205] Local Iraqis became exacerbated with the crime bred by the drugs and the roaming gangs that attempted to procure them. One Iraqi resident lamented such gang-members equated to "Killer[s]for rent." "In Saddam's time, it was very bad. But the best thing Saddam did was be strict with drug users and sellers. They killed them."[206] Health representatives must initiate campaigns and inspect compliance to close private pharmacies that sell drugs illegally and to place more restrictions on prescriptions.

Conclusion

The will to fight is at the nub of all defeat mechanisms. . . One should always look for a way to break the enemy's will and capacity to resist.

Brig. Gen. Huba Wass de Czege

Conflict within and between countries based on tribes, clans, religion, and political ideology is well examined, and the importance and applicability of cultural anthropology to contemporary conflict is understood. General David Petraeus, U.S. Army, recently stated that, at the outset of the operations in Iraq and Afghanistan, "We didn't have the breadth and depth of

---

205 "Drug Crisis Grips Baghdad," http://news.bbc.co.uk/2/hi/middle_east/3156048.stm, accessed October 16, 2009.
206 "Iraq: Iraqi Officials Fear Abuse of Medicines Is Fueling Crime," www.boston.com/globe/, January 30, 2004.

knowledge of the locals we needed."[207] That understanding now needs to be coupled with the roles that drugs play, and the lessons learned must be purposefully examined. With an ethnographic understanding of potential adversaries prior to the first "round being fired" on an irregular battlefield, policy makers and military forces can increase their ability to preserve and protect the innocent while destroying insurgents. By understanding the power and meaning behind what animates "small" warriors, the character of an insurgency can be accessed in a more rigorous manner, and a granular understanding of the situation at hand will follow.

What if the "strong" side could, through information operations, discourage a fight by simply discrediting the drug user? The dilemmas that will arise for the modern soldier, whose Rules of Engagement (ROE) stress a mollifying approach whenever possible and increasingly involve the use of negotiation rather than kinetics, at least in the initial response, demand innovative leaders able to mollify as well as kill, in the words of soft-power scholar Joseph Nye, "co-opting rather than destroying."[208] Action reports from units engaged with drugged combatants need to be

---

[207] Speech at the U.S. Marine Corps Forum on Counterinsurgency Leadership in Afghanistan, Iraq, and Beyond, National Press Club, Washington D.C., September 23, 2009.

[208] Joseph S. Nye, "Soft Power: The Means to Success in World Politics," (Cambridge: *Public Affairs*, 2004), 5.

emphasized post-conflict, and these reports need to be utilized to build a knowledge database for interagency awareness.

The rising phenomenon of drug stimulated "small" players must not be viewed solely as a criminal problem, but a shared criminal-social-military conundrum. Illicit drugs stretch across the blurred crime-war continuum. Solely relegating the implications and effects of this battlefield reality to the realm of law-enforcement resources will grossly retard the development of solutions and inhibit imaginative thought for this cross-regional, multi-agency threat in all its dimensions.

Psychotropic drugs play a fundamental role into bringing individuals into a state of mind to kill or to self-destruct. They also, as we have seen, contribute to breaking down will and abet subjugation to a cause or an act contrary to nature. Consumption of psychoactive drugs, whether licit or illicit, is only likely to increase. Drugs and their patterns of use in asymmetric irregular settings have not been well studied in conflict zones. A cross-agency counterinsurgency plan that does not address insurgent drug use will only prolong the duration and cost of conflict settlements and subvert efforts to build a stable nation in the future.

Contributing Authors

Professor Jeffrey F. Addicott is a Distinguished Professor of Law and the Director of the Center for Terrorism Law at St. Mary's University School of Law, San Antonio, Texas. An active duty Army officer in the Judge Advocate General's Corps for twenty years (he retired in 2000 at the rank of Lieutenant Colonel), Professor Addicott spent a quarter of his career as a senior legal advisor to the United States Army's Special Forces. As an internationally recognized authority on national security law, terrorism law and human rights law, Professor Addicott not only lectures and participates in professional and academic organizations both in the United States and abroad, but he is also a frequent contributor to national and international news shows to include FOX News Channel and MSNBC. Professor Addicott is a prolific author, publishing over 20 books, articles, and monographs on a variety of legal topics. Addicott's most recent book (2009) is entitled: *Terrorism Law: Cases, Materials, Comments, 5th edition.*

Among his many contributions to the field, Professor Addicott pioneered the teaching of law of war and human rights courses to the militaries of numerous nascent democracies in Eastern Europe and Latin America. For these efforts he was awarded the Legion of Merit, named the "Army Judge Advocate of the Year," and honored as a co-recipient of the American Bar Association's Hodson Award. Addicott has served in senior legal positions in Germany, Korea, Panama, and throughout the United States. Professor Addicott holds a Doctor of Juridical Science (S.J.D.) and Master of Laws (LL.M.) from the University of Virginia School of Law. He also received a Master of Laws (LL.M.) from the Army Judge Advocate General's School and a Juris Doctor (J.D.) from the University of Alabama School of Law. Apart form teaching a variety of courses at the law school to include National Security Law and Terrorism Law, Dr. Addicott served as the Associate

Dean for Administration at St. Mary's University School of Law (2006-2007). Dr. Addicott was the 2007 recipient of "St. Mary's University School of Law Distinguished Faculty Award."

Claudia Baisini, M.Sc. and PhD Candidate (registration in process). Attended the University of Milan studying Economics and Law and then moved to Aberdeen King's College, where she focused on Organizational Studies; Cross Cultural Strategy, International Business, and Organizational Change and Learning. Following a term at Copenhagen Business School in Cross Cultural Marketing Strategy, she took her M.Sc. in International Management at the Graduated Business School of the University of Gothenburg, Sweden. Her Master Thesis' was on "Knowledge in knowledge intensive organizations; the case of crime investigation and consulting firms". After working within International Humanitarian Operations, in 2004 she joined the staff of the Swedish National Defense College in Stockholm. The most relevant projects; evaluation of the Planning Under Time pressure method (PUT), research assistant for project STRATMAS (Strategic Management System), a simulation program based on System Dynamics theories , and project leader for MAC, a study focused on Situational Awareness of a squad leader in urban combat. Claudia's current focus is on the development of a method to understand the mindset of relevant actors in the Area of Operations, stemming from how our biases and categorizations influence our own understanding and affect framing. Furthermorc, Claudia works at the development of education and training to enhance observation skills and foster meta-cognition. The project is conducted in cooperation with the FBI Academy (Behavioral Science Unit), Swedish Police, and USJFCOM J9. Claudia is a PhD candidate at the Stockholm Brain Institute (registration in process), where she combines her previous knowledge in organizational theories with Neurosciences in research about learning of creativity and divergent thinking, emotions and role of stress on intuition, and implicit/explicit learning.
Contact information: Claudia.baisini@fhs.se

Erik Bjurström is a researcher PhD at Mälardalen University, Sweden and Swedish Defense Research Agency, with a focus on contemporary challenges to management, control and learning in the face of uncertainty, especially in network constellations. Erik has a background both as a civil academic and consultant as well and has qualified experience as an operational analyst in military planning, research and development. His publications range from civil issues of management control and knowledge management to military intelligence and civil-military harmonization. Given this broad background and his interest in practice, Erik often spans over several theoretical traditions in his quest for practical solutions.

Supervisory Special Agent Andrew J. Bringuel, II, an Agent Supervisor Instructor at the FBI academy, has over 20 years of professional and academic experience, ranging from investigating public corruption, organized crime, and environmental crime cases to the murder of a federal judge and an abortion clinic bombing. Agent Bringuel as acted as an undercover Agent as well as a negotiator working for over 9 years in the field before being promoted to FBI Headquarters as a supervisor in the Counterterrorism Division. After two years at the National Domestic Preparedness Office (NDPO), SSA Bringuel transferred to the FBI Academy in May 2001 and taught in the Investigative Computer Training Unit until May 2005 when he transferred to the Behavioral Science Unit.

Currently Agent Bringuel teaches as an Adjunct Instructor for the University of Virginia, through the FBI's National Academy program. He teaches a graduate level course entitled *Understanding The Mind-set of Terrorists and The Government's Response Tactics*. Agent Bringuel heads up the Terrorism Research and Analysis Project (TRAP) which studies National Security issues and provides operational and case consultation to law enforcement partners.

Agent Bringuel has a Bachelor's degree in Criminology from St. Leo University and a Master's degree in Adult Education from the University of Virginia.
Contact Information: andrew_bringuel@yahoo.com

Steven M. Chermak, (Ph.D., State University of New York at Albany) is a Professor in the School of Criminal Justice at Michigan State University. Dr. Chermak is also a lead investigator affiliated with the The National Consortium for the Study of Terrorism and Responses to Terror (START). First, he has received funding from one of the Department of Homeland Security's Center of Excellence (The National Consortium for the Study of Terrorism and Responses to Terrorism--START) to study the criminal and terrorist activities of domestic far right extremists. This work focuses on identifying pathways to radicalization and escalation towards violence, and comparing the organizational-level differences between violent and nonviolent extremist groups. This project has recently received funding to expand to include information on far-leftists and Jihadists. Second, he received funding (with Drs. David Carter and Edmund McGarrel-MSU) from the National Institute of Justice to study the intelligence practices of State, Local, and Tribal law enforcement agencies. Finally, he has studied the media's role in relation to crime and terrorism issues.
Contact Information: chermak@msu.edu

Kelly R. Damphousse, Ph.D. serves as Associate Dean in the College of Arts and Sciences and Presidents Associates Presidential Professor of Sociology at the University of Oklahoma. He has been studying terrorism since 1994 and is co-director of the American Terrorism Study. His other research interests include voice stress analysis for detection of deception and drug policy research.

Mark G. Frank, Ph.D. is a professor and Director of the Communication Science Center at the University at Buffalo. He received his Ph.D. in Social Psychology from Cornell University in 1989, and afterward, he received a National Research Service Award from the National Institute of Mental Health to do postdoctoral research with Dr. Paul Ekman in the Psychiatry Department at the University of California at San Francisco Medical School. In 1992 he joined the School of Psychology at the University of New South Wales in Sydney, and 4 years later joined the Communication Department at Rutgers University in New Jersey. In 2005 he accepted a position in his hometown at the School of Informatics at the University of Buffalo. He has published numerous research papers on facial expressions, emotion, and interpersonal deception, and has research funding from The National Science Foundation, Homeland Security, and the Department of Defense to examine deception and hidden emotion behaviors in checkpoint and other counter-terrorism situations. He is also the co-developer of an automated computer system to read facial expressions. He has used these findings to lecture, consult with and train virtually all Federal Law Enforcement/Intelligence Agencies, as well as local/state and select foreign agencies. He has also given workshops to US and foreign judges and magistrates. He has presented briefings to the National Academies of Science and the US Congress on Deception and Counter-terrorism.. Finally, he has appeared in over 80 print, radio, and television appearances to talk about his work, including *The New Yorker Magazine, Time Magazine, New York Times, CBS Evening News, CNN, Fox News Channel, National Public Radio, The Learning Channel, the Discovery Channel, the Oprah Show,* and so forth.

Joshua D. Freilich is the Acting Director of the Criminal Justice Ph.D. program and a member of the Criminal Justice Department at John Jay College, the City University of New York. He is a lead investigator for the National Consortium for the Study of Terrorism and Responses to Terrorism (START), a Center for

Excellence of the U.S. Department of Homeland Security (DHS), as well as a member of the Terrorism Research and Analysis Project (TRAP), which is sponsored by the Federal Bureau of Investigation's (FBI) Behavioral Science Unit (BSU). Freilich's research focuses on domestic terrorism as well as criminological theory. His research has been funded by DHS directly as well as through START. Freilich is currently the principal investigator (with Steven Chermak) on the United States Extremist Crime Database (ECDB) study, a large-scale data-collection effort that is building the first-of-its-kind relational database of crimes committed by far-right, Al Qaeda influenced, and animal rights and environmental rights extremists in the United States reported in an open source.
Contact Information: jfreilich@jjay.cuny.edu

Nathaniel T. Fulmer is a Research Fellow for the Center for Terrorism Law, St. Mary's University School of Law; Candidate for J.D. 2010, St. Mary's University School of Law. B.A., University of Texas at Austin, 2007.

Don Gemeinhardt MBA, MSS (Strategic Studies), (USAF Colonel – Retired). He brings an interesting combination of operational intelligence and analysis experience working with various agencies both nationally and internationally and a long history of anti-terrorism program development ending as the Special Assistant for Security Matters for the U.S. Forces in Europe. His program experience has been at various levels in positions from Field work to a base patrolman to various levels of Executive Leadership & Management and Program Director levels in joint Host Nation Support, Coalition Forces, Interagency, Local, State and Federal Agency Intelligence Operations, creation of various Anti-Terrorism efforts, investigating Transnational Terrorism issues, Security Force Protection, Homeland Security, Crisis and Consequence Management, Information Operations, Law Enforcement Management, Training, Investigations and Strategic Planning, Knowledge Management Systems

Applications. Now, he is the Director for Security Solutions Programs at RTI International a non-profit organization involved in a host of Research and Development areas all over the world. He also is the Task Leader for the Assessment and Outreach Areas for the VIMS (Violent Intentions Modeling and Simulations) project with the DHS Institute for Homeland Security Solutions (IHSS). He also continues to be involved in Intelligence, Law Enforcement and Training related areas with various Federal agencies from the FLETC to the FBI Hazardous Device School. Contact Information: Dgemeinhardt@rti.org, (919)-599-8471

Robert C. Gunn is a Research Fellow for the Center for Terrorism Law, St. Mary's University School of Law; Candidate for J.D. 2010, St. Mary's University School of Law. B.A., Rhodes College, 2007.

Jenelle C. Janowicz is an Intelligence Analyst with the Federal Bureau of Investigation and currently works in the Laboratory Division's Terrorist Explosive Device Analytical Center (TEDAC). Prior to her current assignment, she worked in the Weapons of Mass Destruction Directorate, WMD Operations Unit, and as a detailee to the CIA's Counterterrorism Center, Weapons of Mass Destruction Department. IA Janowicz previously worked as an analyst within the FBI's Counterterrorism Division at the Foreign Terrorist Tracking Task Force (FTTTF) and as an intern in the Behavioral Science Unit (BSU). She has a Bachelors of Science degree in Criminal Justice with a minor in Psychology from the University of Scranton, Scranton, PA, and a Masters of Forensic Science with a concentration in crime scene investigation from The George Washington University, Washington, DC. Contact Information: Jenelle.Janowicz@ic.fbi.gov

Gary LaFree is Director of the National Center for the Study of Terrorism and Responses to Terrorism (START) at the University of Maryland, as well as professor in the Department of Criminology and Criminal Justice. In 2005-2006 Dr. LaFree served as President of the American Society of Criminology (ASC). Dr. LaFree has also served as the Past President of the ASC's Division on International Criminology (1991-1993), the chair of the American Sociological Association's Section on Crime, Law and Deviance (1991-1993), the Executive Board of the Harry Frank Guggenheim Foundation (2001-2006), and the Executive Committee of the Justice Research Statistics Association (2000-2001; 1993-1994). Dr. LaFree is a fellow of the American Society of Criminology. He has written over 60 articles and book chapters and three books and is currently on the editorial boards of eight journals. Much of his recent research has dealt with national and international macro-level trends in political and criminal violence. Related work includes studies of U.S. and global homicide trends, global trends in terrorism, the sudden desistance of terrorism, connections between terrorism, democratization and failed states and the effectiveness of responses to terrorism.

Carl J. Maccario is a graduate of Suffolk University Boston Massachusetts. He received his Bachelor of Science in 1982.

Prior to 9/11/01, Carl's served the Commonwealth of Massachusetts Secretary of State's office as an investigator/auditor for the Securities Division. While employed there he was the coordinator for in service training. He attended the Massachusetts State Police Academy for Basic Interview Training. As an investigator Carl conducted hundreds of field interviews and audits as well as numerous investigations regarding possible securities fraud.

Subsequent to 9/11, Carl left his employment with the State and began a career with Virgin Atlantic Airlines Security as a passenger profiler. Carl received training in Behavior Pattern Recognition, Document ID Verification, Deception Detection and Eliciting responses from an Israeli security firm hired by Virgin Atlantic.

Shortly after the Congress created the Department of Homeland Security, Carl began his career with the Federal Government utilizing his knowledge and security experience to help design, develop and implement the first Behavior Screening Program for a major international airport which is now being implemented in airports across the United States. During this development, Carl has trained hundreds of security and law enforcement professionals in Suspicious Behavior Detection, detecting deception and eliciting responses.

Lynn Maskel, M.D. M.S. is the former director of the Forensic Psychiatry fellowship program at Loyola University Medical School in the Chicago area. She is board certified in both forensic as well as child & adolescent psychiatry. She is frequently called upon for consultation and testimony in a variety of criminal matters. Dr. Maskel has an interest in psychopathy, paraphilias, early detection of psychopathology as seen in adolescents and domestic terrorists as influenced by group dynamics. Dr. Maskel, as interim director, is currently developing a new forensic psychiatry fellowship program for the University of California-San Diego in conjunction with Atascadero State Hospital.

Dr. David Matsumoto is an expert in the field of emotion, nonverbal behavior, facial expressions, and culture. Since 1989 Matsumoto has been a Professor of Psychology at San Francisco State University. He is also the Founder and Director of SFSU's Culture and Emotion Research Laboratory. The laboratory focuses on studies involving culture, emotion, social interaction and communication. He is also a Director at Humintell, LLC, a company that provides unique training in the fields of facial expression, gesture, nonverbal behavior, emotion and deception to private and public companies as well as various government agencies. In 2009, Matsumoto was one of the select few to receive the prestigious Minerva Grant; a $1.9 million grant from the US Department of Defense to examine the role of emotions in ideologically-based groups.

Contact Information: dmatsumoto@humintell.com

Jim M. Nyce (PhD, 1987, Brown) is an associate professor in the Department of Anthropology, Ball State University. Nyce studies how information technologies are used in complex workplaces and organizations. A docent at Linköping University, Sweden, he has been visiting professor in military technology and war science at the National Defense College, Stockholm, 1998-2000 and 2005 to present. Since 2005, Nyce has also been scientific adviser to a research project that has focused on the military intelligence function, organizational/ technological change and professional development.

Nyce is visiting professor in Lund University's Master's Program in Human Factors and the university's Leonardo da Vinci Center for Complexity and Systems Thinking. He is adjunct associate professor in Linköping University's Department of Health and Environment, Faculty of Health Sciences and adjunct associate professor, Department of Radiology, Indiana University School of Medicine.

Matthew D. Semel is a lawyer by training and graduated from New York Law School in 1987. He also holds an M.S. in Journalism from Northwestern University. After 13 years as a public defender in the South Bronx, Semel was the staff attorney for the Civil Rights Clinic at Touro Law School and he has also represented capital offenders on appeal. Semel's research interests include capital punishment, terrorism, cultural and crime, and criminal law. He is currently finishing his Ph.D. at John Jay College of Criminal Justice. His dissertation focuses on military and counterterrorism interrogation techniques.

James K. Shearer is a Special Agent with the Federal Bureau of Investigation currently assigned to Pittsburgh Field Division. Since joining the FBI in 2005, Shearer's primary investigative responsibilities have been within the Domestic Terrorism arena, specifically focusing on Animal Rights and Environmental Rights Extremism. Shearer is a certified FBI Police Instructor and served as a National Center for the Analysis of Violent Crime (NCAVC) Coordinator while assigned to the Detroit Division.

He has a Bachelors of Science degree in Public Administration with minors in Political Science and Criminal Justice Administration from Point Park University, Pittsburgh, PA and a Masters of Science in Criminology from Florida State University, Tallahassee, FL.

Pete Simi is an Associate Professor in the School of Criminology & Criminal Justice at the University of Nebraska, Omaha. For the past 13 years he has conducted extensive ethnographic fieldwork with white supremacist groups across the United States. He has published a series of articles that examine the organizational and cultural dimensions of the US White Power Movement. His book manuscript, American Swastika: Inside the White Power Movement's Hidden Spaces of Hate, is scheduled to be published December 2009 and focuses on the relationship between social spaces and extremist violence.

Brent L. Smith is Distinguished Professor and Chair, Department of Sociology and Criminal Justice, and Director, Terrorism Research Center in Fulbright College, at the University of Arkansas. He has directed the American Terrorism Study since it inception in 1988. His research on terrorism has included examination of the temporal and spatial distribution of American terrorism, the pre-cursor behaviors of terrorists and pre-incident indicators of terrorism, prosecutorial and defense strategies in terrorism trials, and the punishment of terrorist defendants. Brent's work has been funded by the National Memorial Institute for the Prevention of Terrorism, the Department of Justice, Department of Homeland Security, and the Department of Defense. Dr. Smith has presented his perspective on American terrorism in various forums, including testimony and briefings before Congressional committees and subcomittees, Los Alamos National Laboratory, Federal Bureau of Investigation, Secret Service, Nuclear Regulatory Commission's Law Enforcement Division, and numerous other agencies and settings.

Erich Henry Wagner is a Lieutenant Colonel in the Marine Corps Reserve currently assigned to AFRICOM. Erich earned his B.S. in History from the United States Naval Academy, and an M.A. in International Relations from The Fletcher School of Law and Diplomacy, Tufts University. In the past decade as an infantry officer he has served in defense of The American Embassy in Panama, trained foreign personnel in Croatia, Australia, Argentina, Korea, Japan, Curacao, and most recently, Iraq. Recently, Erich served as a Congressional Liaison for the Marine Corps to Congress. He has published articles on military history and counterinsurgencies in *The Journal for the Anglo-Zulu War Historical Society*, *The Joint Center for Operational Analysis*, and *Armchair General*.
Contact Information: EHWagner@alumni.tufts.edu

Greg S. Weaver is an Associate Professor in the Department of Sociology, Anthropology and Social Work at Auburn University. He also serves as a reserve deputy with the Lee County (AL) Sheriff's Office. He completed his Ph.D. (Sociology) at the University of Nebraska in 1997. He earned his M.A. in Applied Sociology from the University of Central Florida in 1993. In 1988, he earned a B.S. in Criminology from Auburn University. From 1990-1993, he was employed as a probation officer with the Florida Department of Corrections. Research and teaching interests include lethal violence, homeland security and terrorism, substance use, and research methods. He is a member of the International Association of Crime Analysts, Police Futurists International / Futures Working Group, InfraGard, the Homicide Research Working Group, and the Terrorism Research and Analysis Project.

Index

2

2006 Military Commission Act........... 5
23rd Infantry Division....................... 12

4

4GW............................... 372, 386, 413

6

60 Minutes 15

9

9/11 ...5, 7, 29, 152, 161, 185, 190, 261, 310, 363, 458

A

Abbas Fadhil Mahdi........................ 416
abortions 313
Abu Ghraib4, 11, 14, 15, 16, 17, 18, 19, 28, 298
Abu Musab al-Zarqawi 12, 140
action learning................................. 45
active killing 366, 375
actors.32, 35, 36, 40, 43, 46, 49, 50, 52, 61, 65, 66, 67, 77, 93, 314, 316, 325, 372, 378, 384, 386, 413, 452
Adam Mathes................................. 435
affilative...116, 118, 121, 137, 138, 142
Afghan National Army (ANA) 400
Afghan National Police (ANP) 400
Afghan police................................. 402
Afghanistan...... 16, 24, 25, 27, 51, 294, 298, 344, 384, 390, 391, 397, 398, 399, 400, 401, 402, 407, 408, 409, 410, 411, 412, 414, 416, 435, 439, 440, 442, 444, 445, 447, 448
Al Qaeda.122, 127, 140, 161, 164, 169, 173, 175, 185, 261, 288, 308, 372, 384, 392, 398, 409, 410, 446, 456
Al Qaeda in Iraq (AQI)........... 392, 409
Albert D. Biderman......................... 305
Alex Curtis..................................... 317
Ali Soufan................................ 297, 300
Allure 293
Al-Qa'eda 5, 12, 24
Al-Shabab 389
amateurization................................ 163
Amatzia Baram 395, 396
American Terrorism Study (ATS) .328, 342, 344, 348
amphetamine-laced leaf.................. 387
Amphetamine-Type Stimulants 392
amulets 369, 405, 419
Analytic Strategies 65
anchors... 44, 74, 75, 98, 103, 114, 115, 116, 117, 123, 125, 128, 133, 136, 145
animal rights .. 260, 263, 264, 265, 266, 267, 270, 271, 276, 277, 282, 283, 284, 286, 287, 291, 350, 456
Ansar Al-Islam 398
Anti-Defamation League (ADL)..... 286
army 124, 140, 141, 345, 371, 382, 399, 400
Army War College at Carlisle Barracks 378
Artane 393, 399, 409, 440, 441
Aryan Nations 313, 317
Ashby... 35
Assyrians.. 382
Australian Crime Commission (ACC) 173
Australian Institute of Criminology153, 155, 156, 157, 158, 168, 172, 178, 183, 184
axis of evil....................................... 33
Ayatollah Khomeini....................... 414
Aziz al-Abub.................................. 406

B

Baghdad 14, 396, 410, 426, 447
Bali bombing.................................. 161
Battle of Mogadishu....................... 430
behavioral clue193, 194, 195, 196, 197, 198, 199, 202, 205, 219
Beirut 407
Benjamin Smith 313, 315, 330

Beslan School Siege........................386
Black Hawk Helicopter...................388
body clues.......................................199
British Army...................................401
British Foreign Ministry.................401
brown-brown..................................404
bubbles...................................404, 427
Buford Furrow........ 313, 315, 319, 330
bullets......366, 371, 375, 401, 405, 427, 434, 438
bullets dance........................... 366, 375
Burma...405

C

Callon..38
Center for Iraq Studies at University of Haifa..395
Central Intelligence Agency..............21
Central Java Police..........................412
challenging hypotheses.....................49
change blindness...............................91
Chechnya 384, 407
child soldiers... 403, 405, 430, 442, 445
child troops....................................403
Chinese 8, 173, 302, 303, 305
Cho Seung Hyi........................237, 238
Chris Argyris 47
Chun 88, 89, 90, 91, 106, 107, 108
Chun and Jang...................................88
Clausewitz.................................96, 109
codeine....................................386, 394
cognitive biases.................................49
cognitive restructuring......................44
Colin S. Gray 379
Columbine High School..................330
communication technologies...............9
consciousness... 91, 238, 258, 380, 408, 414, 438
constructivism... 37, 38, 54, 62, 67, 256
contextual cueing.............................89
cookies...406
counterfeiting. 150, 153, 154, 155, 156, 157, 158, 159, 165, 166, 167, 168, 169, 170, 172, 173, 176, 178, 179, 180, 181, 182, 183, 188, 278
counterinsurgency.. 369, 378, 379, 399, 416, 449
Coup d'Oeil..81
courage-inducing 372, 386
Cultural Generic Information Requirements Handbook............377
current operational environment....368

D

Dan Nagourney...............................401
Dane and Pratt...................................83
Darrell Carver 392, 423, 424
Darwin 200, 220, 226, 233, 248, 254
David MacDonald..................400, 444
David Petraeus 447
deception 189, 190, 191, 193, 194, 195, 196, 199, 202, 204, 205, 206, 209, 214, 215, 216, 217, 219, 225, 226, 227, 228, 229, 230, 307, 308, 326, 455, 458, 459
Democratic Republic of Congo.......387
Department of Homeland Security. 155, 261, 314, 343, 347, 350, 363, 436, 454, 455, 458, 461
*Department of Justice*i, 1, 21, 173, 186, 264, 343, 347, 363, 435, 461
Department of Treasury..................436
detainees 11, 14, 15, 16, 19, 21, 414, 441
Dewey, Lewin, Rogers and Freire.....92
DHS START Center of Excellence. 348
Diala..410
Dick Cheney 297
disarmament, demobilization, and reintegration..............................445
disconfirmation .. 47, 48, 49, 57, 60, 61, 65
discrete emotions ... 235, 240, 243, 246, 248
Diyala Province...............................393
domestic security 266, 349
Donald Horowitz.....................133, 419
Donald Schön....................................47
double loop 46, 49
drug trafficking 164, 384, 429, 446
Dylan Klebold................................330

E

Earl Pitts...125

Earth Liberation Front.... 138, 263, 286, 288, 289, 290, 291, 338
East Africa 161, 388
East African Embassy 161
Edgar Schein 44
Egypt... 22
Egyptians 382
Embedded Training Team............... 400
enculturated..................................... 243
Environmental Liberation Front (ELF) 318
environmental rights 259, 261, 262, 263, 264, 265, 266, 268, 269, 271, 273, 274, 277, 278, 279, 280, 282, 284, 350, 456
environmental rights extremists 259, 261, 262, 263, 264, 265, 266, 268, 269, 271, 273, 274, 277, 278, 279, 280, 282, 284, 350, 456
Eric Harris....................................... 330
Eric Hoffer 114, 119
Eric Holder...................................... 297
Eric Robert Rudolph 141
escalation ...85, 237, 246, 252, 277, 454
espoused theory..................... 49, 63, 87
euphoric 409
Extremist Crime Database 273, 287, 328, 342, 348, 350, 360, 363, 455

F

Facial Action Coding System 250
Fallujah..374, 392, 420, 423, 425, 426, 435, 439
far-left 265, 269, 270, 275, 276, 318, 454
far-right...261, 265, 268, 270, 271, 281, 287, 348, 350, 352, 353, 356, 456
FBI Academy...... 37, 65, 138, 452, 453
Fedayeen................................ 392, 411
Federal Bureau of Investigation (FBI) 314
Field Manual 37, 71, 378
Firimbi 388
Flavell 91
fog of war.. 79
Fourth Generation Warfare 372
Frank Ambrose 138
Frank H. Schwable.......................... 302
freedom 6, 19, 51, 52, 132, 140, 272, 367, 376
Freilich and Steve Chermak 160
French Algerian 432
French Legionnaires........................ 406

G

Gaza strip 25
Geneva Conventions 20, 299
George Tiller................................... 313
Gestalt School 42
Global Terrorism Database (GTD) . 261
Government Accountability Office (GAO)....................................... 402
Greeks 382
Green Course 36
Group Analysis Protocol (GAP) 111
group identity (GI) 114, 115
Gulf War 296, 304

H

Hadith 413
hallucinogen.................................... 371
Hamas 24, 25, 173, 175
Hanns Scharff 301
Harbaugh and Khemka 153
Harold G. Wolff.............................. 305
harsh techniques..... 295, 296, 297, 298, 299, 301, 305, 308
Harvard University............. 47, 90, 147
hashish ... 382, 388, 391, 395, 397, 398, 400, 401, 402, 414, 415, 416, 434
hatred 122, 133, 141, 143, 192, 237, 240, 241, 243, 245, 246, 247
Hezbollah ... 24, 25, 164, 166, 169, 173, 175, 185, 406
Hirschi and Gottfredson 277, 278
Holocaust Memorial Museum......... 313
Horn of Africa................................ 409
human performance modification ... 421
human source .... ix, 112, 114, 116, 119, 134, 145, 146, 294
human wave 405
Hussein Al-Ahmad.......................... 398
hypotheses.... 57, 59, 61, 64, 65, 66, 80, 246

I

ideological agenda 6, 172
ideologically-based 243, 459
Illinois State Bar Association.......... 330
illusion 77
imminent.......... 22, 232, 252, 267, 298
impressionistic 220
Inattentional Blindness 90, 109
incongruent 91
indegree 328
indoctrination. 120, 123, 125, 129, 142, 145, 405
Information Operations (IO) 431
ingroup.....233, 238, 239, 242, 245, 254
intergroup emotions 239
internalize 40, 41
International Trade Commission..... 155
INTERPOL 177, 436
interrogators..... 21, 294, 296, 297, 298, 299, 300, 301, 302, 303, 307, 308, 437
intuition...74, 75, 77, 81, 82, 83, 84, 88, 96, 98, 109, 452
IPSG criminal files......................... 177
Iraq12, 13, 14, 15, 16, 21, 23, 140, 294, 298, 304, 310, 344, 389, 390, 391, 392, 394, 395, 396, 398, 399, 407, 409, 410, 412, 414, 416, 417, 420, 429, 432, 434, 437, 438, 440, 446, 447, 448, 462
Iraq Interior Ministry 399
Isandhlwana 370
Ishmael Beah 405
Islam 3, 410, 413, 414, 416, 432, 433
Islamic Jihadi idcology 334
Islamic Movement of Uzbekistan (IMU) 164
Islamic terrorists 4

J

Jack Cloonan........................... 297, 300
Jalal Ammar.................................... 399
James Von Brunn................... 313, 330
Jayish al-Mahdi 393
jeundi 399
Jewish Community Center............. 313
Jim Gray 403
John Jay College.... 149, 259, 293, 341, 348, 350, 455, 460
John Lewis 265
John McCain................................... 304
John Walker 416
Jordan..................... 22, 55, 69, 92, 107
Joseph Paul Franklin 317

K

Kandahar.. 402
Kant 96, 108
Karbala................................... 391, 394
Kashmir.................................. 408, 412
Kati Marton.................................... 405
Khalid Sheik Mohamed 298
Khat 387, 388, 389
kinetics................... 366, 375, 434, 448
Kingdom of Dahomey..................... 430
Kirk 415, 436
Kirkuk 413
Klein 82, 84, 108
Kolb 76, 92, 95, 96, 97, 99, 108
Koran 413
Korean conflict 296
Kosovo Liberation Army (KLA) 164
Krieger 53
Krulak 79, 81, 108
Kurdistan Workers' Party 408
Kurt Lewin 39, 41, 42
Kuwaiti 398, 399, 407
KwaZulu 371

L

Langer 93
Lashkar-e-Taiba 372
Latour.. 38
law enforcement officers (LEOs).... 249
Law of Requisite Variety 35
law of war 5, 10, 11, 13, 18, 19, 20, 26, 27, 28, 451
Lawrence E. Hinkle 305
leaderless resistance 283, 315, 318, 346
learning in action 102
learning space 95
Lebanon War.................................... 25
Levinthal 54, 70, 94, 108
Levinthal and Rerup............ 54, 94, 108

Lewis Carlson 303
Liberians 404
lines of inquiry 59
Lloyd Bucher 304
lone wolf .262, 270, 274, 275, 276, 277, 283, 312, 314, 315, 316, 317, 318, 319, 320, 321, 322, 323, 325, 327, 330, 332, 333, 334
Los Angeles Police Department 169
Louis Beam 317, 336, 346
Louise Richardson 122
Lyon 79
lysergic acid diethylatnide (LSD) ... 372

M

Mahdi militia 395, 426, 427
manipulation 4
manipulator 204
Marc Sageman 132
Marijuana 387
Marine Corps 37, 71, 79, 81, 108, 302, 363, 373, 374, 376, 377, 378, 393, 401, 403, 405, 425, 435, 438, 439, 440, 448, 461
Mark Moyar 440
Marrin 79, 108
Marshall Applewhite 135
mass movements 112, 119, 120, 121, 124, 125, 126, 127, 128, 130, 131, 132, 134, 135, 140, 143, 144, 145
match grade 439
Matt Hale 330
Matthew Alexander 297
media 4, 5, 6, 8, 9, 10, 11, 12, 13, 14, 15, 16, 17, 19, 21, 22, 23, 25, 26, 27, 28, 34, 263, 314, 342, 431, 454
media-savvy 17
Meloy 137, 139, 140, 141, 142, 147
Mental Health at Mazar-iSharif' 397
Merajudin Pathan 435
meta-analysis 202, 219
meta-cognition 74, 75, 91, 96, 452
Methamphetamines 391, 420
Michael Durant 388
Michael Fortier 320
Michael Liguorni 392
Michael Odenwald 388
Michigan State University 149, 259, 311, 341, 348, 350, 454
Mike Cronin 304
Mikhail Bakunin 316
Military Code of Conduct 307
mind-altering 399, 408, 411, 414
mindedness 53, 59
mindfulness . 53, 54, 71, 92, 93, 94, 109
MIT 46, 47, 82, 108
monkey-wrenching 264, 291
Mujahideen 399
Muqtada Al-Sadir's Mahdi Army ... 393
Muqtada al-Sadr 394, 395, 396
Murrah Federal Building. 152, 319, 346
My Lai 11, 12, 18, 28
Mystical Sufi Muslims 414

N

Nader Alemi 397
Najaf 391, 395
Naloxone 442
National Alliance 317
National Defense College 31, 51, 73, 310, 452, 459
navy 391
neo-Nazis 318
new social contract 123
New York Times 15, 297, 310, 385, 391, 394, 399, 408, 441, 455
Nidal Hasan 333
non-ideological 262, 266, 277, 278, 279, 281, 282, 320, 322, 323, 351, 352
Norse Berserkers 381
North Koreans 302, 303, 305

O

Obama Administration 5, 19
Observe-Orient-Decide-Act 102
Oklahoma City 152, 278, 288, 319, 320, 338, 339, 346, 352
Omar Zahed 446
Omerta 127
Operation Smoke Screen 169
Ophelia 380
orbicularis oculi 220
organizational change 41, 42

organizational learning... 45, 46, 54, 70, 291
orphans of martyrs 166
Osama bin Laden 122, 127
Otto Rank.. 45
outgroup..233, 238, 239, 240, 244, 245, 254
overseas contingency operations......... 5

P

Pan Am Flight 103 152
passive-aggressive 141
Paul R. Kan............................ 378, 381
personal identity..... 114, 115, 117, 121, 123, 127, 145
phenylcyclo-hexylpiperidine (PCP) 381
Pictures of Facial Affect 250
Pina e Cunha & Chia................... 78, 95
Pinocchio 193, 195, 221
Potter Stewart.................................. 314
practice theory 76, 92, 93
predicting 77, 205, 232, 234, 255
Probst......263, 267, 270, 274, 283, 289, 318, 338
profiling 64, 290, 334
propaganda. 4, 5, 7, 8, 9, 11, 12, 17, 18, 20, 24, 25, 27, 28, 143, 162, 272, 302, 305, 316, 332
psychological weapon......................... 8

Q

quasi-stationary equilibria................. 43
Queens 424

R

R&G 43, 56, 60, 61, 62
radical4, 5, 25, 115, 271, 286, 290, 291, 319, 320, 321, 334, 346
Ramzi bin al-Shibh 300
Ramzi Hashem Abed 398
Rania.. 412
rank 265, 269, 307, 451
Rapid Recognition Training (RRT) 100
Recognition Primed Decision 82
reconnect... 64
Red & Green 32, 35, 36, 37, 41, 42, 44, 45, 46, 49, 50, 52, 54
Red Bluff 273
Red Cross 16, 50, 52
reflection-in-action 91, 92, 94
Renshaw Recognition Systems 101
repetitive 123
Rerup 54, 70
resist.com 317
rethinking 37, 45, 60
Richard Heuer 64
Richard Kemp 6
Richard Miller................................. 125
Right-Wing Extremism 341
Rima Tannous 408
rip and return.................................. 278
Robert Philip Hanssen..................... 125
Roseneau... 38
Rozin....................... 236, 240, 243, 257
Ruby Ridge 346
rules of engagement 13
Russell Thomas 424

S

Salafi Islamists 132
Salafists... 414
Samuel Renshaw..................... 100, 102
Schlesinger Report 17
Schutz 50
Scott Roeder.................................... 313
Second Bali Bombing 412
Secretary of the Army 346
self consciousness 58, 64
Senate Judiciary Committee............ 349
Sendero Luminoso 164
sensemaking...................................... 38
Shias.. 12
sicaritos... 406
Sierra Leone 404, 405, 422, 443
single loop................................. 46, 47
sixth sense 81
Slobodan Milosevic 446
Small Business Administration 170
small players 384
small wars 367, 373, 378, 379, 428
social interaction .. 38, 39, 62, 134, 459
social learning 278

South Africa.................................... 371
Southern Poverty Law Center 343, 345, 347, 360, 363, 364
Soviets 400, 434
State Department............. 164, 394, 395
stepping out....................................... 45
Steve Kleinman................................ 297
Straight Edge 273
strain 278
strike of the eye................................. 81
suicidal criminal group member (SCGM)..................................... 116
suicidal criminal violent radical true believer (SCVRTB) 115
suicide bomber. 15, 137, 223, 251, 298, 324, 369, 395, 406, 407, 409, 410, 411, 412, 422, 435
summer of hate 313
Sun Tzu... 375
Sunni 218, 389
Sunni Muslim.................................. 218
Swedish Armed Forces ... 32, 35, 36, 67
Swedish Committee for Afghanistan .. 7

T

tactics, techniques and procedures (TTPs).. 379
Tamil Tigers.................................... 164
targeting 145, 271, 280
Taylorian 88
terrorist financing............................ 177
terrorist mindset 32, 34
Terrorists and Other Ideologically Based Groups (TOIBG)............. 247
Terry Nichols 315, 320, 346
tetrahydrocannabinol....................... 371
Theodore Kaczynski (aka the Unabomber).............................. 318
theory in use................................ 50, 87
Thomas Jefferson 26
thwarter-destroyer........................... 242
Timothy McVeigh.. 315, 319, 329, 334, 338, 346
Togo West....................................... 346
Tom Metzger 317
torture......16, 19, 21, 22, 294, 295, 299, 301, 302, 303, 304, 306, 440
Trace Kirk 398, 409, 414, 415, 437
tranquilizers 367, 376, 394, 405
transparency 27
Tri-Border/Triple Frontier Region .. 175
true believer ... 114, 115, 118, 121, 124, 129, 133, 134, 135, 136, 137, 139, 140, 142, 144, 147, 437
tunnel vision........ 49, 57, 64, 66, 74, 75

U

U.S. House of Representatives Judiciary Subcommittee on Crime 349
Ulster Defense Association............. 162
unfreeze........................... 63, 74, 75, 98
United Nations ... 6, 391, 405, 406, 411, 446
University of California Santa Cruz 273
unlearning 42, 45, 67

V

Vanity Fair..................................... 416
Vietnam.. 12, 13, 18, 26, 296, 303, 304, 309, 382
Vietnam War....... 12, 18, 303, 304, 309
violent group member (VGM) 116
violent radical true believer (VRTB) 115
Virginia Tech University 237, 330
Vladimir V. Putin............................ 408

W

Wall Street Journal................ 15, 16, 17
War on Terror .. 4, 5, 10, 14, 15, 16, 28, 29, 187
Washington Post 22, 27, 390, 391, 411, 417
Weapon of Mass Destruction (WMD) 192
Weick and Sutcliffe................... 93, 110
West Side Boys 443
White Patriot Party (WPP)............. 345
white supremacist .. 160, 184, 270, 287, 313, 317, 319, 330, 334, 461
William Dyson 129
William James................................... 92

William Pierce 317
Woolgar 38
World Church of the Creator 313
World War 296, 301, 307, 309

Y

Yanow and Tsoukas............ 93, 94, 110
Yemen.. 409

Z

Zabaydah... 300
Zulu 370, 371, 462
zygomatic................................ 220, 250